TIME
LIFE ®
BOOKS

*This volume is one of a series that explains and demonstrates
how to prepare various types of food, and that offers in each
book an international anthology of great recipes.*

Terrines, Pâtés & Galantines

BY
THE EDITORS OF TIME-LIFE BOOKS

TIME-LIFE BOOKS/ALEXANDRIA, VIRGINIA

Cover: The golden crust of a pâté is sliced to reveal its intricate, layered filling. Strips of dark meats—the tender flesh of hare and game birds—contrast with paler strips of veal, ham and pork fat. These meats are offset by layers of light and dark forcemeats, made by the techniques demonstrated on pages 66-69; a Madeira-flavored jelly is interposed between the filling and the pastry.

Time-Life Books Inc.
is a wholly owned subsidiary of
TIME INCORPORATED

Founder: Henry R. Luce 1898-1967
Editor-in-Chief: Henry Anatole Grunwald
President: J. Richard Munro
Chairman of the Board: Ralph P. Davidson
Corporate Editor: Jason McManus
Group Vice President, Books: Reginald K. Brack Jr.
Vice President, Books: George Artandi

TIME-LIFE BOOKS INC.

Editor: George Constable; *Executive Editor:* George Daniels; *Editorial General Manager:* Neal Goff; *Director of Design:* Louis Klein; *Editorial Board:* Dale M. Brown, Roberta Conlan, Ellen Phillips, Gerry Schremp, Gerald Simons, Rosalind Stubenberg, Kit van Tulleken, Henry Woodhead; *Director of Research:* Phyllis K. Wise; *Director of Photography:* John Conrad Weiser; *Copy Room:* Diane Ullius; *Editorial Operations:* Caroline A. Boubin (manager); *Production:* Celia Beattie; *Quality Control:* James J. Cox (director), Sally Collins; *Library:* Louise D. Forstall

President: William J. Henry; *Senior Vice President:* Christopher T. Linen; *Vice Presidents:* Stephen L. Bair, Robert A. Ellis, John M. Fahey Jr., Juanita T. James, James L. Mercer, Joanne A. Pello, Paul R. Stewart, Christian Strasser

THE GOOD COOK

The original version of this book was created in London for Time-Life International (Nederland) B.V.
European Editor: Kit van Tulleken; *Design Director:* Louis Klein; *Photography Director:* Pamela Marke; *Planning Director:* Alan Lothian; *Chief of Research:* Vanessa Kramer; *Chief Sub-Editor:* Ilse Gray; *Production Editor:* Ellen Brush; *Quality Control:* Douglas Whitworth

Staff for *Terrines, Pâtés & Galantines: Series Editor:* Gillian Boucher; *Series Coordinator:* Liz Timothy; *Text Editor:* Ellen Galford; *Anthology Editor:* Markie Benet; *Staff Writers:* Alexandra Carlier, Sally Crawford, Nicoletta Flessati, Jane Havell, Thom Henvey; *Researchers:* Tim Fraser, Debbie Litton; *Designer:* Michael Morey; *Sub-Editors:* Charles Boyle, Kathy Eason, Aquila Kegan, Sally Rowland; *Design Assistant:* Sally Curnock; *Editorial Department:* Steven Ayckbourn, Kate Cann, Debra Dick, Philip Garner, Theresa John, Lesley Kinahan, Debra Lelliott, Linda Mallett, Molly Sutherland, Julia West, Helen Whitehorn, Sylvia Wilson

U.S. Staff for *Terrines, Pâtés & Galantines: Editor:* Gerry Schremp; *Designer:* Ellen Robling; *Chief Researcher:* Barbara Fleming; *Picture Editor:* Adrian Allen; *Writer:* Leslie Marshall; *Researchers:* Christine B. Dove, Fran Glennon (techniques), Tina Ujlaki (anthology), Denise Li; *Assistant Designer:* Peg Schreiber; *Copy Coordinators:* Nancy Berman, Tonna Gibert, Bobbie C. Paradise; *Art Assistant:* Mary L. Orr; *Picture Coordinator:* Alvin Ferrell; *Editorial Assistants:* Brenda Harwell, Patricia Whiteford

CHIEF SERIES CONSULTANT

Richard Olney, an American, has lived and worked for some three decades in France, where he is highly regarded as an authority on food and wine. Author of *The French Menu Cookbook* and of the award-winning *Simple French Food,* he has also contributed to numerous gastronomic magazines in France and the United States, including the influential journals *Cuisine et Vins de France* and *La Revue du Vin de France.* He has directed cooking courses in both countries and is a member of several distinguished gastronomic and oenological societies, including L'Académie Internationale du Vin, La Confrérie des Chevaliers du Tastevin and La Commanderie du Bontemps de Médoc et des Graves. Working in London with the series editorial staff, he has been basically responsible for the planning of this volume, and has supervised the final selection of recipes submitted by other consultants. The United States edition of The Good Cook has been revised by the Editors of Time-Life Books to bring it into complete accord with American customs and usage.

CHIEF AMERICAN CONSULTANT

Carol Cutler is the author of a number of cookbooks, including the award-winning *The Six-Minute Soufflé and Other Culinary Delights.* During the 12 years she lived in France, she studied at the Cordon Bleu and the École des Trois Gourmandes, and with private chefs. She is a member of the Cercle des Gourmettes, a long-established French food society limited to just 50 members, and is also a charter member of Les Dames d'Escoffier, Washington Chapter.

SPECIAL CONSULTANTS

Richard Sax, who was responsible for many of the step-by-step demonstrations for this volume, was for two years Chef-Director of the test kitchens for *The International Review of Food and Wine.* Trained in New York and in Paris, where he served an apprenticeship at the Hotel Plaza-Athénée, he has run a restaurant on Martha's Vineyard, written articles for a number of publications and conducted cooking courses.
Flight Sergeant Colin Capon, who also demonstrated step-by-step techniques for this volume, graduated from the Royal Air School of Catering in Hereford, England. As a chef with the Royal Air Force in posts around the world, he has prepared many meals for members of the British Royal Family.

PHOTOGRAPHER

John Elliott, based in London, trained at the Regent Street Polytechnic. He has extensive experience in photographing a wide range of subjects for adver-

tising and magazine assignments. His special interest is food photography.

INTERNATIONAL CONSULTANTS
GREAT BRITAIN: *Jane Grigson* has written a number of books about food and has been a cookery correspondent for the London *Observer* since 1968. *Alan Davidson* is the author of several cookbooks and the founder of Prospect Books, which specializes in scholarly publications about food and cookery. FRANCE: *Michel Lemonnier,* the cofounder and vice president of Les Amitiés Gastronomiques Internationales, is a frequent lecturer on wine and vineyards. GERMANY: *Jochen Kuchenbecker* trained as a chef, but worked for 10 years as a food photographer in several European countries before opening his own restaurant in Hamburg. *Anne Brakemeier* the co-author of a number of cookbooks. ITALY: *Massimo Alberini* is a well-known food writer and journalist, with a particular interest in culinary history. His many books include *Storia del Pranzo all'Italiana, 4000 Anni a Tavola* and *100 Ricette Storiche.* THE NETHERLANDS: *Hugh Jans* has published cookbooks and his recipes appear in several Dutch magazines. THE UNITED STATES: *Judith Olney,* author of *Comforting Food* and *Summer Food,* received her culinary training in England and France. In addition to conducting cooking classes, she regularly contributes articles to gastronomic magazines.

Correspondents: Elisabeth Kraemer-Singh (Bonn); Margot Hapgood, Dorothy Bacon (London); Miriam Hsia, Susan Jonas, Lucy T. Voulgaris (New York); Maria Vincenza Aloisi, Josephine du Brusle (Paris); Ann Natanson (Rome). Valuable assistance was also provided by: Janny Hovinga (Amsterdam); Bona Schmid (Milan).

Library of Congress CIP data, page 176.

CONTENTS

Time-honored Luxuries

elebrated for their sumptuous blends of flavors and textures, rrines, pâtés and galantines enhance dining occasions of evy sort, from rustic to elegant. They are the chief delights of ld buffets, picnics and summer suppers, and they also may be vertures to formal dinners or—as is often the case with game tés—epilogues to the roast-meat course. Their French names ggest haute cuisine, yet most terrines, pâtés and galantines e based on commonplace ingredients—pork and chicken are remost among them—prepared by methods that are easily ithin the reach of every cook.

The simplest of the three, the terrine, takes its name from e earthenware mold in which it is traditionally cooked—terne deriving from *terre,* the French word for earth. It is a loaf of eat, seafood or vegetables, blended with elements that flavor d bind the main ingredients. Sometimes a terrine is composed rely of the chopped-meat or puréed-fish mixture known as rcemeat; sometimes it combines forcemeat and solid ingredits—strips of tender meat, morsels of shellfish, coarsely opped nuts or pieces of truffle. Meat terrines can have a marlous complexity of flavor, achieved by seasoning and marinatg ingredients before they are cooked and ripening the mixture r several days afterward; the result is an aromatic richness mparable to the bouquet of a fine wine. Vegetable and fish rrines tend to be lighter compositions; their virtue lies in the eshness and delicacy of their ingredients.

Any terrine mixture can be enclosed and baked in pastry for more formal presentation, in which case it becomes a pâté—terally, a pie. Although the distinction between a terrine and a té is straightforward, and as old as the dishes themselves, the rm pâté is used, incorrectly, for many terrines. The rustic, ounded loaf of coarsely chopped meats popularly known in rance as *pâté de campagne* is a case in point *(pages 18-19).*

A galantine features the same combination of forcemeat and lid ingredients used in terrines and pâtés. However, the conliner is not pastry but a whole boned bird or a large cut of meat, nd the assembly is poached rather than baked. The finished alantine is generally glazed with aspic, made from the poachg liquid, and is always served cold.

The origin of the word galantine is obscure; some people aim it originally meant a dish of aspic jelly, others that it erives from *galline* or *geline*—old French words for "hen." Cerinly the classic dish is chicken galantine, although other birds n be handled in the same way—and the word is now applied to ssemblies made with suckling pig, pig's head, pork shoulder, g of lamb or veal breast.

This book covers the full range of terrines, pâtés and galantines. The following pages introduce basic techniques essential to most of these dishes—the making of gelatinous stocks, the preparation and use of fresh pork fat, the methods for chopping meats for forcemeats and the creation of simple garnishes. This introductory section is followed by three chapters demonstrating meat, vegetable and fish terrines, a chapter on the making of pâtés and a chapter explaining the preparation of galantines and other cold poached-meat dishes. The last part of the book is an anthology of traditional and modern recipes drawn from a plethora of sources.

Many of these dishes have a long history. Country terrines and meatballs, pork pies and the jellied loaves known as brawns have been made for centuries in farmhouse kitchens, evidence of the thrifty use of every scrap of a slaughtered pig. Recipes for meat and fish pâtés are found in medieval and Renaissance cooking manuals. For example, a cookery book by the 14th Century chef Guillaume Tirel, who was known as Taillevent, offers an eel pâté consisting of marinated and sautéed eel fillets layered with a fish forcemeat in a pastry-lined mold; a similar assembly is demonstrated on pages 58-61.

The crust on early pâtés was designed for durability rather than delicacy. In 18th Century England, pies containing concentric layers of small birds stuffed into progressively larger ones *(pages 56-57)* were sent away to friends and relatives at Christmas, with the sturdy pastry acting as a box in which to ship the parcel. In France, the pastry for pâtés eventually became more refined, while the fillings sometimes increased in complexity. A typical example of this is the rich game pâté demonstrated on pages 66-69, which consists of layers of different light and dark meats and forcemeats that are enclosed in a pillow-shaped puff pastry.

The choice of wines to accompany a terrine, pâté or galantine depends on the character of the dish. The light body and simple flavors of a vegetable terrine suggest light, fresh white wines, such as Muscadet. Softer and more complex wines will be well placed with fish terrines: white Burgundy or Hermitage, a mature white Graves or—for the rich flavor of eel—even a light-bodied Sauternes or a cool, young red wine, possibly a Chinon from the Touraine. A rustic terrine needs an uncomplicated wine with a slightly rough edge—a red wine such as California Zinfandel, or perhaps a white Frascati. However, like the terrines, pâtés and galantines themselves, the attendant wines may be varied almost endlessly: Only experimentation and an adventurous palate can produce a perfect marriage of tastes.

Aromatic Stocks and Pellucid Aspics

The wonderful flavor of many a terrine, pâté or galantine derives in part from the full-bodied stock that is included among its ingredients—or used as its poaching liquid. When cool, such a stock sets to a firm and luminous jelly. This jelly, or aspic, provides the glaze for terrines and galantines, closes the gaps between filling and pastry in a pâté, and binds together the meats in a brawn.

For use in meat and vegetable preparations, a gelatinous stock is made by simmering meats and aromatic vegetables in water for many hours to release their gelatin and flavors *(recipe, page 162)*. Among the gelatin-rich meats that may be used are calf's feet, pig's feet, veal shank, pork rind and chicken wing tips.

Seafood dishes or vegetable preparations that are combined with seafood require a stock based on fish *(recipe, page 163)*. Use the bones, heads and trimmings of any lean fish; avoid such oily fish as herring and mackerel, which have too strong a flavor. Because fish bones are very soft, they release their flavor and gelatin within half an hour; if cooked longer, they would make the stock bitter.

To produce a clear jelly with a pure flavor, stock must be prepared with care. As meat or fish nears the boiling point, it releases proteins that would cloud the stock if not removed. Gentle heat draws these impurities to the surface, where they can be skimmed off; boiling would drive them back into the stock.

Most fish have little natural gelatin, so unflavored powdered gelatin must be added to the cooked stock. Use 1 tablespoon [15 ml.] of powdered gelatin to every 2 to 3 cups [½ to ¾ liter] of stock— slightly more liquid than the packet indicates; too much powder will make the aspic stiff and rubbery. Meat stock that is made with gelatinous cuts should set readily. However, before using it as an aspic, refrigerate a spoonful for 15 minutes. If the chilled stock is not firm, stir in softened gelatin, adding 1 tablespoon for each 3 cups of stock.

Both meat and fish stock should be clear. If the stock is cloudy, add whisked egg whites and crushed egg shells *(Step 4, bottom right)*; the impurities will adhere to the egg, forming a solid mass that may be strained off.

Exploiting the Natural Gelatin in Meats

1 **Filling the pot.** Split calf's feet in half lengthwise. Cut pork rind into pieces. To prevent clouding, parboil the feet and rind for five minutes to clean them; drain them, rinse them in cold water, and place them on a rack set inside a large pot. Add other gelatinous meats such as veal shank and chicken wing tips.

2 **Removing scum.** Pour cold water into the pot to cover the meat. Bring to a boil slowly, spooning off the scum that rises to the surface. To prevent the water from boiling, pour in a cup of cold water. Continue spooning off the scum until no more rises, adding more cold water if the liquid begins to boil.

Jelling a Fish Stock

1 **Preparing.** Assemble fish trimmings—the heads and bones of whiting, sole and mullet are shown here. Remove and discard gills. Rinse the fish trimmings under cold water. Set the trimmings on a rack in a large pan. Add a bouquet garni *(Step 3, above)*, sliced carrots, onions and a little salt.

2 **Cooking.** Cover the ingredients in the pan with cold water; bring the water to a boil slowly. Spoon off any scum from the surface. Cover the pan, leaving the lid slightly ajar, and reduce the heat. Simmer for 15 minutes. Pour in dry white wine. Return the stock to a simmer and cook for 15 minutes longer.

3 **Adding aromatics.** Tie together a leek, a celery rib, a handful of parsley, a bay leaf and a thyme sprig to make a bouquet garni. Add the bouquet garni to the stock, along with onions—one stuck with cloves—an unpeeled garlic bulb and carrots. Bring the stock back to the boiling point; skim off any scum.

4 **Simmering the stock.** Place the pot on a heat-diffusing pad. Set the pot lid slightly ajar and adjust the heat to simmer; cook undisturbed for eight hours. Strain the stock through a colander lined with dampened cheesecloth or muslin. Cool the stock and refrigerate it overnight.

5 **Removing fat.** The next day, spoon off the solidified fat from the jellied stock. Wipe off any traces of fat with a towel dipped in hot water and squeezed dry. Refrigerate the stock: It will keep for two or three days, or for a week if boiled every other day. Alternatively, freeze small amounts in plastic bags.

3 **Adding gelatin.** Strain the stock into a deep saucepan through a colander lined with a double layer of dampened cheesecloth or muslin. Mix powdered gelatin with water and let it soak for a few minutes. Add some of the hot stock to dissolve the gelatin, then stir it into the rest of the stock.

4 **Clarifying the stock.** Separate eggs and whisk the whites lightly. Crush the egg shells coarse. Add the shells and whites to the stock, and whisk over high heat as the stock nears a boil. When the egg whites rise, take the pan off the heat. Let the foam settle. Bring the stock to a boil twice more.

5 **Straining the jelly.** Line a strainer with dampened cheesecloth or muslin. Pour in the stock and let it drip through. Let the stock cool; remove any fat. In the refrigerator, the stock will keep for two or three days, or a week if boiled every day. Or the stock can be frozen in small amounts in plastic bags.

A Choice of Textures for Meats

The mixtures of pounded, chopped or ground meats and pork fat known as forcemeats are essential to most of the preparations in this book. Either alone or in combination with other ingredients, such forcemeats fill terrines and pâtés and provide the stuffings for galantines. They may be based on one or more of a variety of meats: Mild pork, veal, chicken or turkey often balance the emphatic flavor of duck, hare or game birds. Pork, veal or poultry livers are frequently included for additional richness and taste.

For a tender forcemeat, any meats chosen must be trimmed of connective tissues and membranes, which stiffen in cooking. Large pieces should be cut into chunks convenient for further handling.

The meats can be chopped in different ways to produce a forcemeat that is fine or coarse in texture. The best way—because it minimizes the loss of juices—is to chop small chunks of meat by hand. Two sharp, heavy chef's knives of equal size and weight will do this most effectively, but you can use one knife.

A second way to chop meats is to pass them through a food grinder (box, below, right). This is faster and easier, but it yields a drier forcemeat. For a coarse forcemeat, chunks of meat are simply pushed through the large-holed disk; for a finer texture, the meats are pushed first through the large-holed disk, then through the disk with the small holes.

Meats chopped with knives or a grinder can be pounded into a smooth forcemeat in a mortar, but the quickest and easiest route to a smooth forcemeat is to use a food processor (Step 1, bottom box). The blades work so fast that the meat is reduced to a paste in seconds. For the smoothest possible texture, a pounded or processed paste may be forced through a drum sieve with a plastic scraper.

A forcemeat need not be uniformly coarse or smooth. You can chop some of the meat coarsely by hand and reduce the rest to a paste in a processor. Or add diced fatback and strips or cubes of tender meat to the forcemeat for contrast.

Wielding Knives to Conserve Precious Juices

1 **Trimming.** Cut meat—here, pork and veal—into chunks. Cut and scrape away connective tissues and membrane; hold the membrane taut as you cut.

2 **Dicing.** Cut the meat into ½-inch [1-cm.] strips; bunch and dice the strips. Remove the rind from fresh fatback. Dice the fat and add it to the meat.

3 **Chopping.** Hold a pair of chef's knives over the meat; bring them down alternately, with a rhythmic action, until the meat is evenly flecked with white.

Taking Advantage of a Processor

1 **Processing.** Trim meat and chicken livers. Cut the meat and fresh fatback into 1-inch [2½-cm.] cubes; then chop them in a food processor.

2 **Sieving.** Push the paste through a drum sieve, a spoonful at a time, with a plastic scraper. Scrape the paste from the bottom of the sieve into a bowl.

Using a Food Grinder

Grinding meat. Trim meat and fat and cut it into cubes. Feed the cubes through a grinder, pushing them with the palm of your hand or a pestle.

Finishing Touches for Forcemeats

In addition to the basic meat mixture, a forcemeat contains ingredients that contribute to its flavor and texture. These elements may vary considerably from one forcemeat to another.

Forcemeats should be well seasoned since they will be used in dishes that are usually served cold—and cold foods need more seasoning than hot foods. Many different flavorings can be added—spices, such as nutmeg and cloves; herbs, such as thyme, marjoram and savory; table wines or fortified wines, such as sherry or Madeira; and spirits, such as brandy or anise-flavored liqueur.

For color and textural contrast, a forcemeat can be augmented by such ingredients as coarsely chopped pistachios or almonds, whole green peppercorns, broiled and peeled red or green peppers, truffle pieces and finely chopped truffle peelings. If you use canned truffles, add their aromatic juices to perfume the mixture.

To lend an especially rich texture, the forcemeat can be enhanced by the mixture of sautéed and sieved chicken livers called *farce gratin (right; recipe, page 63)*. Because the livers are firmed by sautéing, they will produce a much more solid mixture than one containing uncooked livers—which break down virtually into a liquid when sieved.

Generally, eggs are included in forcemeats to bind all of the ingredients together, and bread crumbs are added to lighten the mixture. The bread crumbs are often blended with a little gelatinous stock *(pages 6-7)*, then cooked and reduced to a thick paste called a bread panada *(bottom right)*. The stock in the panada adds flavor and helps to bind the forcemeat by setting into a jelly as it cools. Incorporating the stock into a paste with the bread crumbs also ensures that only a small amount of stock is added; if too much liquid were introduced into the mixture, the forcemeat would be too loose to hold together.

Any forcemeat will improve in flavor if covered and refrigerated for a few hours before the terrine is assembled.

Smoothness from Chicken Livers

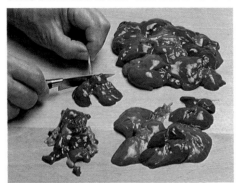

1 **Preparing livers.** With a small knife, trim chicken livers of the connective tissues between the lobes: Grasp the tissue between your thumb and forefinger, and cut away the liver.

2 **Adding brandy.** Sauté chopped shallots in butter for five minutes. Add the livers; increase the heat. After two minutes, add brandy; ignite it with a match. Cook until the flames die.

3 **Pounding the mixture.** Pour the chicken-liver mixture, with its juices, into a mortar. Pound the mixture to a smooth paste with a pestle. Alternatively, chop the mixture in a processor.

4 **Sieving the livers.** Use a plastic scraper to push the paste—a little at a time—through a drum sieve set over a plate. Scrape the purée from the underside of the sieve onto the plate.

A Binding Paste of Bread and Stock

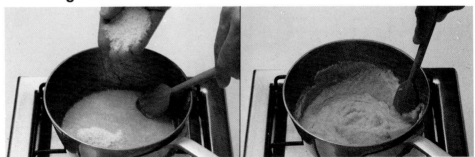

Mixing bread crumbs and stock. Remove the crusts from firm-textured white bread; prepare fine bread crumbs with a grater or in a processor. Heat a little stock in a saucepan. Sprinkle the crumbs onto the stock *(above, left)*. Stirring constantly, cook over medium heat to produce a thick, smooth paste *(right)*.

Mousseline: A Fine Foundation

Mousseline, the most delicate forcemeat, is a purée of tender meats or fish, bound with egg white and enriched with heavy cream *(right; recipe page 164)*. For a sturdier mousseline, the basic mixture can be combined with a flour panada—a paste of flour and egg yolks cooked with milk and butter *(below; recipe, page 164)*. The mild flavor and smooth texture of both types of mousseline make them particularly suitable for terrines, pâtés and galantines based on fish, vegetables, or meats such as sweetbreads.

The meat or fish for a mousseline may be puréed in a mortar *(Step 2, top)* or food processor *(Step 4, bottom)*, but in either case it should be sieved for smoothness. Egg white is added after the flesh is puréed, cream after sieving. Keep ingredients and utensils cold so that the mixture will be firm enough to absorb a large amount of cream. Some mousselines contain whipped cream, but one intended for a pâté, terrine or galantine is best made with unwhipped cream only, to ensure a compact dish that is easy to slice.

An Airy Purée Enhanced by Cream

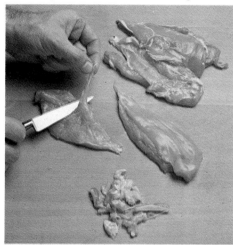

1 **Trimming.** Remove tendons, fat and connective tissue from tender meat—in this case, breasts of chicken—or trim fish fillets of any remaining skin and bones. Cut the flesh into ½-inch [1-cm.] cubes or coarsely chop it.

2 **Adding egg white.** In a mortar, pound the flesh to a paste. Season it with salt, pepper and nutmeg. Gradually add egg white and pound until it is thoroughly incorporated. Alternatively, chop the flesh in a processor, add the seasonings and egg white, and process for 10 to 20 seconds.

A Full-bodied Blend Thickened with Flour

1 **Mixing the panada.** Bring milk to a boil; remove it from the heat to cool slightly. Sift flour into a mixing bowl with salt, pepper and nutmeg. Separate eggs and add the yolks to the center of the bowl. Mixing from the center, work the yolks into the flour. Add melted butter and the hot milk. Stir well.

2 **Cooking.** Pour the panada mixture into a small, heavy saucepan; place the saucepan over medium heat. Stirring the mixture with a whisk, cook the panada until it starts to thicken.

3 **Completing the panada.** Beating with a wooden spoon, continue to cook the panada until it draws away from the sides of the saucepan. Spread the paste onto a plate in a shallow layer and let it cool.

3 **Sieving the purée.** With a plastic scraper, rub the purée through a drum sieve, a little at a time. Place the purée in a metal bowl; press plastic wrap against the surface of the purée to exclude all air. Set the bowl in a larger bowl full of ice. Refrigerate the mixture for at least one hour.

4 **Incorporating cream.** Remove the bowl, still set in ice, from the refrigerator. Pour 3 or 4 tablespoons [45 or 60 ml.] of heavy cream onto the purée. Stirring vigorously with a wooden spoon, work the cream in well. Cover again and refrigerate the mixture for about 15 minutes.

5 **Blending ingredients.** Continue adding cream, a few spoonfuls at a time, working it in thoroughly. When the mixture becomes supple after each addition, beat it well and refrigerate it. When all of the cream is blended in, taste the mousseline for salt. Use the mousseline within a few hours.

4 **Puréeing fish or meat.** Trim fillets of white fish—here, whiting—of skin and bones, or remove tendons and connective tissue from tender meat. Cut the flesh into 1-inch [2½-cm.] chunks. Purée the flesh in a food processor. Add egg white, a little at a time, and process until the whites are incorporated.

5 **Mixing fish and panada.** Put the purée in a bowl and add the cooled panada. Work the two together well; then press the mixture through a drum sieve, a little at a time. Transfer the mixture to a metal bowl and cover it with plastic wrap. Refrigerate it for at least one hour, embedded in a bowl of ice.

6 **Adding cream.** Remove the mixture from the refrigerator; keep it on the ice. Add a little heavy cream and work it in. Cover and chill, still on ice, for 30 minutes. Add the remaining cream, a little at a time, beating the mixture when it becomes supple and chilling it between additions. Use within a few hours.

The Many Uses of Pork Fat

To achieve the moist richness that is one of their most admirable characteristics, terrines, pâtés and galantines must include a generous amount of fat. For preparations usually served cold, fresh pork fat is a particularly good choice. Unlike the fat of beef or lamb, cold cooked pork fat retains a firm, smooth texture and a white color; it neither sticks to the roof of the mouth nor has an intrusive flavor.

Fatback, the most convenient natural form of pork fat, is cubed *(Step 3, box, far right)* to enrich most forcemeats—either by being chopped with the meat or left whole to vary the texture. Strips, or lardons, of fatback *(box, far right)* are often threaded through whole pieces of lean meat, or layered with other ingredients to form a pattern in a forcemeat filling. Thin sheets, or bards, of fatback or pieces of caul—the fatty membrane from the stomach of a pig—can be used to line terrine molds *(below)* and pâtés *(page 60)*.

Fat may also serve to protect rather than to moisten: If melted pork fat—in the form of lard—is poured over terrines, it will create an airtight seal that prolongs their keeping time. Lard may be rendered at home *(box, right)* to separate the pure fat from the tissue of pork fat.

Fresh fatback is obtainable at most butcher shops; the more widely sold salt fatback may be substituted, if it is first blanched for five minutes to eliminate saltiness. Caul can be purchased from specialty butchers. Fresh caul merely needs to be rinsed. Dry-salted caul must be soaked before use, but can be refrigerated safely for several weeks.

Slicing Bards of Fatback

1 **Slicing bards.** Freeze a slab of fresh fatback for an hour to firm it. Set the chilled slab rind side down and press one end against a board to steady it. Working toward the board, slice the fat horizontally into sheets ⅛ inch [3 mm.] thick.

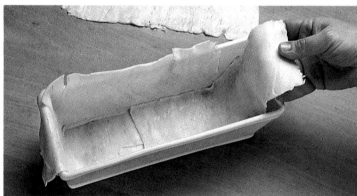

2 **Lining a mold.** Press a layer of bards against the bottom, sides and ends of a terrine mold: Overlap the bards and let the ends overhang the rim of the mold to cover the filling later. Reserve extra bards to finish covering the filled mold.

Dealing with Lacy Caul

1 **Soaking dry-salted caul.** Place caul in a bowl of tepid water to soften it. If the caul has any odor, add a little vinegar or lemon juice to the water.

2 **Drying the caul.** After soaking the caul for 15 minutes, lift it out of the water. Gently spread out the caul on a towel to drain off excess moisture.

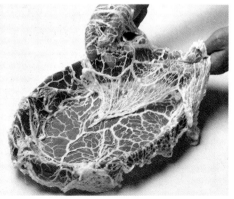

3 **Lining a mold.** Drape a large piece of caul over a mold. Let the caul hang over the rim to cover the filling later. Patch gaps with small pieces of caul.

Rendering Fat into Lard

1 **Adding water.** Cut pork fat—here, fatback, belly fat and suet from around the kidneys—into 1-inch [2½-cm.] cubes. Place the cubes in a heavy pot. Cover the pot bottom with cold water.

2 **Melting down the fat.** Place the pot over low heat. Without covering the pot, cook the fat for about four hours, until the liquid becomes completely clear. Stir occasionally to prevent the pieces of fat from sticking to the pot and to help them melt thoroughly and evenly.

3 **Straining the lard.** Ladle the fat into a strainer that has been lined with several layers of dampened cheesecloth or muslin and set over a dish or pot. Let the fat cool and cover it with foil. The lard will keep for two months in the refrigerator or three months in the freezer. Reserve the solid residue, known as cracklings, to use as a snack or soup garnish.

4 **Using the lard.** Spoon out as much lard as required and melt it in a heavy pan over gentle heat. Ladle the melted lard over the top of a cooled, cooked terrine to cover the mixture completely. As the lard cools, it may shrink, in which case add more melted lard to fill in any gaps.

Cutting Strips and Dice

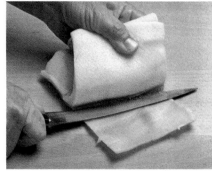

1 **Removing the rind.** Place chilled fatback with its rind side down on a work surface. Using a long, sharp knife, cut into one end of the slab just above the rind and slice along it, lifting away the fat.

2 **Cutting lardons.** Steady the fat with one hand, bending your fingers to protect your finger tips from the knife blade. Cut the fatback into long, straight strips about ¼ inch [6 mm.] thick and wide.

3 **Preparing dice.** Gather several of the strips of fat together, holding the bundle in place with one hand. Slice the lardons crosswise to make ¼-inch [6-mm.] cubes.

Three Colorful Complements

Rich meat terrines, pâtés and galantines need no garnish other than a spoonful of diced aspic or a few sour pickles. However, the more delicate flavors of fish and vegetable terrines invite enhancement with a complementary sauce.

For cold fish and vegetable presentations, the accompaniments may be based on a mayonnaise, a jellied mousse or a simple vinaigrette—all of which are felicitous vehicles for various flavorings *(recipes, pages 164 and 165)*.

Mayonnaise, an emulsion of egg yolks and oil *(Steps 1 and 2, below),* is the richest of these sauce foundations. To ensure that the yolks and oil will blend, bring all the ingredients and implements to room temperature and add the oil slowly; a grooved cork such as the one used here will help to control the flow of oil. Flavor the mayonnaise with chopped capers, sour gherkins and herbs to make a piquant tartar sauce *(Step 4, below).* Or stir in a mixture of fresh herbs and watercress that has been blanched, squeezed and chopped *(Steps 1 and 2, right).*

To achieve a mousse with a suave texture, combine melted meat jelly with flavorings such as watercress *(right);* before the jelly sets, fold in whipped cream to enrich and lighten the mixture. Puréed sorrel, Swiss chard or tomatoes make delicious alternatives to the watercress. Puréed tomatoes are also combined with vinaigrette—a mixture of olive oil and vinegar or lemon juice—for a sauce of brilliant color and robust flavor *(opposite, bottom).* A tomato vinaigrette is a flattering garnish for vegetable terrines particularly those incorporating a mild flavored mousseline *(pages 10-11).*

Vegetable terrines are usually served cold, but fish terrines are often presented hot, along with a hot sauce. Good choices include a flour-thickened velouté sauce based on fish stock, or white butter sauce—a blend of butter, wine, vinegar and shallots *(recipes, pages 165 and 166).*

A Tangy Sauce Based on Mayonnaise

1 **Separating eggs.** Crack each egg and empty it onto your closed fingers; let the white slip through into a bowl. Put the yolks in a large bowl set on a damp towel. Keep the whites for another use.

2 **Adding oil.** Whisk the yolks with salt and pepper until they are smooth and pale. Add vinegar or lemon juice. Whisking continuously, add oil drop by drop *(above, left).* As the mixture begins to thicken, pour in the oil in a thin but steady stream, whisking until the sauce forms soft peaks *(right).*

3 **Chopping flavorings.** Finely chop capers, sour gherkins, and a selection of fresh herbs—in this case, tarragon, chervil, chives and parsley.

4 **Mixing the tartar sauce.** Add the chopped flavorings to the mayonnaise *(above, left).* Stir the mixture until the ingredients are thoroughly combined *(right).* Either serve the tartar sauce at once or cover it with plastic wrap and refrigerate it for up to three days. Before serving it, stir the sauce well.

A Subtle Blend of Watercress and Jelly

1 **Blanching watercress.** Remove watercress leaves from their stems and wash the leaves carefully. Bring a large pan of water to a boil. Drop the leaves into the pan; boil for one minute.

2 **Squeezing watercress.** In a sieve or colander, drain the watercress leaves and refresh them under cold water. Then squeeze the watercress to rid it of excess moisture. Finely chop it.

3 **Sieving.** Melt some jellied meat or fish stock *(pages 6-7)*, and pour it into a metal bowl. Using a pestle, force the chopped watercress through the sieve into the bowl containing the stock.

4 **Stirring over ice.** Whip heavy cream until thick but still pourable; set it aside. Embed the bowl of watercress and stock in a bowl filled with ice. Stir until the mixture begins to thicken.

5 **Folding in cream.** Remove the bowl from the ice. Add the cream to the stock-and-watercress mixture; fold it in well. Taste the mousse for seasoning.

6 **Serving.** Spoon the mousse into a serving bowl, smooth the surface and cover the bowl. Refrigerate the mousse until set—about two hours. Serve it from the bowl.

A Scarlet Sauce with a Sharp Note

1 **Chopping tomatoes.** With a small, sharp knife, cut around the stem of each tomato to remove its core. Chop the tomatoes; then purée them through a sieve.

2 **Making a vinaigrette.** Grind coarse salt in a mortar and add pepper. Add lemon juice to the mortar and stir until the salt is dissolved. Stir in oil.

3 **Adding tomato purée.** Add spoonfuls of tomato purée to the vinaigrette and stir until smooth. Transfer the tomato vinaigrette to a sauceboat and stir thoroughly before serving.

Meat Terrines

The Apotheosis of Meat Loaf

Gentle cooking in a water bath
Weighting terrines for compact texture
Marinating meats to develop flavors
How to seal a terrine with lard
Boning a bird without breaking the skin

A meat terrine is a rich, moist and judiciously seasoned meat loaf—meant, in most cases, to be eaten cold. Traditionally, the cooking is done in a deep, lidded, oval or rectangular mold known as a terrine, which gives the loaf its name. A terrine can be based on many different meats. Pale, delicate veal or chicken and dark, stronger-flavored duck or game birds are all suitable for inclusion, as are sweetbreads, brains, livers and other variety meats. In almost every case, pork, with its mild flesh and firm, white fat, is part of the mixture—and it may also be used alone.

The simplest meat terrine consists solely of forcemeat—a combination of chopped or ground meats and fat that may be either coarse in texture or puréed to a creamy smoothness. For a contrast of textures, forcemeat can be combined with finely chopped vegetables, coarsely chopped nuts or morsels of tender meat. Poultry and game lend themselves particularly well to terrines that display a textural counterpoint: The tender breast or saddle meat can be diced or cut into strips, while the tougher wing and leg meat is chopped or ground up for the forcemeat. Assemblage of the elements for such a loaf can be done in several ways. In the duck terrine on pages 22-25, for example, pieces of duck breast are simply mixed into the forcemeat; in the terrine shown on pages 26-27 the same ingredients are arranged in layers, forming a mosaic that will appear in every slice. Other terrines dispense with forcemeat altogether and consist instead of tightly packed layers of solid meats *(pages 26-27)*.

Whatever the construction of a meat terrine, its ingredients are usually assembled in a mold lined with bards—sheets of fresh pork fatback—or caul *(page 12)* to keep the mixture moist. However, when the mixture is very liquid, as is the case with the chicken liver purée on pages 28-29, the mold is merely buttered and its base lined with buttered paper to facilitate unmolding.

For a uniform texture, a terrine is generally cooked—covered—in a bath of hot water *(page 20)*, which ensures a gentle and even penetration of heat. Notable exceptions are country terrines, which are exposed to the direct heat of the oven to produce a crusty brown exterior *(pages 18-19)*. After cooking, most meat terrines are left to mature for three or four days. However, take the loaf from the refrigerator an hour or so before serving; if it is frigid, its ripened flavors will be muted.

Rings of onion and parsley are strewn over veal scallops to sharpen the flavor of a layered terrine. Bacon lines the mold and is interleaved with veal as the layers are assembled. The two kinds of meat will form colorful stripes in each slice of the terrine.

A Rustic Loaf of Well-seasoned Meats

The simplest of terrines is the sturdy country version shown here. Brown and crusty on the outside, tender and succulent within, it is made from forcemeat— coarsely ground or chopped meats and fat—bound with eggs, lightened with bread crumbs and brightened by lively flavorings. Like most meat loaves, this rustic terrine is baked uncovered. Shaping the meat mixture into a low, slightly mounded loaf ensures that the terrine will cook through evenly. To keep it moist, the loaf is wrapped in caul and topped with strips of fat arranged in an attractive lattice pattern.

For a terrine that is neither too dry nor too fatty, use about twice as much lean meat as fat, including the caul and fatback that cover the mixture. Like most forcemeats, the one shown here (recipe, page 89) is composed mainly of pork—in this case, pork shoulder, pork belly and fatback. Pork liver is another element, contributing smooth texture and hearty taste. And veal is included for its leanness and mild flavor (chicken or turkey could serve in the same role).

Forcemeats can be complemented by many flavorings: aromatics—such as onion or garlic—herbs, spices, and wine or spirits. This terrine is flavored with sautéed onions, a mixture of garlic and parsley known as a *persillade*, dried herbs, nutmeg, cayenne pepper and brandy.

Before committing any terrine to the oven, check the seasoning—keeping in mind that all foods served cold need to be seasoned more highly than hot dishes. Because cooking will alter flavors—and raw pork is unsafe to eat—fry a sample of the forcemeat (Step 5) before tasting it and adjusting the seasonings.

After the terrine has baked for the allotted time, test its doneness by inserting a skewer or meat thermometer into the center of the loaf (Step 8). The terrine should reach an internal temperature of 160° F. [70° C.] before it is taken from the oven; during the first minutes of cooling, the temperature will rise to between 165° and 170° F. [about 75° C.] as heat equalizes throughout the loaf. Cool the baked terrine to room temperature, then chill it overnight to make it firm enough to slice without crumbling. Its flavors will improve if it matures for three to four days.

1 **Preparing meats.** With a sharp knife, remove the rind from the pork shoulder, pork belly and fresh fatback. Trim the membranes and connective tissue from the belly and shoulder; cut away any bloody parts from the fatback. Remove the fat and membranes from a boneless piece of veal—here, a slice of round roast. Cut the meats and fat into 1-inch [2½-cm.] strips, then into cubes. Remove the fat and membranes from pork liver and cube it. Pass the meats, fatback and liver through the coarse disk of a food grinder, or chop them with two knives of equal weight (page 8).

5 **Tasting for seasoning.** Break off a small piece of the forcemeat, and fry it in a lightly oiled skillet over medium heat for three or four minutes, or until its juices run clear, without a trace of pink. Let the fried piece cool for a minute. Then taste it and, if desired, add salt and pepper to the remaining forcemeat.

6 **Forming the terrine.** Line a large, shallow baking dish—an earthenware gratin dish is used here—with prepared caul (page 12), letting the caul hang over the sides. Place the forcemeat in the dish. With your hands mound and smooth the forcemeat.

2 **Sautéing onions.** Melt butter in a pan set over moderately low heat. Add finely chopped onions and cook for 10 to 15 minutes, or until soft but not brown. With a mortar and pestle, pound garlic and coarse salt to a smooth paste. Blend in finely chopped parsley with your finger tips to form a *persillade*.

3 **Assembling ingredients.** In a large bowl, combine the meats, fat, onions and the *persillade* with eggs, fresh bread crumbs, nutmeg, black pepper, cayenne pepper and dried herbs—in this case, marjoram, savory, oregano and thyme. Then pour in a small amount of brandy.

4 **Mixing.** With your hands, mix the ingredients well, squeezing the forcemeat through your fingers several times to make sure that all of its elements are thoroughly combined. If the forcemeat does not cohere, scatter more bread crumbs over it; mix and squeeze the forcemeat again.

7 **Covering with fat.** Slice fresh fatback thin and cut it into strips about ½ inch [1 cm.] wide. Arrange the strips in a crisscross pattern on top of the forcemeat. Lift the overhanging edges of the caul and fold them over the strips of fat. Add more caul, if necessary, to cover the top of the terrine completely.

8 **Baking.** Bake the terrine at 350° F. [180° C.] for one and one half hours. Insert a thin skewer into the center; if the juices run clear and the tip of the skewer feels fairly hot, the terrine is fully cooked. Alternatively, insert a meat thermometer into the center; the terrine is done when its internal temperature reaches 160° F. [70° C.].

9 **Serving.** Let the terrine cool, then cover it with foil or plastic wrap and refrigerate it until thoroughly chilled— at least 12 hours. To improve the flavor, keep it in the refrigerator for three or four days. In either case, remove the terrine from the refrigerator an hour or so before serving. Serve the terrine cut into ½-inch [1-cm.] slices.

Variations on a Simple Theme

To create a terrine of uniform texture, the meat mixture is cooked in a tightly covered mold—a terrine, a casserole or a soufflé dish—on a rack inside a water bath. Called a bain-marie in French, a water bath is merely a large pan or dish filled with enough water to immerse the lower two thirds of the mold. The water moderates the heat around the mold and ensures that its contents cook evenly.

The cover for the mold may be a lid or a piece of foil; for the snuggest fit, use both. A cover holds in most of the steam that rises from the meat mixture, thus hastening the cooking of the top surface without letting it develop a crust. However, the cover should have a hole—as terrine lids do—to let some steam escape and prevent the build-up of pressure or excess moisture inside the mold.

The water bath can be used either in the oven or on top of the stove, in which case the bath, too, should be covered. The water should be almost boiling before it is poured into the bath, and it must be at a simmer throughout cooking.

Once the terrine is cooked, it may be pressed into a compact, easily sliced loaf by allowing it to rest for 20 minutes to reabsorb its juices, then cooling it under weights, and leaving the weights in place overnight. However, very heavy weights will force out juices and make the terrine dry: For best results, use no more than 2 pounds [1 kg.] of weights for a 2- to 3-pound [1- to 1½-kg.] terrine. To distribute the weight, place the weights on a board cut to fit inside the rim of the mold. Or set the weights in a smaller mold of a similar shape on top of the terrine.

The terrine demonstrated here is made with a forcemeat based on pork, veal, fresh pork fat, pork liver and chicken livers (recipe, page 163). Spinach, celery, onion and herbs provide additional color and flavor. You can vary the forcemeat with other leafy vegetables, such as Swiss chard or chicory, and finely chopped variety meats, such as chicken gizzards or beef heart.

As well as providing the filling for a mold, a forcemeat can be shaped into the small meatballs called *caillettes*. Wrapped in caul and baked uncovered, the *caillettes* will acquire a crusty brown surface (*box, opposite; recipe, page 93*).

1 **Preparing spinach.** Trim the stems and thick ribs from spinach. Bring a large pan of salted water to a rapid boil; drop in the spinach leaves and blanch them for one minute. Drain the spinach in a colander, and refresh the leaves under cold running water to stop the cooking and cool them. Squeeze the leaves dry, then chop them fine.

2 **Parboiling celery.** Trim the leaves from two or three small celery ribs and pull off the fibrous strings. Parboil the celery in salted water until almost tender—about three minutes. Remove the celery from the pan with a skimmer. Slice the ribs lengthwise into strips about ¼ inch [6 mm.] wide; cut the strips crosswise into dice.

5 **Cooking in a water bath.** Cover the mold with foil, or foil and a lid. To let steam escape, pierce a hole in the foil with a skewer—if using a lid, insert the skewer through its hole. Set the mold on a rack in a large pan or dish (above); place them in a preheated 350° F. [180° C.] oven. Pour enough almost-boiling water into the pan or dish to cover two thirds of the mold. Cook for one and one half hours. Insert a skewer into the terrine (inset); if the tip is hot to the touch, the terrine is done. Or insert a meat thermometer; it should register 160° F. [70° C.].

Savory Balls of Forcemeat

3 **Preparing forcemeat.** Coarsely chop pork, veal, fatback, pork liver and chicken livers. Sauté a chopped onion in butter until soft. In a bowl, mix the meats, onion, spinach and celery with eggs, chopped garlic and parsley, dried basil and thyme, and ground spices. Fry a sample *(page 18, Step 5)* and correct the seasoning.

4 **Filling the mold.** Line a terrine mold with bards of fatback *(page 12)*. Let the ends overhang the sides. Place the forcemeat in the mold, mounding the center slightly above the rim. To settle the contents, tap the mold on a folded towel. Cover the terrine with bards, folding over hanging ends and adding new bards as needed.

1 **Forming meatballs.** Prepare a forcemeat *(Steps 1 to 3, left)*. Shape handfuls of the mixture into small balls. Cut prepared caul *(page 12)* into pieces about 6 inches [15 cm.] square; wrap each ball in a piece of caul. Pack the balls in a gratin dish; add enough water to cover the bottom.

6 **Weighting.** Place the terrine on a plate or tray and let it rest for about 20 minutes. Leaving the foil in place, cover the top of the terrine with a board that fits inside the rim of the mold. Distribute weights evenly on top of the board. Use scale weights, as shown here, or unopened cans.

7 **Serving.** Cool the terrine for four to six hours. Clean the sides of the mold. Chill the weighted terrine overnight. Remove the weights and the board, but not the foil, and refrigerate the terrine again—preferably for three or four days. Serve the terrine cut into slices about ½ inch [1 cm.] thick. If you like, trim off the frame of white pork fat before serving.

2 **Baking.** Set the dish, uncovered, in a 450° F. [230° C.] oven; bake for 25 minutes. Place the dish under a preheated broiler for about five minutes to brown the meatballs. Serve them hot, or chill them overnight to let their flavor develop and serve them cold.

Making the Most of a Bird

Giving a terrine a variegated texture is simply a matter of mixing the forcemeat with solid ingredients: Pieces of raw and cooked meats, whole pitted olives, and whole or coarsely chopped nuts, morels and truffles are just a few of the many options. In the demonstration here and on the following two pages, marinated cubes of duck breast, diced ham and fatback, and peeled pistachios are added to a forcemeat that is flavored with brandy (recipe, page 108).

Poultry and small game such as rabbit or quail are well suited to terrines of mixed textures, since no part of their meat need be wasted. The tender fillets are left in relatively large pieces, and the tougher meat and the giblets are incorporated into the forcemeat. Even the bones have a use: They are simmered in a gelatinous stock until they have released their flavor; then the stock is reduced and added to the terrine.

Removing the raw flesh from the bones of poultry or small game is surprisingly easy if you use a small, sharp knife and always cut close to the bone. The breast of a bird—or the saddle of a rabbit—readily comes away from each side of the bone in one piece, but it should be handled carefully to prevent tearing. Less care is needed in boning the rest of the bird or animal, because this flesh becomes part of the forcemeat.

The forcemeat for the terrine can be either coarse or smooth in texture. If you want a coarse mixture, chop the meats by hand or put them through a food grinder. For a smoother texture, purée them in a food processor, or pound them in a mortar and—in order to achieve maximum smoothness—press them through a sieve. If you like, combine contrasting textures in a single forcemeat mixture by chopping some of the meats and reducing the rest to a purée.

So that its flavors develop, the cooked terrine should be kept for at least three days before it is served. However, you can keep it for a longer period if you replace the covering sheets of fatback with an airtight layer of lard (page 13). Under this protective seal, the flavor will continue to improve and the terrine will remain in prime condition for two weeks.

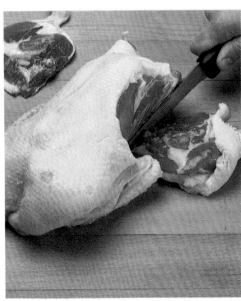

1 **Removing the legs.** With a sharp knife, cut through the skin between the body and one thigh of a bird—in this case, a duck. Bend the leg outward and away from the body to release the ball of the joint from its socket. Cut through the connective tissue of the joint, and the flesh beneath it, to free the leg. Remove the other leg in the same way.

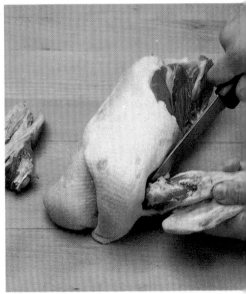

2 **Removing the wings.** With your fingers, locate the ball-and-socket joint beneath the skin at the base of one wing. Swing the wing away from the body and cut through the joint to separate the ball and socket, then cut through the skin at the base to separate the wing from the body (above). Free the other wing in the same way.

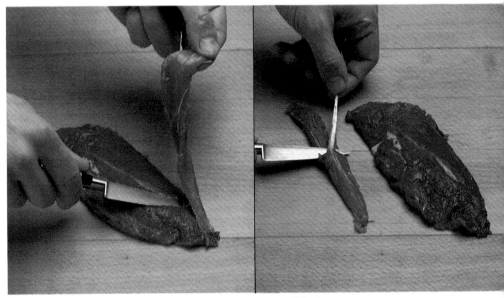

5 **Removing the tendon.** With your fingers or a small knife, carefully separate the large and small fillets that constitute each breast half (above, left). To remove the tendon that runs along the length of the smaller fillet, cut the tip of the tendon free. Lifting the tendon with your fingers, slide the knife between tendon and fillet to separate the two (right). Remove all of the surface membrane.

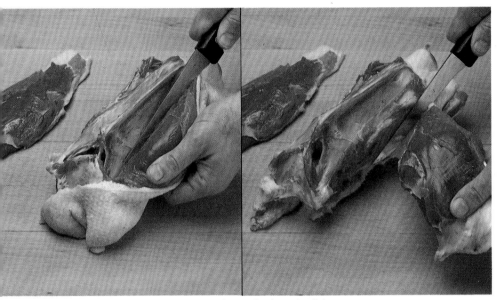

3 **Freeing the breast.** Make an incision down the length of the breastbone, cutting just to one side of the central ridge of bone. Keeping the blade close to the bone, cut through the connective tissue between the flesh of one breast half and the bone, scraping the flesh away *(above, left)*. Cut the breast half free at the neck end. Draw the knife along the length of the body, close to the ribs, to separate the breast half from the rest of the body *(right)*. Cut the other half of the breast free in the same way.

4 **Skinning the breast.** If the skin of the breast half comes away easily, peel it off with your fingers. If not, lay each half with its skin side down and cut into the connective tissue joining the flesh to the skin. Then, lifting the flesh and keeping the knife close to the skin, cut through the tissue to free the flesh.

6 **Dicing the breast meat.** Slice the breast meat into ½-inch [1-cm.] strips, then into cubes *(above)*. In a shallow dish, mix the cubes with a marinade—in this case, white wine, oil, thyme, marjoram, oregano, savory, crushed bay leaf, salt and pepper. Cover the dish with plastic wrap and refrigerate for several hours or overnight.

7 **Trimming the leg meat.** Peel the skin away from one leg. Holding the base of the leg bone, scrape away the meat with a small, sharp knife *(above, left)*. Remove all of the membranes from the flesh. Remove the tendon by grasping the tip of it in one hand and scraping the flesh away from the tendon with the knife *(right)*. Scrape the meat from the other leg and both wings in the same way. Remove all connective tissues. ▶

8 **Enriching a stock.** In a pot, combine gelatinous meat stock *(pages 6-7)* with a bouquet garni, bay leaf, carrot and an onion stuck with two cloves. Add the duck bones. Bring slowly to a boil; spoon off the scum. With the lid ajar, simmer for three hours. Strain the stock through a colander lined with damp muslin or cheesecloth; skim off fat.

9 **Reducing the stock.** Return the stock to the pan, set on the side of the heat, and bring the stock back to a boil, skimming off the fatty skin that forms on the cooler side. Reduce the stock by half, stirring occasionally. Transfer it to a small pan and reduce it until syrupy. Make a panada with the reduced stock *(page 10).*

10 **Making the forcemeat.** Chop the leg and wing meat from the duck with veal, fresh pork fatback, chicken livers, and the duck heart and liver *(page 8).* Put the mixture in a bowl; add diced ham, diced fatback, eggs, the panada, brandy, spices and dried herbs. Mix together.

14 **Filling the terrine.** Line a terrine mold with bards of fatback *(page 12).* Fill the mold with the forcemeat and smooth the surface. Place a folded towel on the work surface; tap the mold on the towel several times to settle its contents. Put two bay leaves on top of the forcemeat. Cover the terrine with a layer of fatback.

15 **Cooking.** Cover the mold with foil or a lid; if foil is used, pierce a hole in it to let steam escape. Cook the terrine in a water bath *(page 20)* in a 350° F. [180° C.] oven for one and one half to three hours, depending on the size and shape of the mold. Insert a skewer through the hole in the foil; if the tip feels hot, the terrine is cooked.

16 **Removing the top fat.** Put the terrine on a plate. Place a board on top and weight it *(page 21, Step 6).* Cool the terrine. Refrigerate it overnight; then remove the weights. If desired, leave it in the refrigerator for three or four days. For a more attractive presentation, peel off the top bards.

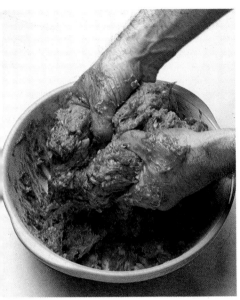

11 **Mixing ingredients.** Continue to mix the forcemeat ingredients thoroughly by repeatedly squeezing the forcemeat through the fingers of both hands until everything is amalgamated.

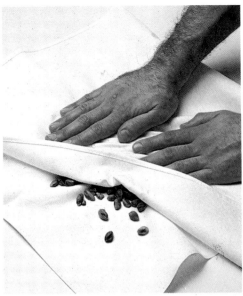

12 **Peeling pistachios.** Bring a pan of water to a boil. Drop in pistachios and blanch them for one minute. Drain the nuts and rub them vigorously between the folds of a towel to loosen their skins. Peel away any remaining skins with your fingers. If you like, coarsely chop the pistachios.

13 **Garnishing.** Drain the diced breast meat and add it to the forcemeat; add the nuts to the mixture. Combine the ingredients thoroughly, taking care not to crush the breast meat. Fry a piece of forcemeat *(page 18, Step 5)* and taste it; add seasoning as needed.

17 **Sealing.** To preserve the terrine for up to two weeks, peel off the top bards and wipe the meat with a damp towel. Ladle melted lard over the terrine to form a layer at least ½ inch [1 cm.] deep. Chill the terrine to set the lard; it will shrink away from the mold. Ladle in more melted lard to completely seal the terrine.

18 **Serving the terrine.** Remove the terrine from the refrigerator about an hour before serving. With a sharp knife, cut the terrine into slices ½ inch [1 cm.] thick. Peel away the covering of lard and the frame of fatback from each slice before you present it.

Layering Ingredients for Patterned Effects

Arranging the ingredients of a terrine in horizontal layers creates a loaf whose attractive pattern is revealed in every slice. You can assemble the terrine from layers of forcemeat and solid ingredients, or you can omit the forcemeat and base the terrine on two or more different solid meats. In either case, the solid ingredients should be positioned lengthwise in the mold so that each slice of the terrine is patterned similarly.

Consider colors as well as flavors when selecting and arranging the ingredients. You could include white strips of fatback *(page 12)* or vivid strips of ham or cooked corned tongue. Black truffle pieces will stand out in relief against a background of pale forcemeat. In the top demonstration, pieces of marinated duck breast are sandwiched between layers of pistachio-flecked forcemeat to produce an intricate mosaic *(recipe, page 108)*. In the terrine demonstrated below, alternating slices of veal and bacon show up in cross section as colorful stripes *(recipe, page 87)*.

If you are assembling a terrine with alternate layers of lean meat and forcemeat, be sure to begin and end with forcemeat. The fat in the forcemeat will prevent the lean meat from drying out as the terrine cooks. At the same time, the fat will seal the ingredients in a firm block.

Similarly, the first and last layers of the veal-and-bacon terrine should consist of bacon, which takes the place of fatback as a lining for the mold and moistens the slices of lean veal within it. When the cooked terrine is chilled, the bacon fat will solidify and the natural gelatin in the veal will set. However, because the veal-and-bacon terrine has no forcemeat to cement its solid ingredients together, it—and other terrines that do not contain forcemeat—must be cooled under weights to compact it.

Carefully composed terrines such as these will look even more impressive if they are glazed with a meat aspic *(pages 6-7)* before serving. However, aspic keeps no more than two or three days, so it is essential that the terrine be glazed the day before it is served.

Creating a Mosaic of Meats

1 **Layering.** Bone a duck *(pages 22-23)*. Cut the breast into strips and marinate. Chop the remaining meat; mix it with chopped veal, fatback, chicken livers, ham, pistachios, bread panada *(page 9)*, Madeira, eggs, brandy and seasonings. Line a mold with bards *(page 12)*; layer it with forcemeat and duck strips.

Achieving a Striped Cross Section

1 **Lining the mold.** Lay slices of bacon lengthwise in the bottom and against the sides of a terrine mold to line it completely. Press the slices firmly to the mold so that they adhere.

2 **Layering the terrine.** Cut thinly sliced veal scallops into strips and gently flatten them with a mallet. Mix chopped onion and parsley with pepper. Cover the bottom layer of bacon with veal; press it down firmly and sprinkle in the onion mixture. Continue layering bacon, veal and the onion mixture. End with a layer of bacon.

3 **Adding wine.** Place a bay leaf and some thyme sprigs on top of the terrine. Pour in a little white wine. Cover the mold with foil or a lid. Cook it on a rack in a water bath in a 350° F. [180° C.] oven for one and one half hours—or until the tip of a skewer inserted in the center feels hot or the terrine reaches a temperature of 160° F. [70° C.].

2 **Glazing.** Cover the forcemeat with a bay leaf, bards and foil. Cook the terrine in a water bath *(page 20)* in a 350° F. [180° C.] oven until a skewer inserted into it feels hot. Weight, cool, then chill the terrine overnight. Remove the top bards; wipe the terrine with a damp towel. Ladle in melted aspic *(pages 6-7)*.

3 **Serving the terrine.** Refrigerate the terrine at least overnight to set the layer of aspic into a firm glaze. Remove the terrine from the refrigerator about an hour before serving it. Cut the terrine into slices for serving.

4 **Weighting.** Put the terrine on a plate; set a board, cut to fit inside the mold, on top of the foil. Place two or three weights on the board *(above)*. Cool the terrine, then refrigerate it—still weighted—overnight. Remove the weights, but keep the terrine in the refrigerator until you serve it: The terrine will be easier to slice when chilled.

Crafting an Even-textured Loaf

For silken-textured terrines, livers are an ideal ingredient. Because of their tenderness, livers are easily puréed by chopping them or, as in this demonstration, by grinding them in a processor. Extra smoothness is achieved by sieving the puréed livers to rid them of membrane.

The terrine shown here is made with chicken livers, but any kind of poultry or meat liver may be used—either alone or in combinations. Chicken and turkey livers are mildest in flavor; goose and pork livers are most assertive. In this version, the livers are bound with eggs and a bread panada *(page 10),* enriched with marrow and cream, and flavored with garlic, herbs, cayenne pepper and brandy *(recipe, page 95).* Bread crumbs could replace the panada; butter could serve as enrichment. Alternate flavorings include sautéed chopped onions, ginger or nutmeg, red wine or bourbon.

After the cooked terrine is taken from the oven, it will shrink slightly from its mold; when it is tepid, it will slip out easily. Chilling makes it easy to slice.

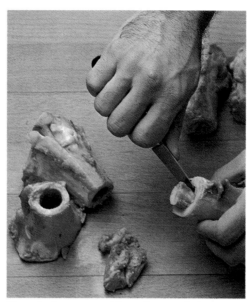

1 Prying marrow from bones. Ask your butcher to saw a beef marrowbone into sections 3 to 4 inches [8 to 10 cm.] long. To remove the marrow from each section, insert the tip of a knife between the marrow and the bone, then lever out the marrow.

2 Puréeing chicken livers. Trim chicken livers of surface connective tissue. Make a stiff panada of stock and bread crumbs. Pound garlic to a paste in a mortar; mix it into the panada. Place the livers in the bowl of processor. Add the panada, marrow, salt, black pepper, cayenne pepper and mixed dried herbs. Purée them.

6 Filling the mold. Pour the terrine mixture into the mold. Cover it with foil or a lid. Place the terrine in a water bath; pour in almost-boiling water. Cook the terrine in a preheated 350° F. [180° C.] oven for about one hour, until the top is firm to the touch.

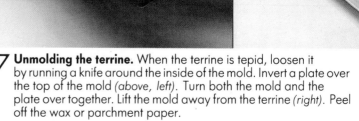

7 Unmolding the terrine. When the terrine is tepid, loosen it by running a knife around the inside of the mold. Invert a plate over the top of the mold *(above, left).* Turn both the mold and the plate over together. Lift the mold away from the terrine *(right).* Peel off the wax or parchment paper.

3 **Sieving.** To remove all membranes from the purée, use a pestle to push it through a sieve into a bowl. With a spatula, scrape off any purée that sticks to the underside of the sieve. Add the scrapings to the bowl.

4 **Adding eggs and cream.** Whisk eggs, cream and brandy into the sieved purée. Poach a spoonful of the mixture gently in a small skillet of simmering water for one or two minutes—until it is firm to the touch. Let the sample cool, then taste it. Adjust the seasoning of the remaining mixture as necessary.

5 **Preparing the mold.** Butter a terrine mold generously. To facilitate unmolding the cooked terrine, cut a piece of wax paper or parchment paper to fit into the bottom of the mold. Set the paper in place and brush the top with softened butter.

8 **Chilling and serving.** Cover the terrine tightly with plastic wrap to keep the surface from drying out. To firm it, refrigerate the terrine for at least 24 hours, but no longer than four days. An hour before serving, remove it from the refrigerator. Just before serving, peel off the plastic wrap. Serve the loaf cut into thick slices *(right)*.

Two Strategies for Handling Brains

Because calf's or lamb's brains are unfamiliar meats to most cooks, they may seem unlikely ingredients for terrines. However, their combination of mild flavor and creamy texture yields terrines of singular delicacy and lightness. Depending upon the way you prepare brains, you can achieve either a perfect smoothness *(top demonstration; recipe, page 102)* or a chunky but still-velvety consistency *(bottom demonstration; recipe, page 103)*. Calf's and lamb's brains are used interchangeably, although those of a calf are about twice as large. Because brains are highly perishable, only specialty butchers and large supermarkets sell them—and then sometimes only when ordered in advance. They should be cooked at once; brains cannot be kept refrigerated for more than 24 hours—and will become spongy in texture if frozen.

Before they are cooked, brains must be freed of the thin membrane that surrounds them and then soaked to remove all blood. To whiten the meat, acidulate the soaking water by adding 1 tablespoon [15 ml.] of vinegar to each quart [1 liter] of cold water. For a smooth brain terrine, the brains are puréed raw. For a coarser texture, the brains are left intact, parboiled to firm them, braised with flavorings and cut into cubes.

After they are puréed or cubed, the brains must be bound with eggs. Other ingredients can then be added to furnish counterpoints of flavor and texture. Here, cubes of precooked corned tongue and chopped scallions are added to the puréed brains; chopped pistachios speckle the cubed-brain terrine.

Brain terrines may be unmolded and served hot—with a meat velouté or a tomato sauce *(recipes, pages 165 and 166)*—or chilled and served cold. Tightly covered with foil or plastic wrap, the cooked terrines can be safely stored in the refrigerator for about four days.

A Creamy Amalgam Flecked with Color

1 **Peeling.** Immerse the brains in a bowl of cold water for a few minutes to loosen their thin outer membrane. Peel it away, working between the ridges and dipping the brains in the water occasionally. To remove blood, soak the brains for one hour in several changes of acidulated water.

2 **Puréeing.** Purée the brains with eggs and chopped garlic in a processo as here, or press them through a food mill and stir in eggs and garlic. Seasor with salt, white pepper and nutmeg. Make a paste of bread crumbs and he milk, and add it to the purée with a knob of butter. Purée again.

A Cake Marbled with Herbs and Pistachios

1 **Blanching the brains.** Peel and soak the brains *(Step 1, top)*. Fill a saucepan with enough water to cover the brains. Add salt and vinegar and bring the water to a boil. Reduce the heat and gently lower the brains into the pan. Simmer them for five minutes, then drain them on a towel.

2 **Preparing a braise.** With your hands, gently separate the brains' two lobes. Heat oil in a skillet over low heat; sauté finely chopped onion, parsley and chives in the oil for about fiv minutes without browning them. Add the brains. Pour in white wine and simme until it evaporates—about 10 minutes.

3 **Cooking.** Place the purée in a bowl, add cubed cooked tongue and finely chopped scallions. Stir well. Poach a sample (page 29, Step 4) to test the seasoning. Pour the mixture into a buttered mold. Cover the terrine and cook it in a water bath (page 20) in a 325° F. [160° C.] oven.

4 **Unmolding.** As soon as the terrine is firm to the touch—after about 45 minutes—remove it from the oven. Let it cool slightly. Loosen the terrine by running a knife blade around the inside of the mold. Invert a serving plate over the terrine; reverse plate and mold together and lift off the mold.

5 **Serving the terrine.** Let the unmolded terrine cool completely, then cover it tightly with plastic wrap. Refrigerate the terrine for at least three hours, but remove it from the refrigerator about half an hour before serving it. Slice the terrine and, if you like, garnish it with black olives.

3 **Cutting up the brains.** In a large bowl, lightly beat eggs. With a slotted spoon, remove the brains from the skillet; reserve the braising mixture and taste it for seasoning. With a sharp knife, cut the brains into ¾-inch [2-cm.] cubes. Blanch pistachios (page 5, Step 12); coarsely chop them.

4 **Assembling the terrine.** Butter a terrine mold or, as here, a soufflé dish. Add the brains, pistachios and the contents of the skillet to the eggs in the bowl and mix gently. Pour the mixture into the mold. Set the terrine on a rack in a water bath (page 20, Step 5) and cook it in a preheated 325° F. [160° C.] oven.

5 **Serving.** When the terrine has set— after about 55 minutes—remove it from the oven. Let it cool slightly. Unmold it onto a serving board or plate (Step 4, top). If you like, garnish the terrine with lettuce; serve it in wedges, like a cake.

A Boned Bird Packed with Forcemeat

Surprisingly, perhaps, it is easy to bone poultry, or game birds such as pheasant, without splitting the skin. The skin then becomes a capacious pouch that can be stuffed with forcemeat and neatly contained within a terrine mold. If you use a goose or, as here, a duck, its fat will melt during cooking, moistening and flavoring the forcemeat.

The bones are removed through the neck opening. To do this, scrape around the bones with a small, very sharp knife and roll back the surrounding flesh and skin—turning the bird inside out. The exposed flesh can be left in place or removed to be added to the forcemeat. You then turn the skin right side out again and stuff the pouch.

In this demonstration, the forcemeat is made with the chopped flesh of the bird as well as with pork and fatback. The duck liver is included and its richness supplemented by chicken livers (recipe, page 112). For a compact shape, cook the stuffed bird in an oval terrine mold that holds it tightly.

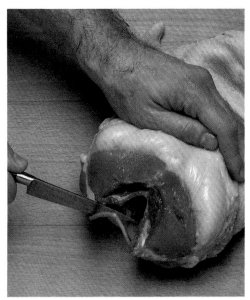

1 **Freeing the wishbone.** Remove all loose globs of fat from the bird. Cut off each wing tip at the first joint. Pull back the skin from the neck and shoulders. With a small, sharp knife, cut around both sides of the wishbone to free it from the breastbone. Snap the wishbone free from the shoulder joint.

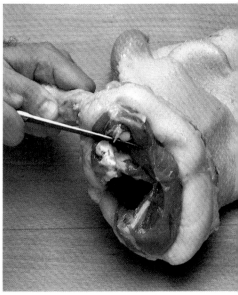

2 **Severing the wing bones.** Pull back one wing so that it comes away from the collarbone and shoulder blade. With the tip of the knife, cut through the strong sinews that connect the wing bone to these other bones. Free the other wing bone of the bird in the same way

6 **Removing the carcass.** Bend the leg away from the bird to pop the ball out of its socket. Free the leg bones in the same way you freed the wing bones (Step 4). Separating the rest of the flesh from the carcass, cut off the carcass at the tail (above). Remove any small bones that remain embedded in the flesh.

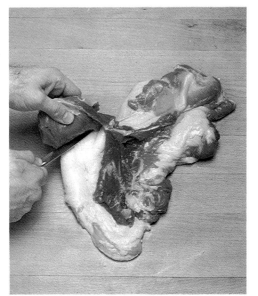

7 **Removing flesh.** Cut through the connective tissue between the flesh and the skin's fatty lining, lifting away the freed flesh. Turn over the pouch and cut away the flesh from the underside. If the bird is fatty, cut away as many layers of fat as possible without piercing the skin. Starting at the neck end, turn the pouch skin side out.

8 **Stuffing the skin.** Chop the duck flesh, lean pork, fatback, chicken livers and the duck's own liver (page 8). Mix the meats thoroughly with brandy, spices, eggs, salt and pepper. Fill the pouch with this forcemeat (above), then fold the neck flap over the opening. Place the stuffed bird in a terrine mold that holds it tightly.

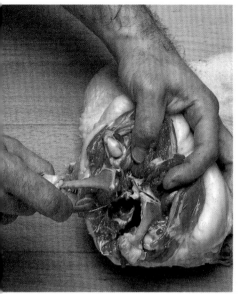 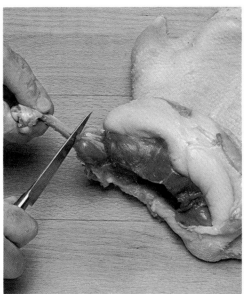 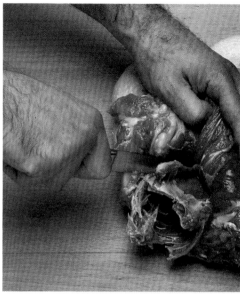

3 **Freeing the collarbones.** Locate the collarbones with your fingers. Scrape the flesh from the bones with the knife. Snap each collarbone away from the breastbone. Scrape the flesh from the shoulder blade, which is attached to the other end of each collarbone; then remove the collarbones and shoulder blade together.

4 **Boning the wings.** Holding the wing bone by the joint exposed in Step 2, cut the flesh away from the top of the bone and scrape the remaining flesh from the bone with the knife. The bone will gradually come out of its pocket of skin and flesh. Remove the bone from the other wing.

5 **Exposing the carcass.** Pull back the flesh to reveal the top of the rib cage. With your finger tips, separate the flesh from the breastbone and ribs. Use the knife tip to free flesh that does not come away easily. Work on one side, then on the other, turning the bird over to scrape the flesh away from the back.

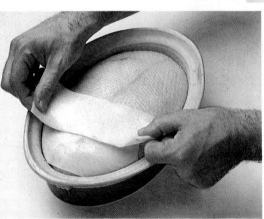 

9 **Cooking and serving.** To keep the top moist, lay bards over the bird *(above)*. Cover the mold with foil or a lid, and cook in a water bath in a 350° F. [180° C.] oven until the tip of a skewer inserted into the center feels hot or the terrine reaches an internal temperature of 160° F. [70° C.]—one and one half to three hours. Weight the terrine *(page 21)*, cool it and chill it overnight. Remove the weights, but keep it refrigerated for at least 24 hours before serving *(right)*.

2
Vegetable Terrines
Freshness and Color from the Garden

he final layer of chicken mousseline
or a terrine is carefully smoothed over
eat rows of broccoli florets. The
roccoli surmounts layers of carrot strips,
reen beans, halved zucchini, sliced
rtichoke bottoms and halved morels,
ach separated by equal portions of
ousseline (pages 38-39). In the even
eat of a water bath, the mousseline
ill set to a firm cream, binding the
egetables in place.

Fresh vegetables yield terrines that are beguilingly delicate and color-ful. As preparation for this role, vegetables are individually cooked—usually by boiling or by sautéing in butter—to tenderize them and re-move any excess moisture. They then are bound with eggs or mousseline, and the assembly is finished in a water bath, which serves mainly to set the binding agents.

Vegetable terrines offer endless opportunities for imaginative combi-nations of flavors, textures, shapes and colors. Almost any sort of vegeta-ble can be used, from mild mushrooms and celeriac to assertive fennel and Swiss chard. Because they are treated so simply, the vegetables should be the most perfect of specimens—the artichokes and beans crisp and bright-colored, the peas and peppers plump and ripe, the carrots and broccoli young and firm.

A terrine can be composed from only two or three vegetables, or from a greater number. Depending on the vegetables you choose and the ef-fects you want to create, you can purée them or chop them, cut them into even-sized pieces or leave small ones intact. The modes of assemblage are even more diverse. For example, a random mixing of six or seven vegeta-bles produces an attractive complexity of tastes and textures; each slice of the cooked terrine will reveal a mosaic of shapes and colors (pages 36-37). For a more formal terrine, vegetables of contrasting colors may be patterned in alternating layers with a mousseline that has been tinted to different hues. To increase the drama of the presentation, a multicolored assembly of vegetables and mousseline can be concealed within a shiny casing of vine leaves; when cut into slices, the terrine reveals the delight-ful surprise of its bright interior (pages 40-41).

Vegetable terrines are generally chilled and then brought almost to room temperature before being served—usually as a first course or as an addition to a buffet. They can be garnished with a colorful sauce that is piquant enough to offset, but not overshadow, their delicate flavors—green mayonnaise, perhaps, or a bright tomato vinaigrette (recipes, pages 164 and 165).

Terrines based on vegetables do not improve with keeping; for great-est enjoyment of their fresh ingredients, plan to serve them on the day after they are made.

A Kaleidoscopic Vegetable Loaf

Distributing whole vegetable pieces randomly throughout a vegetable purée produces a terrine that will display a different mosaic pattern in every slice. Eggs bind the vegetables and purée together so that they become a compact loaf when cooked in a water bath *(page 20)*. At the same time, bread crumbs serve to lighten the mixture and absorb any moisture released by the vegetables.

The terrine shown here *(recipe, page 124)* is based on a green purée of sorrel and chopped spinach, fortified with a purée of cooked dried beans. The starchy beans give extra body and smoothness to the loaf. Textural contrast is provided by adding diced carrots, cut green beans, and the mixture of sautéed mushrooms, onion and parsley known as a *duxelles*. Elbow macaroni furnishes unexpected highlights against the dark background of the purées.

Virtually any vegetable can be included in simple terrines of this type, although strong-flavored varieties such as cabbage or rutabaga would tend to overwhelm the other ingredients unless used sparingly. Because the gentle heat of the water bath serves only to set the eggs, the terrine's vegetable elements must all be precooked to make them tender and develop their flavors. Soft, moist vegetables—sorrel, mushrooms and leeks, for example—need to be sautéed in butter to drive off excess water. Spinach, romaine or Swiss chard leaves need to be parboiled, squeezed dry and chopped. Firm vegetables such as carrots, green beans or snow peas can be just parboiled or, for a sweeter effect, parboiled and then tossed in butter.

After a vegetable terrine is cooked, it is cooled, covered, and chilled thoroughly—for at least 12 hours—to allow its flavors to merge and mellow. However, before serving, the terrine should be allowed to warm to room temperature so that its taste will not be muted by cold.

1 **Puréeing beans.** Soak dried navy beans overnight. Bring to a boil in three times their volume of fresh water. Skim; add a carrot, clove-studded onion and bouquet garni. Cover, and simmer until tender—about two hours. Discard the aromatics, drain the beans and purée them through a food mill.

2 **Making a duxelles.** Sauté finely chopped onion in butter over low heat for 10 minutes, until soft but not brown. Finely chop mushrooms and parsley; add the mushrooms to the onion and increase the heat. Stir until the mushrooms exude no more liquid. Add the parsley, lemon juice, salt and pepper

5 **Mixing bread and garlic.** Pound peeled garlic cloves to a paste in a mortar. Remove the crusts from stale white bread and soak it briefly in hot water. Squeeze the bread dry and mix it well with the garlic in the mortar.

6 **Combining ingredients.** Put the bean purée into a bowl together with the *duxelles*, carrots, green beans, macaroni, the bread-and-garlic paste, softened butter and eggs. Add the spinach, sorrel and dried herbs—here savory, marjoram and thyme. Mix the ingredients and season with salt and cayenne pepper.

3 **Preparing vegetables.** Strip the stems off sorrel and shred the leaves; remove the stems of spinach. Peel carrots, slice them into strips and cut the strips into dice. Top and tail green beans and cut them into 1-inch [2½-cm.] lengths. Blanch, refresh, squeeze and chop the spinach (page 20, Step 1). Cook the sorrel in butter—do not use an aluminum or iron pan, since sorrel reacts chemically with these metals. Stir occasionally, until the sorrel is reduced to a purée—about 10 minutes.

4 **Parboiling carrots and beans.** In a large pan of boiling salted water, cook the carrots for about 10 minutes, until just tender. Drain the carrots (left). Bring the water to a boil again and cook the green beans for five to eight minutes, or until still slightly crisp. Remove and drain the beans (right). If necessary, add water to fill the pan. Add salt and a dash of oil and bring the water to a boil. Stir in elbow macaroni and cook for about seven minutes—until tender but firm. Drain the macaroni.

7 **Filling the mold.** Pack the vegetable mixture into a buttered terrine mold. Tap the mold on a cloth-covered surface to settle the mixture. Cover the terrine with foil or a lid, and cook it in a water bath (page 20) in a 350° F. [180° C.] oven for one and a half hours. Cool under weights (page 21) for two hours. Remove the weights and chill overnight.

8 **Serving the terrine.** Remove the terrine from the refrigerator and allow it to warm to room temperature for about one hour. Serve the terrine in slices. Accompany it, if you like, with green mayonnaise or a tomato vinaigrette (recipes, pages 164 and 165).

A Rainbow of Colors in Formal Array

A highly decorative terrine may be constructed by embedding vegetables of varied colors and shapes in a creamy chicken mousseline. The vegetables can be cut into large pieces and arranged in layers—as shown here—to produce a pattern that is repeated in every slice. Or, for a more informal presentation, the vegetables can be diced and mixed randomly into the mousseline.

Choose vegetables that will stand out in bold relief against the pale mousseline—the terrine in this demonstration includes zucchini, green beans, carrots, broccoli, artichoke bottoms and morels *(recipe, page 125)*. To protect the fragile mousseline, which tends to separate if it gets too warm, chill the cooked vegetables before assembling the terrine.

For additional color, the mousseline itself can be tinted: Powdered saffron turns it yellow, puréed tomatoes turn it pink, and chopped watercress turns it green. If you like, tint some mousseline and leave the rest plain, then alternate the mousselines in the terrine.

1 **Preparing vegetables.** Soak dried morels in warm water for 30 minutes to soften them. Trim their stem tips and slice each morel lengthwise. Cut off the ends of small zucchini and halve them lengthwise. Top and tail green beans. Peel carrots and cut them into strips. Break broccoli into florets and cut off the stems. Parboil each fresh vegetable separately until just tender—about three minutes for the zucchini and broccoli, five minutes for the beans, 10 minutes for the carrots. Drain and chill the vegetables.

5 **Starting the layers.** Butter a long, rectangular terrine mold. Trim wax paper to fit the bottom of the mold. Press the paper into place and butter the top. Spoon all of the green mousseline from the mortar into the mold. Arrange the carrot strips on the mousseline. Do not push the vegetables down too far; the layers should remain distinct.

6 **Adding layers.** Cover the carrots with a thin layer of white mousseline and lay the halved zucchini on top of it, running lengthwise. Cover the zucchini with a thin, smooth layer of mousseline and place the morel halves on top of it. Continue filling the terrine with alternate layers of mousseline and the remaining vegetables.

7 **Cooking.** When the last layer of vegetables—here, the broccoli florets—has been placed in the mold, complete the terrine by spooning in a final layer of mousseline. Cover the terrine with buttered foil or a lid. Cook the terrine in a water bath *(page 20)* in a preheated 300° F. [150° C.] oven until firm—30 to 45 minutes.

2 **Trimming artichokes.** Break off the stems of artichokes. Snap off the tough outer leaves. Using a stainless-steel knife, cut off the top half of each artichoke and discard it. Pare away the tough green exterior of the artichoke bottom. Moisten the artichoke bottom with lemon juice to prevent discoloration.

3 **Removing the chokes.** Bring a pan of lightly salted water to a boil. Add the artichoke bottoms and cook them until tender—15 to 35 minutes, depending on size. Drain them, upside down, on a paper towel. Scoop out the fibrous chokes and cut the bottoms into ½-inch [1-cm.] slices. Chill.

4 **Tinting mousseline.** Prepare a mousseline from chicken or a delicately flavored fish *(pages 10-11).* Blanch watercress and squeeze it dry *(page 15).* Chop it fine and pound it to a paste in a mortar. Spoon in about one seventh of the mousseline and stir until it is green-flecked. Chill all the mousseline.

3 **Serving.** Let the terrine cool, then chill it overnight. Run a knife around the inside of the mold, invert the terrine onto a plate and remove the wax paper. Gently turn the terrine right side up. Slice the terrine *(above),* and serve it with tomato vinaigrette *(page 15)* garnished with herbs such as mustard cress *(right).*

A Leaf-encased Surprise

A glossy casing of vine leaves enhances the dramatic effect of a layered vegetable terrine. In each slice, the light colors of the terrine's interior are framed with dark leaves whose tartness parries pleasantly with the delicate flavors of mousseline and fresh vegetables.

As with any vegetable terrine, the vegetables should be chosen for color, flavor and textural variety. In this demonstration, the terrine includes parboiled peas, green beans, zucchini and carrots, and sweet red peppers that have been broiled and peeled *(recipe, page 127)*. Among other appropriate candidates are snow peas, corn kernels and broccoli.

Any meat or fish mousseline *(pages 10-11)* can be used to bind the vegetables. Here, they are held together by an especially light variation of mousseline in which bland peanut oil takes the place of the heavy cream conventionally used. Because it is so delicate, this mousseline must be kept chilled until it is ready for use, and the other terrine ingredients must also be chilled before assembly.

Fresh vine leaves bring a unique gloss to the casing and need only be parboiled briefly to soften them before they are fitted into the terrine mold. When fresh vine leaves are unavailable, preserved leaves—obtainable from stores that sell gourmet and Middle Eastern foods—can be used instead if thoroughly rinsed to attenuate their briny taste. Other types of leaves—for example, Swiss chard, romaine and spinach—may also be substituted; these should be trimmed of stems and thick ribs before they are used.

1 **Preparing vegetables.** Shell peas. Top and tail green beans. Peel small carrots. Cut off the ends of zucchini. Parboil each vegetable separately and refresh it in ice water to stop the cooking. The carrots will need about 10 minutes of cooking, the green beans and zucchini about five minutes, and the peas from two to 10, depending on age. Broil sweet red peppers, turning them frequently, for seven or eight minutes to char their skins. Peel off their loosened skins, then halve, derib and slice the peppers. Cut the zucchini into strips. Refrigerate all of the vegetables.

5 **Layering ingredients.** Spread a layer of the chilled mousseline over the bottom of the mold *(left)*. Continue filling the terrine, alternating layers of vegetables and mousseline and arranging the vegetables to create an attractive pattern. Here, peppers and beans are used for the first vegetable layer *(right)*, carrots and peas for the second layer and zucchini and peppers for the third. Finish with a layer of mousseline. Cover the top with vine leaves, fold in the overhanging leaves and cover with a piece of buttered foil or a lid.

2 **Dicing ham.** Place a large mixing bowl and either the container and the blade of a food processor or the container of a blender in the freezer to chill. Separate eggs, reserving the whites in a small bowl. Cut sliced cooked ham into dice. Refrigerate the ham.

3 **Making the mousseline.** Put the cold ham in the chilled food processor or blender container; add lemon juice, salt and pepper. Grind the mixture briefly, then blend in egg whites. Blend in peanut oil *(above)*, adding only a little at a time. Working quickly, use a spatula to scrape the mousseline into the chilled mixing bowl. Refrigerate.

4 **Lining the mold.** Prepare vine leaves—parboil fresh leaves for five minutes or rinse preserved ones in hot running water—and spread them on paper towels. Pat the leaves dry and let them cool to room temperature. Butter a terrine mold and line its sides with the leaves, dull surfaces inward. Then line the bottom of the terrine with leaves.

6 **Cooking and serving.** Cook the terrine in a water bath *(page 20)* in a 350° F. [180° C.] oven until firm—about 30 minutes. Cool the terrine, then chill it overnight. About an hour before serving time, unmold the terrine onto a serving plate and, if you like, garnish the top with strips of avocado. Serve the terrine in slices, accompanied by a vinaigrette *(recipe, page 165)* enriched with puréed tomato or avocado.

3
Fish Terrines
Delicate Flavors from River and Sea

A fish terrine, with its silky texture and sophisticated nuances of taste, is a particularly felicitous dish to precede main courses based on the robust flavors of meat or game. Such a terrine can be made with a wide variety of fish and shellfish. Its delicacy depends chiefly on the freshness of the ingredients. Fish should have bright eyes, shining skin and clear red gills. Shrimp and scallops should smell fresh and sweet, and other shellfish should be alive when purchased.

All of the terrines in this chapter begin with a forcemeat based on raw fish, which breaks down easily into a purée. The puréed fish is bound with eggs and enhanced with diverse ingredients: cream for smooth texture, herbs and spices for flavor, and dissolved saffron for color. When whole eggs are the binding agent, the result is a rich mousse. Although separating the eggs and beating the whites before adding them will lighten the mousse, the most delicate terrine filling of all—a mousseline—relies on egg whites alone to bind it.

Some fish terrines are composed mainly of forcemeat, but even this fundamental approach can be elegant. On pages 44-45, for example, a salmon forcemeat sandwiches an equally creamy mixture of puréed peas to produce a striking assemblage in pastel shades of orange and green. Combining morsels of fish and shellfish with forcemeat creates an interplay of texture as well as color and flavor: In the terrine on pages 46-47, shrimp, scallops and mussels are built up in alternate layers with a light fish forcemeat, yielding pleasingly patterned slices when the cooked terrine is served. Whole fillets of fish can also play a part; they are flexible enough to wrap around a forcemeat, or to curl into a tube that can be filled and surrounded with forcemeats of different hues *(pages 48-51)*.

Fish terrines are generally cooked in the gentle heat of a water bath *(page 20)*. Because fish is innately tender, an hour is often time enough to firm the mixture and cook it through. Fish terrines can be served directly from their containers or unmolded, and are delicious hot—presented with fish velouté or white butter sauce *(recipes, pages 165 and 166)*. When chilled before serving, these terrines may be complemented with tartar sauce, or a jellied mousse flavored with watercress or tomato. For a dazzling effect, an unmolded terrine can be glazed with aspic. Fish terrines do not keep well: Serve them within two or three days.

A whiting-based mousseline, flavored with saffron and pistachios, is spooned into a terrine mold lined with fillets of sole. More fillets will be laid on top, and the overhanging fillets folded over to encircle the mousseline. Once it is cooked and unmolded, this terrine *(pages 48-50)* will be glazed with aspic.

Juxtaposing Mousses of Different Hues

Any smooth raw-fish or shellfish purée bound with whole eggs and enriched with cream makes a simple and delicate terrine. During cooking, the eggs set and transform the mixture into a velvety mousse that is firm enough to slice.

If this fish mixture is juxtaposed with another mousse based on a green vegetable such as spinach, watercress or peas, the result will be a lively interplay of flavors and colors. In this demonstration, a layer of pea mousse, flecked with sorrel, chives and parsley, is sandwiched between two layers of salmon mousse (recipe, page 128); when the cooked terrine is sliced for serving, broad bands of pale orange and green are revealed.

Salmon's highly esteemed flesh lends the terrine an exquisite flavor. But any fish, even a less luxurious variety such as whiting, is a fitting choice for a mousse. Also appropriate are shellfish, including shrimp, scallops, crabs and lobsters.

After the seafood is shelled or the fish filleted and skinned (Steps 1 and 2), it can be pounded to smoothness with a mortar and pestle. However, a food processor lightens the work of turning it into a purée. Before puréeing vegetables for the second mousse, you must precook them to make them tender. Then you can pass them through a food mill or purée them in a processor; in either case, the purée should be sieved to make it perfectly smooth.

For layering, the two mousses should be of approximately the same consistency. To achieve this, mix each purée with the same number of eggs—here, three were used to bind each mixture—and a spoonful or two of cream. If one mixture is heavier, lighten it with a little extra cream to prevent it from sinking too deeply into the other mousse. When you have assembled the layers, cook the terrine in a water bath in the oven (page 20).

The terrine may be served hot, either as a first course or as a light main dish, accompanied by a fish velouté (recipe, page 165). If the terrine is to be served cold, let it cool, cover it, and refrigerate it overnight. Garnish the chilled terrine with a green mayonnaise or tartar sauce (page 14), if you like.

1 **Filleting the salmon.** Lay the salmon—here, a section cut from the tail end—on a board. Holding the fish steady, cut along the back to expose the backbone. With the knife, scrape the exposed bone to detach the upper fillet; cut it free at the tail. To free the other fillet, scrape underneath the backbone.

2 **Skinning fillets.** Lay a fillet skin side down. At the tail end, cut away about ½ inch [1 cm.] of flesh, leaving behind a small flap of skin. Holding the flap, insert the knife beneath the flesh at the tail and cut away from yourself until the fillet is free. Skin the other fillet.

5 **Adding eggs and cream.** Wash, dry and chop sorrel, parsley and chives. Add the herbs to the pea purée. Add eggs, cream, salt and pepper. With a wooden spoon, beat the ingredients together until they are amalgamated. Or blend the mixture in the processor.

6 **Layering the terrine.** Butter a mold and pour in half of the salmon mousse. Add the pea mousse, then the remaining salmon mixture. Smooth the surface with a spatula. To keep the surface moist, cover the mousse with buttered parchment or wax paper. Place the mold on a rack in a large pan. Add boiling water to cover the mold by two thirds.

Making a salmon mousse. Cut the salmon into 1-inch [2½-cm.] squares and purée them in a food processor, as here; or coarsely chop the salmon and pound it in a mortar. Add eggs, paprika, salt, pepper and cream to the purée; blend the mixture in the processor or beat the ingredients together in a large bowl.

Puréeing the peas. Shell peas and drop them into a large pan of boiling salted water. Boil them over high heat until tender two to 10 minutes, depending on their age. Drain the peas colander and then refresh them with cold water to stop cooking. Press the peas through a food mill fitted with a disk *(above, left)*, or purée them in a food processor. To remove any skins, spoon the purée into a sieve, then push the purée through the sieve, using a wooden pestle *(right)*.

Cooking and serving. Cook the terrine in the water bath in a 350° F. [180° C.] oven for about one hour, or until its surface is firm and it has shrunk slightly from the sides of the mold. To serve it cold, peel off the buttered paper, let the terrine cool, cover it with plastic wrap and refrigerate it overnight. Unmold the terrine and serve it in slices—accompanied, if you like, with a green mayonnaise *(recipe, page 164)*.

Nuggets of Shellfish in a Tender Mousse

Intermingling small, solid pieces of sea-food with a smooth fish mousse will endow a terrine with a pleasing contrast of textures. The elements can be mixed together randomly or, as here, assembled in alternating layers of mousse and solid morsels—arranged lengthwise to make a uniform design *(recipe, page 130)*. To ensure a moist richness and to form a firm loaf, the mold is lined with caul *(page 12)* and the assembly begins and ends with a layer of mousse.

The mousse used in this demonstration is based on puréed sole, enriched with a bread paste and cream. For a particularly tender, airy mousse, the eggs are separated and the whites are whisked before being folded in.

Any firm-textured fish can replace the sole. And the solid morsels can include any fish or shellfish, filleted or shelled and—if necessary—cut into pieces. Excess liquid would make the mousse too moist, so the fish or shellfish morsels should be precooked and well drained before they are added to the terrine.

1 Preparing shrimp. Bring fish stock or water flavored lightly with lemon juice and salt to a boil. Add raw shrimp and simmer uncovered just until they turn pink—one to two minutes. Drain the shrimp and peel off their shells. Use a small knife to cut along the back of each shrimp, then pull out and discard the intestinal veins. Chill the shrimp.

2 Cleaning mussels. To make sure that mussels are alive, slide closed she laterally (they should not move) and tap slightly open shells against a bow (they should shut). Discard any dead specimens. Soak the remaining musse in ice water for 10 minutes to refresh them, then scrub the shells with a brus and pull off the ropy beards *(above)*.

6 Preparing forcemeat. Separate eggs; add the yolks to the fish purée and reserve the whites. Chop fresh herbs fine—chives are used here—and add them to the purée. With a wooden spoon, beat the mixture until it is a smooth paste. Add brandy, salt, pepper and spices; stir well.

7 Adding bread. Remove the crust from a slice of firm-textured white bread and immerse the bread in milk. Squeeze the bread dry. Beat the bread with softened butter and blend the resulting paste into the forcemeat mixture. Chill the mixture for one hour, then beat in cream.

8 Folding in egg whites. Beat the egg whites until they form soft peaks. Using a rubber spatula, gently fold about one quarter of the whites into the forcemeat mixture to lighten it. Then fold in the remaining whites. Chill the mousse for 30 minutes.

3 **Steaming mussels.** In a large pot, melt a little butter over high heat. Add the cleaned mussels, cover, and cook for about five minutes, shaking the pan periodically. When the mussels open, drain them. Discard any that have failed to open. Remove the rest from their shells. Chill the mussels.

4 **Sautéing scallops.** Stirring constantly, sauté fresh scallops and finely chopped shallots in butter for about two minutes. Add warmed brandy *(above)*. Then tilt the pan and hold a long match to the liquid to ignite the brandy. When the flames die, drain the scallops. Chill them.

5 **Puréeing fish.** Cut skinned fish fillets—in this case, sole—into small pieces. Purée the fish in a food processor or pound it, using a mortar and pestle. To make the purée smooth, rub it through a drum sieve, a little at a time, using a plastic scraper.

9 **Assembling the terrine.** Butter a terrine mold and line it with pieces of prepared caul, letting the edges overhang. Spread a ½-inch [1-cm.] layer of the chilled fish mousse over the bottom of the mold. Add a layer of shellfish, arranged in neat rows. Continue to fill the mold with alternating layers of mousse and shellfish, finishing with a layer of mousse. Cover the surface with the overhanging caul. Then cover the mold with foil or with a lid.

10 **Cooking and serving.** Set the mold on a rack in a water bath *(page 20)*. Cook the terrine in a preheated 350° F. [180° C.] oven for about one hour, or until the surface feels firm. Let the terrine cool, then cover it with foil or plastic wrap and refrigerate it overnight. To serve, cut it into slices about ½ inch [1 cm.] thick, transferring each slice to a plate with a spatula. Accompany the terrine, if desired, with chilled watercress mousse *(page 15)*.

A Roulade of Fillets

Slender, flexible fish fillets can be combined with delicate mousselines *(pages 10-11)* in a variety of striking and ingenious presentations. An overlapping row of fillets, for example, can enfold a mousseline inside a rectangular mold; in this demonstration and on page 50, sole fillets encase a mousseline that has been tinged with saffron and studded with pistachios.

Assembled in a different way, the same basic components can create another intriguing geometrical pattern: The fillets can be curled around a core of watercress-flavored mousseline and this cylinder embedded in saffron-colored mousseline *(page 51)*. When sliced, the terrine reveals a circular core of green ringed with white, inside a golden square.

In assemblies of this type, both the fillets and the forcemeat offer opportunities for imaginative variation. Firm-textured fillets of all sorts are suitable, and instead of limiting your choice to one type of fish, you can combine fillets of two different colors. Lining a mold with alternating fillets of sea trout and salmon, for

example, will produce pale orange and white bands around the filling.

The mousseline filling can be transformed—in color, texture and flavor—by the addition of such ingredients as chopped fresh herbs, tiny cubes of parboiled crayfish or shrimp, blanched and chopped spinach or puréed tomatoes. You can even replace the mousseline itself with another mixture; the green core of the terrine on page 51, for example, could be made with puréed romaine lettuce bound with egg yolk and bread crumbs.

The manner of presentation depends on the design of the assemblage. The terrine with a circular core has a plain exterior; its visual impact lies in its cross-section, and it can be served directly from the mold. But the mousseline contained in a lining of fillets will be most impressive if it is unmolded to display the contours of the fish that surrounds it. An aspic glaze will enhance its appearance; for extra flavor, stir a splash of fortified wine—Madeira or dry sherry, for example—into the tepid aspic before it sets.

1 **Skinning sole.** Lay the sole dark side uppermost. Slit the skin where the [tail] joins the body and pry up a small flap of skin. Hold the tail down firmly with cloth. Pull the skin toward the head. When you reach the jaws, turn the fish over. Hold the head and continue pulling the skin until you reach the tail. Cut off the tail and the attached skin.

5 **Lining the mold.** Butter a long, narrow mold—a 5-cup [1 ¼-liter] terrine is shown. Reserve the smallest fillets; lay the rest crosswise in the mold, positioning them membrane side up, overlapping each other slightly, with their tips hanging over the rim. Press the fillets gently against the mold so that they take on its shape. Chill the mold.

6 **Preparing the filling.** Make 2 pounds [1 kg.] of fish mousseline *(recipe, page 164)*—here, whiting is used. Peel ⅓ cup [75 ml.] of pistachios and coarsely chop them. Dissolve ½ teaspoon [2 ml.] of powdered saffron in a little hot water, and add it to the mousseline. Add the nuts and mix well.

7 **Filling the mold.** Poach a spoonful of the mousseline in simmering water for a minute or so to firm it; cool and taste it for seasoning. Pack the mousseline in the mold. Smooth the surface with a spatula. To settle the contents, tap the mold gently on a folded towel. Cut the reserved fillets to fit across the top and lay them in the mold.

2 **Filleting the sole.** Using a very sharp knife with a flexible blade, cut through the exposed flesh of the fish from head to tail down the backbone. Starting at the head end, and keeping the knife almost flat against the ribs, cut the left-hand fillet free *(above)*. Remove the right-hand fillet. Turn the fish over and repeat the process.

3 **Trimming the fillets.** To remove any specks of blood from the fillets and ensure their whiteness, soak all of them—the fillets from three soles are used here—for about 15 minutes in a bowl of cold water. Drain them on a towel. With the blade of a wide knife, flatten the fillets slightly. On a board, trim each fillet of any fins or ragged edges.

4 **Scoring the fillets.** Position the sole fillets on the board with their thin membrane uppermost. During the cooking, the membrane will shrink; to prevent the flesh from becoming distorted, ease the tension of the membrane by making three or four shallow, diagonal incisions across the surface of each fillet.

8 **Cooking the terrine.** Fold the overhanging fillets over the top and cover the terrine with buttered wax or parchment paper. Set the mold on a rack in a water bath *(page 20)* and cook the terrine in a preheated 325° F. [160° C.] oven for about 50 minutes, or until the filling is firm and springy to the touch.

9 **Draining the juices.** Lift the terrine from its water bath and let it cool until tepid. Place a rack on top of the mold. Grasp the mold and rack together and invert both quickly over a tray to collect the juices. When the juices have drained, turn the mold and rack over.

10 **Unmolding the terrine.** Lift away the rack. Place a long serving platter over the mold and turn both over together. Lift away the mold. With paper towels, blot up any juices on the platter and clean the surface of the terrine. Cover the unmolded terrine with plastic wrap and place it in the refrigerator overnight. ▶

11 **Glazing with aspic.** Prepare fish aspic (pages 6-7). When it is tepid, add two or three spoonfuls of Madeira or sherry. Spoon a little aspic into a small bowl—preferably made of metal—and embed the bowl in ice. Stir the aspic until it turns syrupy. Spoon it quickly over the top and sides of the chilled terrine. The aspic will form a thin layer over the terrine and a lake of jelly around it.

12 **Completing the glaze.** Chill the terrine for about 10 minutes before adding another layer of syrupy aspic. Repeat th process several times. In another bowl, mix chopped parsley with enough aspic to make a thin paste; stir over ice until thick Spoon a strip of jellied parsley along the top of the terrine. Chill. Add two more coats of aspic, chilling after each addition

13 **Serving.** About half an hour before serving time, remove the terrine from the refrigerator. Garnish it, if you like, with a chiffonade of thinly sliced lettuce leaves. With a sharp knife, cut the terrine into ½-inch [1-cm.] slices; use a spatula to transfer the slices to individual plates. Serve some jelly with each slice.

Geometric Effects in Green and Yellow

1 **Making a filling.** Parboil the leaves from five bunches of watercress for one minute. Drain the leaves, refresh under cold water, squeeze them dry and chop them. Prepare fish mousseline and put about one fifth of it in a bowl. Stir in the watercress, an egg yolk and a handful of bread crumbs. Sieve the mixture and chill it.

2 **Lining the mold.** Beat saffron and chopped pistachios into the remaining mousseline *(page 48, Step 6)*. Place half of the mixture in a long, well-buttered mold. With the back of a spoon, make a trench the length of the mold. Prepare fillets *(pages 48-49, Steps 1 to 4)*; lay them crosswise, membrane side up and overlapping slightly, along the mold.

3 **Adding the filling.** Spoon the watercress filling along the center of the row of fillets to form a strip about 1 inch [2½ cm.] wide *(above)*. With a knife, smooth the filling to give it a rounded shape. Fold the ends of the last fillet that you laid in the terrine over the filling; then fold over the neighboring fillet.

4 **Cooking.** Fold over the fillets in turn; fill the mold with the remaining saffron mousseline. Cover with buttered paper; cook in a water bath at 325° F. [160° C.] for 50 minutes.

5 **Serving.** Leave the terrine until tepid; then drain *(page 49, Step 9)*. Cover and chill overnight. Slice the terrine and serve from the dish, with a tartar sauce—as here—or a green mayonnaise.

4

Pâtés
Golden Crusts of Pastry

Revealing bold layers of contrasting meats and forcemeat beneath its shell of hot-water crust, a halved goose pie is cut into serving slices. To make the pâté, a boned chicken, stuffed with a cooked beef tongue, was put into the cavity of a boned goose, and the spaces were filled with forcemeat (pages 56-57). Encased in pastry dough, the goose provides a firm structure to hold the filling together during its long cooking.

A wrapping of pastry transforms any terrine into a pâté—a stately, savory pie that invites decoration. The surfaces can be scored with the tines of a fork or adorned with cut-out dough shapes; alternatively, the pie can be baked in a patterned mold that will leave its impression in the dough. A glaze of egg will give a rich, golden color to the dough while it bakes into a crisp pastry that provides a delicious contrast of texture to the tender filling within.

Generally a pâté is constructed from raw dough and raw forcemeat. During baking, the forcemeat shrinks and the dough swells. To close the gaps between the pastry and its filling, melted aspic is poured in through holes in the pastry lid after the pâté cools. When it sets, the aspic unites the pastry with the filling and provides a third textural element.

Because neither pastry nor aspic stays at its best for long, a pâté should be served as soon as the aspic has set—ideally, the day after the pie is baked. Fish or vegetable fillings do not, in any event, profit from longer keeping. But because a meat filling will taste better if left to mature for three or four days after cooking, some pâté makers prepare the filling separately as a terrine, chill it until it reaches the peak of its flavor, then enclose it in dough for baking (pages 66-69).

The choice of dough for the case depends mainly on the flavor and texture desired, but also varies with the firmness of the filling: A moist filling tends to leak out of a fragile pastry. Hot-water crust—a very strong, dense dough made from flour and melted lard or butter (pages 54-55)—can be fashioned into a raised pie that will stand up by itself and contain even a very juicy forcemeat. Short-crust dough, made from flour, bits of chilled butter, and an egg for binding, is less strong, but it has a more delicate flavor and a flaky texture. If the filling is a soft mousseline or liver purée, short crust needs the support of a metal mold during baking (pages 58-60). But if the filling is firm, such dough can be wrapped around it to make a freestanding pâté (pages 62-63). Rough puff dough, made with a large proportion of butter and repeatedly folded for a light texture, is more tender and best reserved for enclosing a precooked forcemeat or for use as a decorative lid (pages 68-69). Puff pastry—the most delicate dough of all—should only be used to wrap precooked fillings or the lightest of raw forcemeats (pages 64-65).

Melted Fat for a Robust Dough

Hot-water crust—a simple dough made with fat melted in hot water—can be shaped around a mold to produce a free-standing case strong enough to hold even the moistest of fillings. Pliable when warm, the dough *(recipe, page 166)* is especially firm when cool, because the molten fat bonds so totally with the flour.

To make the dough, bring lard or butter and water to a boil and pour the mixture—while still hot—over the dry ingredients: The heat will burst some of the starch granules in the flour, turning it sticky; the moisture will activate the flour's gluten proteins, forming an elastic mesh. As a result, the dough will be claylike when ready for molding.

Any straight-sided jar or crock will serve as a mold. To prevent sticking, coat the mold with fat and flour. After the dough is shaped and cooled, use a cloth drenched with hot water to melt the fat so the mold will slide out. The crust is then ready to be filled—here, with layers of pork forcemeat and apple slices *(recipe, page 133)*—and baked.

1 **Melting fat with water.** Cut butter or, as here, lard into cubes and add them to cold water in a pan. Bring the water and fat to a boil over medium heat; immediately remove the pan from the heat. If some cubes are still solid, stir the contents of the pan so that all of the fat melts and the liquid becomes clear.

2 **Mixing the dough.** While the fat is melting, sift flour and salt into a large bowl. If you like, add a little sifted confectioners' sugar to sweeten the dough and to help it brown. Make a well in the middle of the dry ingredients. Pour the hot fat-and-water mixture into the well, stirring until the ingredients are thoroughly combined.

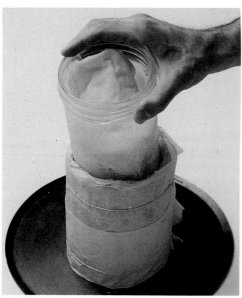

5 **Removing the mold.** Wrap several thicknesses of wax or parchment paper around the sides of the dough case and tie the paper with string. Refrigerate the case until it is firm—at least one hour. Stuff a cloth inside the jar and pour in some hot water. After a minute, lift the jar out of the case, twisting it gently upward.

6 **Filling the case.** Finely chop lean pork and fresh fatback; add a chopped onion, salt, pepper and nutmeg. Toss slices of peeled apple with lemon juice. Spoon alternate layers of forcemeat and apple into the case, beginning and ending with forcemeat. Pour in hard cider and shape the top of the filling into a dome.

7 **Sealing.** Roll the remaining dough to a thickness of ½ inch [1 cm.]. Brush the rim of the case with beaten egg. Set the lid in place and firmly press down the edges. Crimp the edges of the lid and the case to seal them. Glaze the lid with beaten egg.

3 **Cooling the dough.** When the dough has cooled enough to handle, gather it into a ball with your hands. Cover the bowl with a cloth. Leave the dough until it feels firm but can still be molded into shape—about 30 minutes.

4 **Molding the dough.** Smear a tall, straight-sided jar with lard or butter, then dust it with flour. Set aside about one fifth of the dough for a lid. Place the rest on a greased baking sheet and shape it with your hands into a round. Flatten the middle of the round to a thickness of ½ inch [1 cm.]. Place the jar in the center and, with your hands, mold the dough around the sides of the jar *(left)*. Press the dough upward, keeping the thickness uniform, until you have a case of the height you want *(right)*; stop before you reach the rim of the jar. Pat the surface smooth. Trim the top edge.

8 **Decorating.** Cut a hole in the lid; decorate with dough scraps and glaze the lid again. Place a rolled cardboard tube in the hole; bake at 375° F. [190° C.] for one and a quarter hours, or until the internal temperature is 160° F. [70° C.].

9 **Serving.** Remove the paper and glaze the sides of the case. Bake for 15 minutes. Chill overnight. Pour in melted meat aspic *(pages 6-7)* and chill for three hours. Cut into wedges and serve.

Sumptuous Treats in a Sturdy Case

Because of its malleability, hot-water crust *(pages 54-55)* is the wrapper of choice for that Renaissance extravaganza—a whole boned bird stuffed with another bird *(recipe, page 134)*. The dough needs no rolling or trimming: It can be pressed a handful at a time directly onto the surface of the outermost bird and molded to retain the contours of the bird in the finished pâté. Furthermore, the bonding of flour and fat in hot-water crust makes the dough almost impermeable, enabling it to seal in the juices of the birds during the lengthy cooking.

Since any kind of small bird can be fitted inside a larger one, the possible combinations may be varied according to availability and taste. A quail or partridge, for instance, will slide neatly inside a roasting chicken or guinea hen; a pheasant or duck inside a turkey. In the demonstration at right, a roasting chicken is stuffed into a goose.

To give the pâté a firm and flavorsome core, the smaller bird may be stuffed with forcemeat or a piece of cooked meat such as the corned beef tongue shown here. The rich red color of beef tongue makes a striking contrast with the pale chicken meat and the darker goose meat; veal liver or ham could be substituted.

Forcemeat can be used to close any gaps between the solid meats, thereby unifying the layers of the assembly. As a finishing touch, the cooled pâté also can be enriched by pouring tepid gelatinous meat stock *(pages 6-7)* through the steam hole in the lid to fill the spaces between the outermost bird and the pastry crust. The stock will set to a firm, translucent aspic when the pâté is refrigerated to mellow overnight.

1 Preparing tongue. To remove excess salt, soak a corned beef tongue in cold water for an hour and then blanch it in fresh water for 15 minutes. Simmer the tongue in fresh water until tender—about three hours. Cool the tongue in the liquid. Then remove the bones at the base; peel off the skin and trim the tongue into a neat shape.

2 Marinating the birds. Bone a goose and a chicken through the neck opening, leaving them turned inside out *(pages 32-33, Steps 1-6)*. Place the birds on a tray with the breast meat facing upward. Sprinkle them with salt, pepper and dried herbs, and dribble brandy over them. Cover the birds and leave them to marinate.

6 Covering with dough. Prepare a hot-water crust dough *(recipe, page 166)* and let it cool just enough so that you can handle it. If you like, spread it out on a tray to cool it more quickly. Press large, flattened handfuls of dough over the back and sides of the goose, molding and sealing the dough into an even layer about ¾ inch [2 cm.] thick.

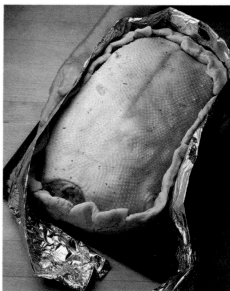

7 Protecting with foil. Turn the goose over and place it on a lightly oiled baking sheet. To help prevent the sides of the pâté from collapsing during cooking, wrap several thicknesses of foil around the sides. Tie string tightly around the foil to secure it.

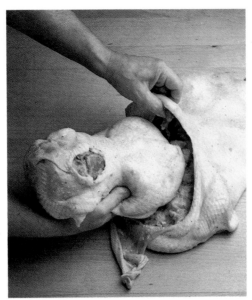

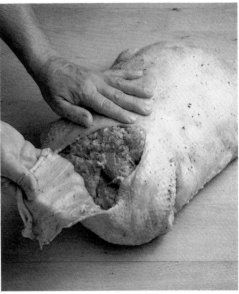

3 **Stuffing the chicken.** Prepare a basic forcemeat *(recipe, page 163).* Finely chop the livers, hearts and gizzards of both birds; add them to the forcemeat. Smear some forcemeat over the tongue. Turn the marinated birds skin side out; slide the tongue inside the chicken through the neck opening.

4 **Stuffing the goose.** Position the goose breast side up. Spread a layer of forcemeat inside the boned goose. Slip the chicken into the goose. Fill any remaining spaces around the chicken with the rest of the forcemeat.

5 **Closing the goose.** Smooth the outside of the goose with your hands to give it an even shape. Grasp the flap of skin at the goose's neck and lay it over the opening to cover the chicken. Refrigerate the stuffed assembly for about two hours to firm it.

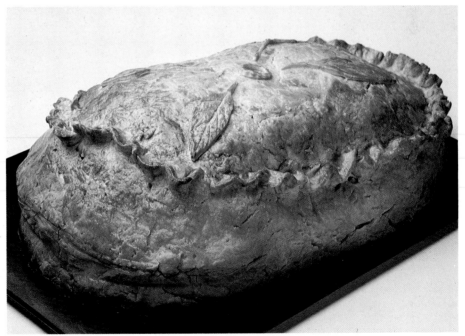

8 **Decorating.** Press dough onto the breast of the goose until the bird is entirely encased. Crimp the side edges to seal them. Glaze the lid with egg yolk beaten with water. Cut a hole in the lid for steam to escape. Set a ring of dough around the hole and decorate the lid with dough leaves. Glaze the ring and leaves.

9 **Baking.** Bake the pâté for 15 minutes in a 400° F. [200° C.] oven. Reduce the heat to 325° F. [160° C.] and bake for four hours. After 45 minutes, cover the pâté with foil to keep it from browning too fast. After three hours more, remove the foil and glaze the pâté with beaten egg so that it will brown. Cool the pâté, then chill it overnight. Serve it sliced *(page 52).*

PÂTÉS

The Shaping of a Short-Crust Mold

The simplest dough for a flaky pâté crust is a butter short crust enriched with eggs. The butter gives the pastry a good flavor and a crisp texture; the eggs strengthen the dough so that it forms a firm container for the forcemeat within.

Making the short-crust dough is easy: Flour is mixed with butter in a ratio of four parts flour to one part butter (recipe, page 167). To prevent the butter from becoming oily, which would result in crumbly pastry, be sure it is very cold and either cut it into the dough with two knives or a pastry blender, or rub it in rapidly with your finger tips. Bind the dough with eggs, adding just a little water if the dough is still too dry to cohere. To make the pastry sturdy and flexible, knead the dough briefly to develop its microscopic meshwork of gluten proteins.

Traditionally, pâtés made with short crust are baked in molds. The dough is rolled out into a large sheet and dropped into the mold in one piece to eliminate side and bottom seams that might allow leaking. Molds specifically designed for

pâtés—the rectangular one at right and the eye-shaped one shown on page 60, for example—are available where fine kitchen supplies are sold. All have removable sides so that the baked pâté can be unmolded easily. Lacking a mold, you can bake a pâté in a metal loaf pan lined with buttered parchment paper.

To nourish the forcemeat filling and prevent its juices from seeping into the pastry, line the dough with bards of fatback (page 12). Then add the filling—in this case, a fish mousseline layered with eel fillets (recipe, page 142). Because eels deteriorate quickly when killed, it is best to buy them live and dispatch them at the last minute (Step 4).

Top the filled mold with a dough lid and cut a hole in the lid to let steam escape. During baking, the filling will shrink, leaving a gap between the forcemeat and the crust. Once the pâté is cool, melted aspic can be poured through the hole to fill the gap. It will set to a translucent jelly that provides a delicious contrast to the filling and the crisp pastry.

1 **Making the dough.** Chill butter so that it is firm. Sift flour with salt into a large mixing bowl. Cut the butter into small cubes and add them to the bowl. Holding a table knife in each hand, cut the butter into the flour with a scissorlike action until the mixture resembles coarse bread crumbs.

5 **Filleting the eel.** Using cloths to grasp the flap and hold the body, pull off all of the skin. Cut off the head. Slit the belly from the neck to the vent; pull out and discard the entrails. Rinse the eel. Cut along its length just above the spine. Cut and pry the spine away from the bottom fillet. Pull out any small bones. Cut the fillets in half.

6 **Firming the flesh.** Sauté the fillets in butter for about three minutes. Add finely chopped shallots and mushrooms; turn the fillets over and sprinkle them with parsley. Cook for two to three minutes, or until the fillets are just firm. Transfer everything to a dish, add dry white wine, brandy, oil, pepper and salt, and marinate for an hour.

7 **Making anchovy butter.** Pound anchovy fillets in a mortar. Add softened butter and continue to pound until a thick paste is formed. Push the paste, a little at a time, through a sieve with a scraper or wooden spoon.

58

2 **Enriching with eggs.** Break eggs into the bowl. Using a fork, stir the mixture until the eggs are amalgamated. Stir in cold water, a spoonful at a time, until the dough just begins to cohere.

3 **Kneading the dough.** With your hands, gather the dough into a ball and place it on a work surface. With the heel of your hand, press the dough and push forward to stretch it. Fold it back, turning it at the same time. Repeat three or four times until the dough is smooth. Enclose it in plastic wrap and refrigerate for at least one hour.

4 **Killing an eel.** Using a cloth, hold an eel firmly just behind the head. Rap the head smartly against the work surface to stun the eel; pierce its head with a sharp knife. Cover the head with the cloth, grasp it firmly and cut through the skin all the way around the body, just behind the head. Loosen a generous flap of skin with pliers.

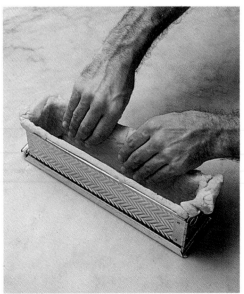

8 **Trimming the dough.** On a cool, floured surface, roll three quarters of the short-crust dough into a rectangle about ⅓ inch [1 cm.] thick. Trim the long edges to measure slightly more than the mold's length plus twice its height, and the shorter edges to slightly more than the mold's width plus twice its height. Reserve the dough scraps.

9 **Lining the mold.** Butter the inside of the mold. With both hands, lift the rectangle of dough and lower it carefully into the mold so that it covers the bottom and sides evenly.

10 **Making a close fit.** Gently press the dough against the bottom and sides of the mold. Make sure that the dough lining is of an even thickness, with no cracks or gaps. Trim off any overhanging dough so that the edges are flush with the top of the mold. Reserve the dough scraps. ▶

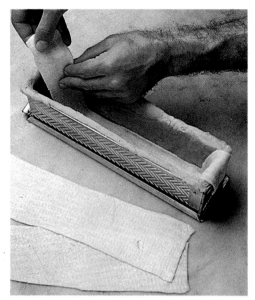

11 **Lining with fatback.** Freeze bards of fatback *(page 12)* for 15 minutes to firm them, then cut them so that they will fit neatly inside the dough case. Press them against the dough so that the bottom and sides of the case are securely lined with a thin layer of fat.

12 **Filling the mold.** Drain the marinated eel on a towel, but do not wipe off the flavorings. Prepare a fish mousseline *(pages 10-11)*; beat in the anchovy butter and some of the eel marinade. Spread mousseline over the bottom of the mold. Add alternate layers of eel and mousseline, ending with a layer of mousseline.

13 **Covering the filling.** To settle the contents of the mold, tap the base on a folded towel. Lay more bards over the filling. Roll out the remaining dough and trim it to fit over the top. Brush the rim of the dough case with water and fit the lid in place, pressing the edges down firmly.

Lining an Eye-shaped Mold

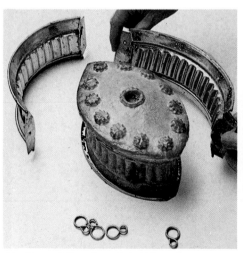

1 **Folding the dough.** On a cool, lightly floured surface, roll three quarters of the dough into a rectangle ⅓ inch [1 cm.] thick. The long edges should be slightly longer than the mold's length, the short edges slightly more than its width plus twice its height. Moisten the long edges. Fold the rectangle in half, pressing the wet edges to seal them.

2 **Lining the mold.** Lift the resulting pocket of dough and position it in the mold so that the sealed edges align with the joints of the mold's curved sides. Press the dough firmly against the sides and bottom, then line it with fatback. Fill, cover, glaze, decorate and bake the pâté *(Steps 12 to 15)*.

3 **Unmolding the pâté.** When the pâté is cooked, allow it to cool until tepid. Remove the clips that hold the mold's sides together and gently pull the sides away. Using a spatula, free the pâté from the base of the mold and put it on a plate. Refrigerate it overnight and fill it with aspic *(Step 17, right)*. Serve it cold.

4 **Glazing the dough.** In a bowl, lightly beat an egg yolk with a few drops of water. Brush the lid with this glaze. In the lid, cut a round hole big enough to hold a tube of rolled cardboard or a small cutter. With small cutters or a knife, make decorations from the dough scraps to fit around the hole in the lid.

15 **Preparing for cooking.** Using a fork, pattern the edge of the lid, then glaze the top again. Place a tube of cardboard or—as above—a deep cutter in the central hole. Place the pâté on a baking sheet and bake at 375° F. [190° C.] for 15 minutes, then at 350° F. [180° C.] for one hour.

16 **Unmolding.** If the crust browns too quickly, drape it with foil or parchment paper. Let the cooked pâté cool until it is tepid. Then remove the cardboard tube or cutter. Place the mold on a plate and slide out the base. Remove the mold's securing pins and draw the sides away. Chill the pâté overnight.

7 **Adding aspic.** Melt fish aspic (pages 6-7), cool it until tepid and add dry sherry. Set a funnel in the steam hole and ladle in aspic to fill the gap under the lid (below). If the pâté leaks, chill the remaining aspic until syrupy before adding it. Chill the pâté for at least four hours; serve cold.

A Rough-Puff Lid for a Freestanding Pâté

Lighter and far crisper than short crust, rough puff pastry will impart a luxurious finish to almost any pâté. Rough puff dough *(recipe, page 167)* contains a high ratio of butter—one part butter to two parts flour—and the butter is kept in pieces instead of being thoroughly united with the flour as it is for short crust.

Once mixed, a rough puff dough is repeatedly rolled, folded and chilled—a process that forms thin leaves of butter separated by layers of dough. The oven's heat turns the moisture in the dough to steam; the steam, together with air that is trapped between layers, separates the layers of dough to form a puffy crust.

Because rough puff must be unimpeded if it is to rise well, it should not be contained in a mold. Although it can enclose a freestanding pâté with a cooked filling *(pages 66-69)*, rough puff dough does not seal in a raw filling as well as an egg-enriched short crust. Here, these problems are solved by wrapping raw filling in short crust and saving the rough puff for the lid of the pâté, where it can rise freely to form a tempting crown.

1 Preparing the dough. With two table knives, cut chilled butter cubes into flour and salt until the butter is in tiny pieces. Stir in cold water with a fork. Gather the dough into a ball, cover it with plastic wrap and chill it for an hour. On a cool, floured surface, gently beat the dough with a rolling pin to flatten it. Roll it out into a rectangle.

2 Folding into layers. Fold the ends of the dough to meet in the middle, th fold these two layers in half to create four layers. Give the dough a quarter t so that the folded edges are at the sides; roll out the dough into a rectang again. Repeat the folding. Wrap the dough and chill for 30 minutes.

6 Shaping the filling. Flatten and shape the forcemeat into a rectangle covering the center third of the bards; the ends of the rectangle should be at the rimless edges of the baking sheet. Arrange half of the marinated meat on top of the forcemeat. Add another third of the forcemeat, then the remaining meat strips. Finish with forcemeat.

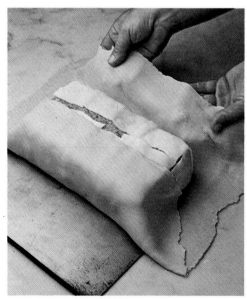

7 Wrapping the filling. Smooth the filling, sloping the sides slightly inward at the top. Press short bards of fatback against the ends; fold up the long bards to cover the filling. Lift the two long edges of dough over the filling; trim them so that they just meet along the top.

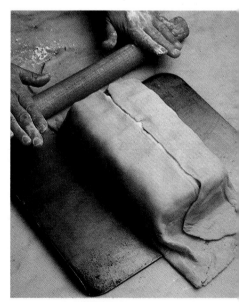

8 Sealing the pâté. Roll out the folded ends of the dough thin: Each e should measure about half the length of the pâté plus its height. Trim the en and, if desired, cut excess dough fron the corners. Brush the top and rolled-c ends with water. Fold each end over the top; trim the edges so that they ju meet in the middle.

3 **Rolling out the dough.** Place the dough on the floured surface with the folded edges at the sides. Roll it out into a rectangle; fold it again. Turn, roll and fold the dough a fourth time. Rewrap the dough and chill it for another 30 minutes. Then unwrap it and repeat the rolling-and-folding sequence twice more. Wrap and chill the dough again.

4 **Rolling short crust.** Prepare a short-crust dough *(recipe, page 167)*. Roll it out into a 2-foot [60-cm.] square about ¼ inch [6 mm.] thick. Wrap it around a long rolling pin to transfer it without damage to a rimless baking sheet. Unroll the dough onto the sheet.

5 **Arranging bards.** Marinate strips of ham, fatback and veal in herbs and brandy. Prepare forcemeat—here, a mixture of pork, veal and chicken livers *(recipe, page 163)*. Lay chilled fatback bards *(page 12)* over the dough, placing them lengthwise above the baking sheet. Spoon one third of the forcemeat across the center of the bards.

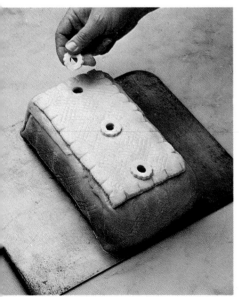

9 **Adding a lid.** Roll the rough puff ¼ inch [6 mm.] thick; cut it to fit the top of the pâté. Brush the top with water; set the lid in place. Use egg and water to glaze the pâté—but avoid the sides of the lid lest it fail to rise. Score the lid with a fork; cut steam holes and ring them with dough. Glaze the pâté again and chill it for 20 minutes.

10 **Cooking and serving.** Place a cardboard tube in each hole. Bake the pâté for 15 minutes at 425° F. [220° C.], then at 325° F. [160° C.] for one and one half hours, or until the tip of a skewer inserted into the center of the pâté through a hole comes out hot. Chill overnight, pour in stock, chill for four hours to set it, and serve.

A Buttery Wrapping of Classic Puff Pastry

Puff pastry is the most time-consuming dough to prepare *(recipe, page 167)*, but it produces the lightest and most delicate of coverings for pâtés. The strategy for making it is similar to that used for rough puff dough: Repeated rolling and folding entraps air between alternating layers of dough and butter so that the pastry swells and crisps as it bakes. For puff pastry, however, most of the butter is added in the form of a sheet, which is then dispersed uniformly through the dough to create more than 700 discrete, paper-thin layers. As a result of this process, puff-pastry dough rises two or three times higher than rough puff dough.

Most butter—unless hand-churned—has a high water content that may make the pastry gummy. For this reason, the butter that is used in sheet form must be kneaded on a lightly floured work surface for about five minutes, until it is waxy and dry. After kneading, the butter should be chilled to firm it before it is shaped and incorporated into the dough.

Puff-pastry dough includes not only all-purpose flour, but also cake flour, which is low in gluten and therefore does not toughen in the frequent handling required. Even so, the dough must be chilled after each rolling-and-folding sequence to relax the gluten in the all-purpose flour as well as to firm the butter. As the dough is repeatedly worked, the chilling periods should be progressively lengthened to ensure that the puff pastry is tender.

Because of its delicacy, puff pastry should be used only to encase fillings that are already cooked *(pages 66-69)* or light forcemeats that bake fairly quickly. In this demonstration, the dough is used for individual pâtés shaped in tartlet pans. The filling shown is a salmon forcemeat *(recipe, page 144)*, but a creamy mousseline made from tender meat or fish could be substituted. Unlike most pâté fillings, these fragile mixtures do not require chilling to firm them; the pâtés can be served hot or at room temperature.

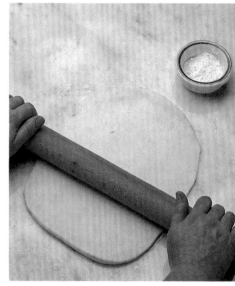

1 **Preparing the dough.** Mix together all-purpose flour, cake flour, salt, chilled butter and cold water to make a preliminary puff-pastry dough. Refrigerate the dough for about 30 minutes. On a lightly floured cold surface, roll the chilled dough into a square about ½ inch [1 cm.] thick. Use quick, light strokes to flatten it evenly.

5 **Finishing the dough.** Turn the dough so that its folded edges are at right angles to the rolling pin, and repeat Steps 3 and 4. Wrap the dough and chill it for an hour. Repeat the rolling-and-folding process two more times, doubling the chilling time after each repetition.

6 **Preparing the forcemeat.** Chop skinned fish fillets—in this case, salmon. Combine the fish with chopped shallots, scallions and parsley, bread crumbs, cream and seasonings. Using a blender or a food processor, purée this mixture in small batches. Beat in egg yolks and softened butter. Then taste for seasoning.

7 **Lining the molds.** Roll the dough out about ¼ inch [6 mm.] thick. Using cutter, stamp out rounds the same diameter as the tops of small tartlet pans; set these lids aside. Use a cutter about 1 inch [2½ cm.] larger to cut rounds to line the tartlet pans. Gently press a large dough round into each pan.

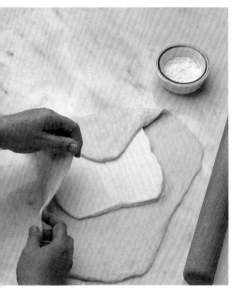

2 **Enclosing butter.** Between two pieces of wax paper, flatten chilled, kneaded butter into a square about ¾ inch [2 cm.] thick. Place this square diagonally on the rolled-out dough. Fold the corners of the dough over the butter, leaving a ½-inch [1-cm.] margin all around it. Gently press the seams of this envelope together.

3 **Rolling the dough.** Pressing lightly to avoid squeezing out the butter, roll the dough into a rectangle three times as long as it is wide. Smooth the edges of the dough by patting them with the sides of your hands. Do not add flour, lest it make the pastry tough and dry.

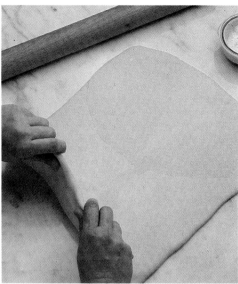

4 **Folding the dough.** Fold one end of the rectangle over the center, then fold the other end over the first, aligning them so that they form a three-layered package of dough that is about one third the size of the original rectangle. Press the edges of the dough lightly with the rolling pin to seal them.

8 **Filling the pâtés.** Spoon the forcemeat into the lined pans and smooth the tops. Set the pans on a baking sheet. Brush the rims of the pâtés with an egg glaze and gently press the lids in place. Set decorative shapes, cut from the leftover dough, on top. Lightly glaze the tops—but not the sides—of the lids. Chill for 30 minutes.

9 **Cooking and serving.** Bake the pâtés in a 400° F. [200° C.] oven for about 30 minutes, or until the tip of a skewer inserted into the center of a pâté feels hot when withdrawn. Serve the pâtés immediately or after they cool to room temperature.

A Ripened Terrine in a Delicate Crust

The meat assemblies that fill pâtés improve in flavor if refrigerated for a few days after they are cooked. But neither pastry nor aspic benefit from lengthy keeping, so a pâté is best served the day after it is baked. The contradiction can be resolved: To produce a dish that combines the beauty of a pâté with the flavor of a ripened terrine, the filling can be made in advance—as a terrine—and left to mature before it is wrapped in dough.

The method is particularly advantageous for large pâtés. In a freestanding assembly, the mass of uncooked forcemeat might spread and lose its shape before the oven's heat firmed it. Even in a mold, the pâté might burn on the outside before the forcemeat cooked through. By contrast, precooking firms the filling into a solid block, and the pâté needs only enough baking to crisp the pastry.

Although any filling can be used, a large pâté invites a complex arrangement of many ingredients. The multi-tiered pâté demonstrated here and on the following pages combines game—rabbit, quail and wild duck—with chicken, veal and ham. For all its lavishness, the pâté, called Lovely Aurora's Pillow *(recipe, pages 144-145)*, makes full use of each component. The tender strips of pale rabbit, chicken and veal and darker quail and wild duck are steeped in different marinades to intensify their special flavors. The tougher meats from the game and chicken are added to the forcemeat mixtures. And their bones enrich the wine-flavored aspic that fills the gaps in the baked pâté.

After the filling has been assembled in a mold—juxtaposing layers of light and dark forcemeat with marinated meats—it is cooked, given time to mature, then wrapped for a secondary baking in short-crust or more fragile rough puff or puff-pastry dough; rough puff is used here.

From start to finish allow approximately a week for preparing the pâté. On the first day, marinate the meats and prepare stock for the aspic. The next day, make the terrine. Let it mature for three or four days. The day before serving, prepare the dough, bake the pâté and chill it. Several hours before serving, pour in the aspic and rechill the pâté. The spectacular results will amply repay your effort.

1 Filleting a rabbit. Place a skinned and eviscerated rabbit on its belly on a chopping board. With a sharp knife, cut along one side of the spine, from the top of the hind leg to the shoulder. Carve around the rib cage to detach the flesh from each side of the body; cut each fillet free at the shoulder and leg. Reserve these loin—or saddle—fillets.

2 Removing flank fillets. Turn the rabbit over. On each side of the carcass cut away the triangular flank section that runs from the rib cage to the hind leg. Reserve these flank fillets for the dark forcemeat mixture you will make later.

5 Marinating light meats. Slice the rabbit loin and tenderloin fillets into strips and put them in a bowl. Add strips of boneless veal and lean ham. Bone a chicken, using the techniques shown on pages 22-23, and slice the breast into strips *(above)*; reserve the remaining meat, the bones and the liver. Soak the breast strips with the other light meats in wine marinade.

6 Marinating dark meats. Slice the quail and duck breasts into strips and place them in a bowl with a marinade of Madeira, Cognac, oil, salt and pepper. Cover both dishes of meat strips with plastic wrap, and marinate the refrigerator for about 24 hours, turning the strips occasionally.

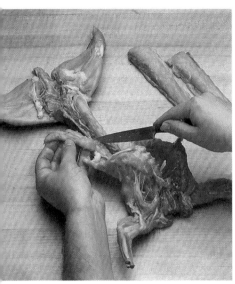
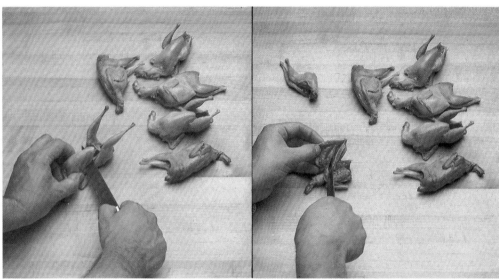

3 **Removing tenderloins.** With the rabbit upside down, use a sharp knife to cut away the small tenderloins that lie on either side of the spinal column. Set the tenderloins aside with the loin fillets. Cut all of the remaining meat from the legs and body of the rabbit and reserve it for the dark forcemeat mixture. Reserve the bones for the stockpot.

4 **Filleting quail breasts.** Slide a small, sharp knife behind the rib cage of each quail to detach the breast section from the back and legs (left). Turn each breast over and carve around the bone to detach the breast fillets (right). Reserve these fillets for dark meat strips. Remove any meat from the quails' legs and back and reserve it for the dark forcemeat. Reserve the bones for the stockpot. Bone a duck (pages 22-23)—here, a wild duck; reserve the breast fillets for dark meat strips, the remaining meat for the dark forcemeat, the bones for the stockpot and the liver for a purée.

7 **Enriching meat stock.** Prepare a gelatinous meat stock (pages 6-7). Roast all of the reserved game and chicken bones in a preheated 375° F. [190° C.] oven for 20 to 30 minutes. Place the bones in a large pot and pour the stock over them. Bring to a boil slowly, skimming frequently. With the lid ajar, simmer gently for four hours. Strain, cool and degrease the enriched stock.

8 **Making light forcemeat.** Grind the reserved chicken meat together with some veal, lean pork and fresh pork fatback to make a light forcemeat. Sauté, pound and sieve the reserved chicken and duck livers, together with some additional chicken livers, to make a smooth purée (page 9). Add half of the liver purée to the light forcemeat and mix thoroughly.

9 **Making dark forcemeat.** Grind the reserved duck, quail and rabbit together with some lean pork and fatback to make a dark forcemeat. Add the remaining liver purée. Drain the marinade from the light meat strips into the light forcemeat; then drain the marinade from the dark strips into the dark forcemeat. Fry a sample of each forcemeat (page 18, Step 5) and taste for seasoning. ▶

10 **Dark forcemeat.** Line the base and sides of a large terrine mold or baking dish with bards of fatback *(page 12)*. Spread a layer of the dark forcemeat ½ inch [1 cm.] thick over the bottom of the mold; smooth the forcemeat with the back of a spoon.

11 **Light meat strips.** Form a second layer, using the marinated strips of light meats—rabbit, chicken and veal—and strips of ham. Alternate the various meats to make a variegated pattern. Sprinkle the meat strips with chopped pistachios.

12 **Light forcemeat.** Cover the light meat strips with a ½-inch [1-cm layer of the light forcemeat mixture. Then smooth the forcemeat with the back of the spoon.

16 **Trimming.** Press the top rectangle of dough against the sides of the terrine. Cut around the bottom of the terrine to trim any excess from the top rectangle of dough; take care not to cut through the bottom rectangle. Trim the bottom rectangle of dough to form a margin of about 2 inches [5 cm.] all around the terrine.

17 **Sealing the pâté.** Brush the seam between the top and bottom dough rectangles with beaten egg and press it gently to seal it. Fold the margin of the lower rectangle up against the seam and then down again to make a double rim around the base *(above, left)*. Crimp the lower rim with a fork; make a series of indentations around the upper rim to give it a frilled effect. With scissors, make a shallow cut on both sides of each indentation *(right)* to ensure that the frill keeps its shape during baking. Cut five steam holes in the top and place a ring of pastry around each hole. Brush the pâté with egg and chill it for about an hour.

3 **Dark meat strips.** Form a fourth layer with strips of dark meats—quail and wild duck—arranging the meats alternately. Sprinkle pistachios over the strips. Continue to fill the mold, following the same sequence of layers. Finish with a layer of light forcemeat. Lay bards over the terrine and cover the mold with foil or a lid.

14 **Cooking.** Cook the terrine in a water bath *(page 20)* in a 325° F. [160° C.] oven for four hours, or until the juices run clear. Cool the terrine for 45 minutes, weight it *(page 21)* and chill overnight. Remove the weights, but refrigerate the terrine for three or four days. Unmold the terrine and scrape away the fatback and any traces of jelly.

15 **Rolling the dough.** Prepare rough puff dough *(pages 62-63)*. Roll out one third of the dough into a rectangle about ¼ inch [6 mm.] thick and 2 inches [5 cm.] larger on all sides than the terrine. Transfer the dough to a buttered baking sheet; place the terrine in the center. Roll out the remaining dough and lay it on top.

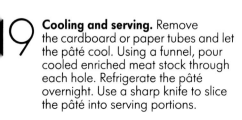

18 **Cooking.** Insert a rolled cardboard or parchment paper tube in each hole. Bake in a preheated 425° F. [220° C.] oven for 10 minutes. Reduce the heat to 375° F. [190° C.] and cook for one and one half hours. Cover the dough with foil if it browns quickly.

19 **Cooling and serving.** Remove the cardboard or paper tubes and let the pâté cool. Using a funnel, pour cooled enriched meat stock through each hole. Refrigerate the pâté overnight. Use a sharp knife to slice the pâté into serving portions.

5
Galantines and Aspics
A Spectrum of Effects from Poaching

Glistening wine-flavored aspic is spooned around a slice of succulent poached pork liver *(page 74)*. Lardons of fatback were threaded lengthwise through the liver to nourish the meat during poaching, and the liver was wrapped in cloth to give it a neat cylindrical shape.

Aspic-glazed galantines and meats embedded in aspic are among the most delectable and inviting of all cold presentations. Like terrines and pâtés, they often contain forcemeat and usually employ such assembly techniques as layering ingredients to create attractive cross sections when sliced. But instead of being cooked in the oven, these preparations are poached slowly on top of the stove in a liquid that barely trembles. Afterward, the meats are cooled and finished with gelatinous stock that sets to a translucent aspic.

At their simplest, such presentations are made by ladling the stock over cut-up or whole poached meats, such as the pork liver shown opposite. To produce the brawn demonstrated on pages 72-73, chunks of meat are seasoned with vinegar and spices before they are immersed in stock; the result is the tangy jellied loaf often known as headcheese for the selection of meats—tongue, pig's ears and the like—that it contains.

More elaborate advance work is required for galantines, which are made by stuffing a firm forcemeat into a suckling pig or—more typically—the skin of a bird. For a galantine of suckling pig *(pages 75-78)*, partial boning is necessary to ensure that the finished dish retains the animal's original shape. However, for a poultry galantine *(pages 79-82)*, the bird is completely boned, and its skin and meat are shaped into a roll to enclose layers of forcemeat and other fillings.

All of these presentations depend on gentle heat to keep the meat succulent and allow it to cook evenly. For successful poaching, it is essential that the liquid never nears a boil. To make sure the liquid for a galantine stays at about 175° F. [80° C.], suspend a cooking thermometer inside the cooking vessel and check it often. For brawn, the meats are simmered on the bone at a slightly higher temperature to draw out the gelatin; even so, the liquid should never go above 190° F. [90° C.].

Either stock or water can be used for poaching. Stock will exchange flavors with the meat during cooking to become an especially rich jelly. With small items, such as a liver or chicken, stock is the logical cooking medium. Larger cuts, such as suckling pig, are more economically poached in water; after cooking, the meat can be glazed with a separately prepared aspic. In either case, a jellied meat dish should be kept refrigerated and served within two or three days: The aspic deteriorates quickly.

Meats Embedded in a Jellied Stock

When gelatinous cuts of meat are simmered for several hours, they transform their cooking liquid into a full-bodied stock. If the stock is poured over chunks of meat that have been removed from these cuts and flavored with vinegar and spices, it will set to encase the meat in a firm, translucent jelly. The end result is brawn, a shimmering loaf of contrasting textures and piquant flavor.

Brawns may be prepared from many different meats, but they are particularly well suited to the inexpensive, gelatin-rich cuts of pork and beef that are usually reserved for the stockpot. The traditional brawn shown here is based on pig's head and feet, but other cuts, such as beef cheek meat and shank, calf's feet, pig's snout or ears, or pork rind, can be added or substituted (recipes, pages 150-152).

The availability of these meats depends on where you live. Supermarkets carry them occasionally, but specialty butchers and ethnic markets are more likely sources. You may need to order the meats in advance.

If you are using a head, ask the butcher to saw it into equal-sized pieces that will cook evenly. Reserve the brain for another dish, but include the tongue in the brawn. Leave the meats on the bones; the meat will be much easier to remove after cooking.

Salting pork overnight before cooking it will improve its flavor. The salt will draw juices from the pork, forming a brine; both the brine and the salt should be rinsed off before the pieces are added to the pot. Aromatics and wine or hard cider will contribute flavor to the cooking liquid, but the stock should not be salted until after it has reduced (Step 5); it may contain sufficient salt from the pork.

The meats should be simmered for several hours to release their gelatin. The heat must be kept low to prevent the flesh from becoming dry and stringy.

Once assembled, the brawn can be kept in the refrigerator for two or three days.

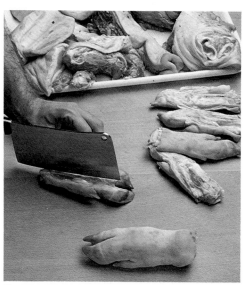

1 **Splitting feet.** With a small knife, scrape off the hairs from pieces of pig's head; to singe off remaining hairs, hold the pieces over an open flame. Use a knife to clean the ears. With a cleaver, split the pig's feet in half lengthwise. Rinse all of the meats well.

2 **Salting the pork.** Put a layer of coarse salt in the bottom of a large gla or glazed earthenware dish. Rub the pieces of head and feet with coarse s (above) and place them in the dish. Sprinkle more salt between the layers pork to make sure all of the pieces are well coated. Cover the dish with plasti wrap or a lid and refrigerate overnight

6 **Boning the pork.** Using a small knife and your fingers, remove the bones from the base of the tongue and peel the tongue. Take the meat and rind off the remaining bones. Discard the rind.

7 **Adding flavorings.** Cut the pork into chunks about 1 inch [2½ cm.] squa and place the chunks in a large bowl. Add ground black pepper, ground mac and cayenne pepper, and grate some nutmeg onto the meats. Pour in a little wine vinegar. To coat the chunks of pork evenly, toss them with the wine vinegar and spices.

3 **Filling the pot.** Rinse the pork pieces under cold running water. To prevent the meats from sticking, put a wire rack in a large pot and place the pork on the rack. Add enough cold water to cover the meats and set the pot over low heat. Bring the liquid slowly to a boil, skimming off the scum that rises.

4 **Cooking the meats.** Add carrots and onions—one stuck with two cloves—an unpeeled garlic bulb, allspice berries and a bouquet garni. Pour in white wine. Bring the stock back to a boil. Skim off any scum. Decrease the heat and set the pot lid ajar. Simmer the meats for at least four hours, or until they are tender.

5 **Degreasing.** Transfer the meats to a bowl; discard the aromatics. Skim off the fat and strain the stock through a colander lined with dampened cheesecloth. Return the stock to the pot. Set the pot half off the burner and simmer, skimming off any skin, for 45 minutes, or until a spoonful sets firm when refrigerated for 15 minutes.

8 **Ladling in stock.** Strain the reduced stock through the colander lined with fresh cheesecloth. Taste the stock and, if necessary, add salt. Place the cut-up meats in a mold and ladle in enough stock to cover them.

9 **Serving the brawn.** To set the stock, cover the mold tightly with foil or plastic wrap and refrigerate it overnight. Remove any fat from the surface of the jelly with a teaspoon or the tip of a knife. Serve the brawn in slices, accompanied by pickles (above).

Larding a Liver for Succulence and Flavor

Marinating the large lobe of a pork liver in an herbed wine marinade, then poaching it slowly in a gelatinous stock modulates its aggressive flavor while preserving its tenderness and succulence. When the liver is glazed with aspic derived from the cooking liquid, its transformation into an impressive cold presentation is complete (recipe, page 154).

Because pork liver contains no natural internal fat, seasoned lardons (page 13) should be threaded through the meat to flavor it and keep it moist during the 40 to 50 minutes of poaching it requires. To mold it into a neat shape as it cooks, the liver must be rolled in prepared caul or, as demonstrated here, enclosed in a piece of cheesecloth.

Beef, veal and lamb liver invite the same preparation. However, beef livers need one and one half hours of poaching time, and veal and lamb livers—because of their small size—should be poached for only 30 to 40 minutes.

1 **Preparing lardons.** Chill fresh fatback to firm it. Cut it into ¼-inch [6-mm.] lardons (page 13). Toss the lardons in a blend of ground mixed herbs, salt and pepper. To secure a lardon to the larding needle, open the clip at the wider end of the needle and place one end of the lardon on the pin inside. Close the clip to hold the lardon in place.

2 **Larding the liver.** Trim the large lobe of a pork liver to a neat shape. Remove all connective tissue. Thread lardons crosswise through the liver at ¾-inch [2-cm.] intervals. Trim the ends of the lardons, leaving about ½ inch [1 cm.] on either side of the liver

3 **Wrapping the liver.** Immerse the liver in a marinade of white wine, sliced shallots, a garlic bulb halved horizontally, thyme, bay leaves, whole allspice and parsley. Cover and chill overnight. Remove the liver and roll it up in muslin or cheesecloth, with the lardons running along the length of the roll (above). Tie the ends of the roll with string and snip off surplus cloth.

4 **Poaching the liver.** Place the liver in a snug-fitting pot. Add the marinade and cover the liver with meat stock (pages 6-7); pour in Cognac. Bring slowly to a boil; skim. Reduce the heat, set the lid ajar and poach the liver for 40 to 50 minutes. Leave it in the stock to cool; when tepid, transfer it to a plate.

5 **Straining the stock.** Strain, degrease and reduce the stock (page 24, Step 9). Unwrap the liver, wipe it with paper towels and put it in a close-fitting mold. Pour the reduced stock over the liver. Refrigerate overnight. The next day wipe off any fat from the surface of the aspic with a towel dipped in hot water. Serve the liver in slices (page 70).

A Suckling Pig in a Shiny Coat

An impressive galantine for a special occasion is a whole suckling pig, stuffed, poached and coated with aspic cream, a velvety glaze known in French as *chaud-froid*. The grandeur of the galantine will repay every minute spent assembling it.

Suckling pigs—eviscerated and ready to be cooked—are sold at butcher shops and ethnic markets; you may need to order the pig a week or two in advance. If only a frozen pig is obtainable, allow two days for it to defrost in your refrigerator.

Start the preparation of the pig two days before you plan to serve the galantine. To facilitate carving, remove the breastbone, ribs, spine and pelvic bone; let the skull, leg bones and tail bones stay in place to preserve the pig's natural shape. Then dry-salt the pig overnight to improve the flavor of its meat. The next day, stuff the pig and poach it for eight hours. Chill it overnight; it will then be ready for glazing and serving.

Almost any forcemeat can be chosen to fill the pig; the stuffing used in the demonstration here and on the following pages is a veal, pork and liver mixture *(recipe, page 163)* enlivened with spinach. A pig weighing 12 pounds [6 kg.]—which will provide about 40 servings for a first course or buffet—requires about 5 pounds [2½ kg.] of forcemeat.

To enclose the stuffing, sew up the opening in the underside of the pig. Then bind the pig in cloth to keep it intact during the lengthy poaching, and use more cloth to secure it to the rack of a large fish poacher. If you lack a poacher, use an oversized roasting pan.

The pig should cook in water that barely trembles: Clip a thermometer inside the poacher to make sure that the water temperature never rises above 175° F. [80° C.]. Because of the poaching vessel's size, you will have to place it across two burners of the stove to disperse the heat evenly; use heat-diffusing pads to help control the poaching temperature.

The aspic cream *(demonstration, page 7; recipe, page 165)* is a velouté enhanced with jellied stock and cream. It gives the galantine a creamy sheen while providing an opaque coating to conceal any blemishes or tears in the pig's skin.

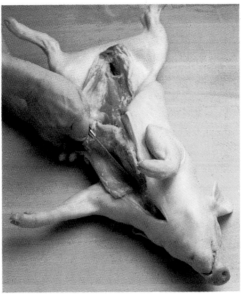

1 **Opening the pig.** Scrape or singe hairs from the pig. Clean the ears, nostrils and feet with a small knife and a dampened paper towel. Wipe the pig inside and out with a cloth. Lay the pig on its back; make a cut from the belly opening to the throat. Cut and scrape the flesh from the breastbone and ribs, keeping the blade against the bones.

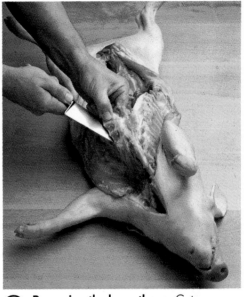

2 **Removing the breastbone.** Cut through the cartilage that joins the belly ribs and back ribs on one side *(above)*. Make a second cut through the cartilage on the opposite side of the rib cage to free and remove the piece of breastbone and the belly ribs.

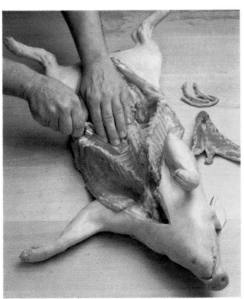

3 **Cutting between back ribs.** To separate each back rib in turn, make a cut in the flesh on both sides of it; keep the knife close to the bone and cut only as deep as the rib itself so that as much meat as possible is left behind. Then cut along both sides of the spine through the cartilage that connects the spine to the ribs.

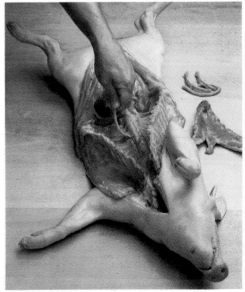

4 **Twisting ribs free.** Starting at the lower end of the rib cage, lift up a rib and slide the knife under it to detach the rib from the flesh. Twist the rib to separate it from the spine. Remove the remaining ribs on both sides of the spine in the same way. ▶

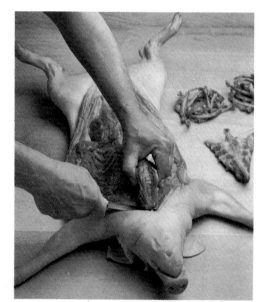

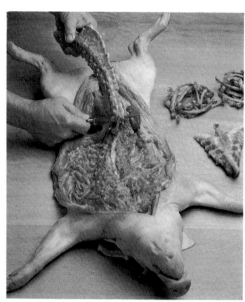

5 **Detaching the upper spine.** Cut through the connective tissue on either side of the spine—working from the neck toward the bottom of the rib cage to free the flesh from the protruding bones. Locate the top of the spine where it joins the skull and sever the cartilage between the skull and spine, lifting the spine as you do so (above).

6 **Removing the upper spine.** Pull up the spine with one hand and cut through the connective tissue that joins it to the back. When the spine is freed as far as the end of the rib cage, cut through the vertebrae (above) and remove this section of spine. Cut out the two kidneys, if still in place; reserve them for another dish.

7 **Freeing the lower spine.** To remove the rest of the spine, work between the fillets of lean flesh and the spine, cutting the connective tissu if necessary. Cut the flesh away from the remaining portion of spine (above) and lift it out.

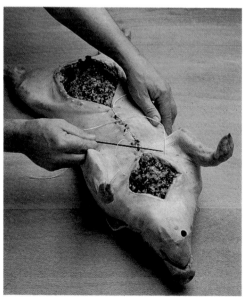

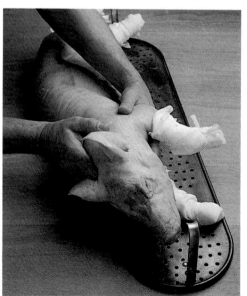

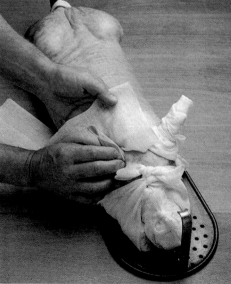

10 **Sewing.** With a trussing needle and string knotted at the end, make a stitch across the middle of the pig. Working toward the head, stitch across the pig at ¾-inch [2-cm.] intervals; pull the needle back through the loop of string after each stitch. At the neck, knot the string. Sew up the lower half of the pig the same way.

11 **Wrapping the legs.** Cut four bands of muslin or cheesecloth about 8 inches [20 cm.] wide and 36 inches [90 cm.] long; fold them in half lengthwise and wrap one around each foot and leg of the pig. Tie thin strips around each leg. Roll the pig onto the rack of a fish poacher, belly down, tucking the legs underneath.

12 **Wrapping the pig.** Wrap the pig's snout in a band of cloth. Rest th snout on the forelegs, then tie a doubled band of cloth around the sno and forelegs to keep them in position. Wrap the tail in cloth; secure the band with a thin strip. Curl the pig's ears inward and bind them with cloth (above); tie with thin strips.

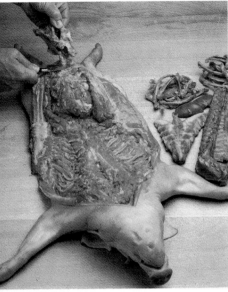

8 **Removing the pelvic bone.** Cut around the pelvic bone, severing the tendons that connect it to the thigh bones; bend the legs back if necessary to find the joints. When the pelvic bone is freed, remove the small vertebrae beneath it that link the tail to the spine. Leave the bones in the tail.

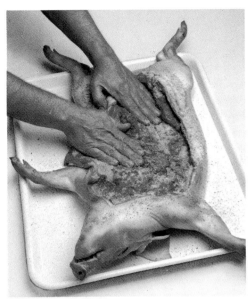

9 **Salting.** Turn the pig over and rub coarse salt and herbs—here, thyme, marjoram, oregano and savory—into the skin. Lay the pig on its back on a tray and rub the salt mixture into its cavity. Cover the pig and chill overnight. The next day, rinse the pig and dry it inside and out with paper towels. Fill the cavity loosely with forcemeat.

A Union of Cream and Aspic

1 **Preparing a velouté.** Melt butter. Stir in flour to make a roux; cook for three to four minutes. Whisk in meat stock. Set the pan half off the heat; as it simmers, repeatedly remove the surface skin.

2 **Adding cream.** When the sauce is thick, add jellied stock, a little at a time. Reduce the sauce after each addition, until it coats a spoon. When all the jelly has been added, gradually stir in heavy cream.

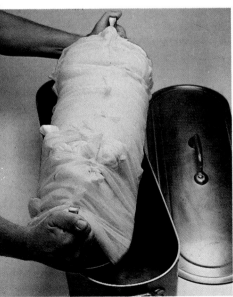

13 **Poaching the pig.** Wrap cheesecloth or muslin around the pig and rack; make sure the whole pig is covered. Tie strips around the wrapped head. Fold back the ears; tie them down with a strip. Put the pig into the poacher. Cover the pig with water; add salt. Heat the water until it just trembles; with lid ajar, cook for eight hours.

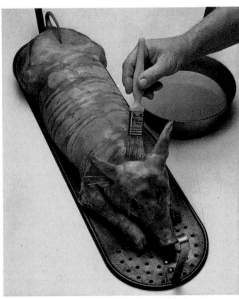

14 **Glazing.** Lift the rack out; empty the poacher. Free the ears but do not unwrap them; insert skewers behind them to prop them up. Refrigerate the pig overnight. Unwrap the pig and wipe off fat with hot, damp towels. Remove skewers; prop the ears open with toothpicks. Paint the pig with aspic cream *(box, right)*. ▶

3 **Chilling.** Reduce the sauce again, until it coats the spoon. Take the pan off the heat and set it in a bowl of ice. Stir the aspic cream as it cools; remove it from the ice when it starts to thicken.

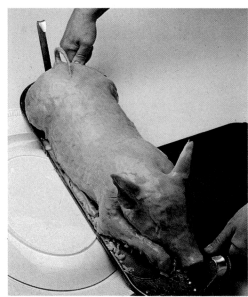

15 **Moving the pig to a platter.** Chill the pig in the poacher over ice, or in the refrigerator, to set the sauce. Apply more coats of sauce until the pig is well covered, chilling between coats. Chill a large platter with a smaller one inverted inside it. Place the rack on the edge of the inverted platter. With wide spatulas or, as here, a spatula and baking sheet, slide the pig onto the inverted platter.

16 **Serving.** Present the pig sprinkled with chopped herbs and surrounded with chopped aspic. To carve the pig, first free one hindquarter by cutting along the center of the back and then crosswise. Move this section to a board and slice it *(right)*. Carve the meat off the hind leg. Carve the other hindquarter, then carve the forequarters. Slice the meat from the snout and ears. Accompany each serving with some of the aspic.

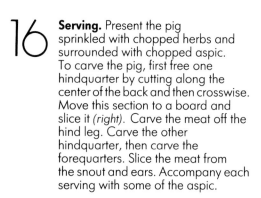

A Poultry Parcel Filled and Glazed

Any kind of poultry or large game bird can be boned and turned into an elegant galantine. The skin-covered flesh of the bird—a chicken is chosen for the demonstration at right and on the following pages—serves as a delectable container for forcemeat and other flavorings. After is shaped into a roll, this assembly is poached in meat stock, cooled, glazed with aspic and served partly sliced to reveal the pattern of good things inside (recipe, page 155).

When a bird is boned for a galantine, it is split down the back and opened out to form a flat sheet of skin and flesh. Piercing the skin would let the filling escape: keep the blade of the knife close to the bones and proceed carefully.

The ingredients within the galantine should be selected for visual effect as well as for flavor. In this demonstration, the forcemeat and solid morsels are layered. The skin and chicken meat form the first layer, which is covered with a layer of forcemeat. The forcemeat is topped with a row of truffle halves flanked by strips of ham, tongue and fatback.

The elements of the forcemeat can, of course, be varied: Here, pistachios and chopped truffle trimmings provide flecks of green and black, but soaked raisins or cubed poached carrots could be used. The solid ingredients of the galantine could include veal or duck breast, and the truffles might be replaced by morels or pitted ripe olives. Whatever foods are chosen, they will form a circular mosaic in cross section when the chicken is rolled up.

Wrap muslin or cheesecloth around the roll to keep its shape during poaching; the flavors of the stock will easily penetrate the cloth. After cooking, cool the bird in the stock so that it absorbs more flavor from the liquid. Then weight the roll to compact the filling and flatten it slightly to form a stable base.

The stock can subsequently be transformed into an aspic to coat the galantine, and the glazed assembly may be further embellished in many ways. In this demonstration, the galantine is decorated with a flower design of calendula petals, tarragon leaves and tomato (page 2), but you can improvise patterns with such ingredients as olives, hard-boiled eggs, carrots and peeled, seeded peppers.

1 Cutting along the back. Place a bird—in this case, a chicken—breast side down. With a sharp knife, slit through the skin to the bone, starting at the neck end and cutting down the center of the back toward the tail end.

2 Freeing flesh. With the knife blade against the backbone, cut down through the flesh on one side of the carcass. Sever the connective tissue between the flesh and the bone. Cut away the shoulder blade, leaving it embedded in the flesh. As you cut, lift the skin and flesh with your other hand to expose the next bit of connective tissue.

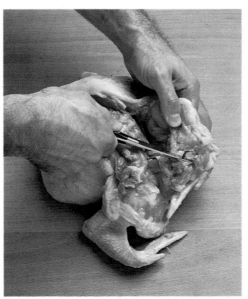

3 Cutting the wing and leg. Grasp one of the wings and bend it outward so that the ball in the joint between the wing and shoulder pops out of its socket. Cut between the ball and socket (above). In the same way, free the leg on the same side of the bird, severing the ball-and-socket joint that connects the thigh to the body.

4 Separating flesh from bone. Cut the flesh away from the rib cage of the bird, working from the neck; keep the knife blade against the carcass as you work. Take care not to pierce the skin when you reach the ridge of the breastbone: There is no flesh between the skin and bone at this point. ▶

5 **Removing the carcass.** Repeat Steps 2 to 4 to free the flesh and skin from the other side of the bird. Locate the wishbone at the neck end and snap it away from the breastbone, leaving it embedded in the flesh. Cut beneath the carcass along the ridge of the breastbone (above). Lift away the carcass, cutting off the tail.

6 **Removing the collarbones.** With your fingers, locate the shafts of the wishbone and the shoulder blades and collarbones attached to each side of the wishbone. Use the knife to cut the collarbones and shoulder bones out of the flesh. Remove the wishbone.

7 **Removing the wing bones.** Hold down a wing to steady it, and cleave through the upper bone just above the joint with the wing tip. Working from the inside of the bird, cut the flesh away from the wing bone and pull the bone out, leaving the skin and flesh of the wing turned inside out. Pick out fragments of bone. Remove the other wing bone.

11 **Layering the filling.** Prepare a veal-and-pork forcemeat. Cut ham, cooked tongue and fatback into ½-inch [1-cm.] strips. Peel and trim truffles, halve them and add the chopped trimmings to the forcemeat. Spread half the forcemeat over the bird; arrange the meat strips across it, alternating the different types.

12 **Forming the roll.** Spread the rest of the forcemeat over the strips of meat. Arrange the halved truffles in a row down the center of the forcemeat. Holding one end of the cloth, lift one side of the chicken and fold it to the center; lift and fold the other side to meet the first at the center, forming a cylinder.

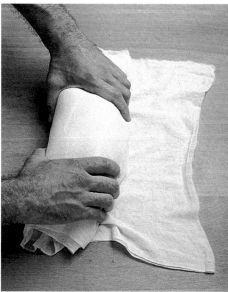

13 **Wrapping in cloth.** Pull the flaps of skin at the neck and tail of the bird neatly over the ends of the roll of meat. Roll the cylinder in the cloth. Twist the ends of the cloth and tie them with string; trim excess cloth.

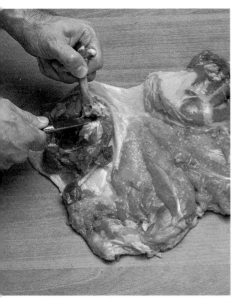

8 Removing the leg bones. Starting from the inside and holding the top of the bone, cut the flesh away from it. When you reach the joint of the thigh and drumstick, cut between the two bones (above). Free the drumstick bone. Remove the bones from the other leg. Leave the boned leg and wing flesh turned to the inside.

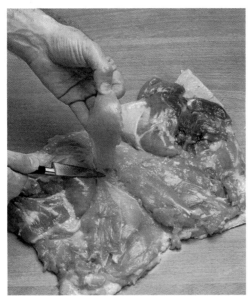

9 Trimming the flesh. So that the flesh will form a uniform layer over the skin, cut some of the thick flesh from the leg and wing areas and reserve it. Locate the two narrow fillets of flesh that are easily separated from the rest of the breast; lift them away and reserve them (above). Remove tendons from the flesh that has been removed.

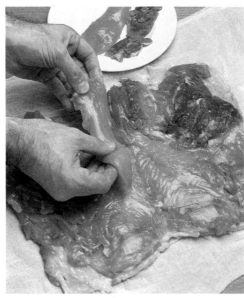

10 Redistributing the flesh. Cut cheesecloth or muslin into a rectangle about 3 by 2 feet [90 by 60 cm.]. Fold it in two so that it measures 1 1/2 by 2 feet [45 by 60 cm.]. Lay it on the work surface and place the chicken on it skin side down. Arrange the reserved flesh over the bird to form an even layer of flesh.

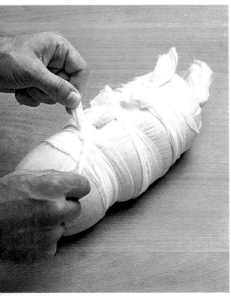

14 Securing the roll. To fasten the bundle securely without cutting into the galantine, use three strips of cloth about 1 1/2 feet [45 cm.] long. Wrap one strip round the middle of the roll and tie it with a knot. Tie the other two strips on each side.

15 Poaching. Place the roll on a rack in a snug-fitting pot. Ladle in enough boiling meat stock (pages 6-7) to cover the roll. Over medium heat, bring the stock to the boiling point; reduce the heat and set the lid ajar. Poach at 175° F. [80° C.] for one and three quarters hours, or until the roll feels firm.

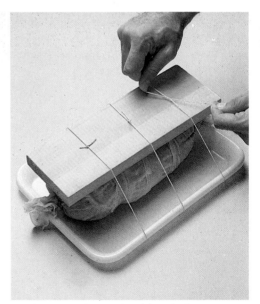

16 Weighting. Cool the chicken in the stock until lukewarm. Lift it out of the pot and onto a tray. Place a board on top of the roll and tie the board to the tray. Place a 2- to 2 1/2-pound [1-kg.] weight on the board and refrigerate the roll overnight. If the stock in the pan is cloudy, clarify it; chill the stock. ▶

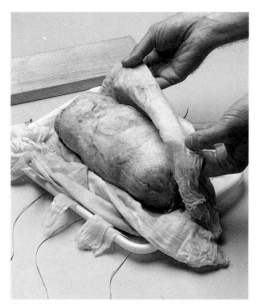

17 **Unwrapping the roll.** The next day, remove the tray from the refrigerator and take the weight off. Cut the strings and remove the board. Snip the cloth ties and gently peel the cloth off the roll. Dip paper towels in hot water and wipe all fat from the surface of the chicken skin.

18 **Glazing the roll.** Place the roll on a rack set over a tray. Spoon any fat from the chilled stock. Melt the stock; when barely tepid, add some Madeira. Ladle some stock into a metal bowl and set it in ice in a larger bowl. Stir until the stock turns syrupy, then spoon it rapidly over the galantine. Chill to set this aspic.

19 **Decorating the roll.** Apply several layers of aspic, chilling for a few minutes between applications. Blanch tarragon leaves in boiling water for a few seconds; drain on a towel. Dipping each piece in syrupy stock to make it sticky, create a flower with the leaves, calendula petals and a disk of tomato.

20 **Serving the galantine.** Cover the decorated galantine with another layer of aspic and refrigerate it until about half an hour before serving time. Use two spatulas to lift the galantine onto a platter. Slice part of the roll to reveal the pattern inside. Surround the roll with chopped aspic, and serve some with each slice.

Anthology
of Recipes

Drawing upon the cooking literature of more than 10 countries, the editors and consultants for this volume have selected 189 published recipes and augmented these with standard preparations for the Anthology that follows. The selections range from the simple to the complex—from a basic terrine made by merely blending cooked-and-puréed chicken livers with butter to an elaborate presentation based on pike and salmon, enriched with truffles and green peppercorns, formed into a cylinder for poaching and served with a mustardy sorrel sauce.

Many of the recipes were written by world-renowned exponents of the culinary art, but the Anthology also includes selections from rare and out-of-print books and from works that have never been published in English. Whatever the sources, the emphasis in these recipes is always on fresh, natural ingredients that blend harmoniously and on techniques that are practical for the home cook.

Since many early recipe writers did not specify amounts of ingredients, sizes of pans or even cooking times and temperatures, the missing information has been judiciously added. In some cases, clarifying introductory notes have also been supplied; they are printed in italics. Modern recipe terms have been substituted for archaic language; but to preserve the character of the original recipes and to create a true anthology, the authors' texts have been changed as little as possible.

In keeping with the organization of the first half of the book, most of the recipes are categorized according to the ingredients and the technique. Recipes for standard preparations—stocks, sauces and a selection of pastry doughs among them—appear at the end of the Anthology. Unfamiliar cooking terms and uncommon ingredients are explained in the combined General Index and Glossary.

Ingredients are listed within each recipe in order of use, with both the customary United States measurements and the metric measurements provided. All quantities reflect the American practice of measuring such solid ingredients as flour by volume rather than by weight, as is done in Europe.

To make the quantities simpler to measure, many of the figures have been rounded off to correspond to the gradations on U.S. metric spoons and cups. (One cup, for example, equals 237 milliliters; however, wherever practicable in these recipes, the metric equivalent of 1 cup appears as a more readily measured 250 milliliters—¼ liter.)

Similarly, the weight, temperature and linear metric equivalents have been rounded off slightly. Thus the American and metric figures do not exactly match, but using one set or the other will produce the same good results.

Meat Terrines

Pork Terrine with Swiss Chard and Cream

Pâté de Porc aux Blettes et à la Créme

To make about 4½ pounds [2¼ kg.]

¼ lb.	chicken livers, trimmed	125 g.
¼ cup	bourbon or Cognac	50 ml.
	freshly ground pepper	
1 lb.	boneless fatty pork, coarsely ground	½ kg.
½ lb.	boneless ham, coarsely ground	¼ kg.
¼ lb.	bacon, coarsely ground	125 g.
2 lb.	Swiss chard leaves, parboiled for 5 minutes, refreshed, drained, squeezed dry and coarsely chopped	1 kg.
2	garlic cloves, finely chopped	2
4	eggs, beaten with 1 cup [¼ liter] heavy cream	4
1¼ tsp.	salt	6 ml.
1 tbsp.	fines herbes	15 ml.
1 tbsp.	chopped fresh tarragon leaves	15 ml.
	cayenne pepper	
	freshly grated nutmeg	
⅓ cup	port	75 ml.
3	thin strips fresh pork fatback	3
¼ lb.	prosciutto in 1 piece, cut into long strips	125 g.
1	bay leaf	1
	flour-and-water paste	

Marinate the chicken livers in the bourbon or Cognac with a few generous grinds of pepper for two hours. Drain them, set them aside and reserve the marinade. Combine the ground meats with the chard, garlic, eggs, seasonings, herbs, port and the reserved marinade. Fry a spoonful of this mixture and taste it for seasoning.

Line the sides and bottom of a 7-cup [1¾-liter] terrine mold with the fatback strips. Pack in one third of the meat mixture, then arrange down the center half of the chicken livers and half of the prosciutto strips. Layer another third of the meat mixture on top, add the remaining livers and strips of prosciutto, and top with the last of the meat mixture. Give the mold several solid taps against the work surface to help settle the contents and top with the bay leaf. Put on the lid and seal it with the flour-and-water paste. Place the mold in a pan, and pour boiling water around it to reach about halfway up the sides. Cook it in a preheated 375° F. [190° C.] oven for one and one half hours. When the terrine is pricked, the juices should run clear and not rosy.

Remove the mold to a rack, break away the flour seal, and place a good weight on top to pack the terrine down as it cools. When it is cold, place it in the refrigerator, where it will keep very well for at least two weeks.

It is really best to wait for two or three days before serving the terrine, when the flavors will be richer and the texture more settled. Serve directly from the mold or unmold it onto a platter.

SIMONE BECK
NEW MENUS FROM SIMCA'S CUISINE

Pork Terrine

Terrine de Porc

To make about 3 pounds [1½ kg.]

2½ lb.	fresh pork belly, ground	1¼ kg.
½ lb.	pork liver, trimmed and ground	¼ kg.
1	onion, finely chopped	1
2	garlic cloves, finely chopped	2
2	branches fresh rosemary or 2 tsp. [10 ml.] dried rosemary	2
1	egg	1
2 tbsp.	brandy	30 ml.
	salt and freshly ground black pepper	
1	pig's foot, split and blanched for 5 minutes	1

Mix the ground meats with the onion, garlic and the leaves of one branch of rosemary. If you are using the dried herb, crumble it fine and add it all to the meats. Beat the egg with the brandy and add them to the meats with plenty of salt and pepper. Blend all of the ingredients together well. Fry a small piece of the mixture and taste it for seasoning.

Spoon the mixture into a greased 6-cup [1½-liter] earthenware or other ovenproof terrine. Press the pig's foot into the center, together with the second branch of rosemary, if using. Place the terrine in a water bath in a preheated 425° F. [220° C.] oven. After 15 minutes, reduce the heat to 375° F. [190° C.] and cook for another one to one and one half hours, until the meat shrinks away from the sides of the terrine and the juices run clear.

Take the terrine out of the oven, remove the pig's foot and the branch of rosemary and smooth over the top. Place a weight on top of the terrine and let it cool.

Refrigerate it for at least one day before serving.

HELGE RUBINSTEIN
FRENCH COOKERY

Pork Cake Terrine

Northumbrian Mitton of Pork

To make about 2 pounds [1 kg.]

1½ lb.	sausage meat	¾ kg.
6 to 8 tbsp.	chopped mixed fresh parsley, thyme, chervil, chives, marjoram and a little sage	90 to 120 ml.
about ¾ lb.	lean salt pork with the rind removed, blanched for 3 minutes, drained and thinly sliced	about 350 g.
	salt and freshly ground pepper	

Test the sausage meat by frying a small piece; alter the seasoning, if necessary, to your own taste. Make small flat cakes of this meat and roll each one in the chopped herbs.

Line a greased 4-cup [1-liter] terrine with slices of salt pork and put in a layer of sausage-meat cakes, a layer of salt-pork slices, and so on, until both are used up, seasoning lightly as you go. Fit foil directly on top of the meat and put a weight on top of that to keep the meat pressed down while it is cooking.

Stand the terrine in a water bath and cook for about one hour in a preheated 350° F. [180° C.] oven, removing the weight and the foil for the last 15 minutes. You can drain off the surplus fat, but the terrine will keep longer if you do not. This can be eaten hot, and often is, but it is also good cold (put a weight on it as it cools).

SIMONE SEKERS
PÂTÉS, TERRINES AND POTTED MEATS

Pork and Spinach Terrine

To make about 1½ pounds [¾ kg.]

1 lb.	spinach or chard, parboiled for 3 minutes, drained, squeezed dry and coarsely chopped	½ kg.
1 lb.	boneless fatty pork, ground	½ kg.
1 tbsp.	salt	15 ml.
½ tsp.	freshly ground black pepper	2 ml.
¼ tsp.	mixed spices	1 ml.

Combine all of the ingredients. Fry a spoonful of the mixture and taste it for seasoning. Turn the mixture into a 3-cup [¾-liter] earthenware terrine mold or loaf pan. On top put a piece of buttered parchment paper. Stand the mold or pan in a baking dish half-filled with water. Cook the terrine in a preheated 325° F. [160° C.] oven for 45 minutes to one hour, until it is firm but not browned.

This terrine can be eaten hot as a main course, but I prefer it cold, as a first dish, with bread or toast.

ELIZABETH DAVID
SPICES, SALT AND AROMATICS IN THE ENGLISH KITCHEN

Cheap and Good Terrine

Pasztet Tani a Dobry

To make about 7 pounds [3½ kg.]

2 lb.	fresh pork fat, cubed	1 kg.
1½ lb.	boneless ham, cubed	¾ kg.
2 lb.	boneless lean veal, cubed	1 kg.
⅓ cup	dried wild mushrooms, soaked in warm water for 30 minutes, drained, stems cut off	75 ml.
2	onions, 1 grated	2
1	parsnip	1
¼ lb.	celeriac, in 1 piece	125 g.
15	small sweet red peppers, halved, seeded and deribbed	15
20	peppercorns, crushed	20
1	bay leaf	1
3	hard rolls, crumbled	3
one 1½ lb.	pork liver, trimmed and cut in half	one ¾ kg.
2½ tsp.	freshly grated nutmeg	12 ml.
5	eggs	5
8 tbsp.	butter, melted	120 ml.
	salt and freshly ground pepper	
	lard	
	dry bread crumbs	

Fry the pork fat in a large saucepan until the cubes have rendered their pure fat and are lightly browned. Add the ham, veal and mushrooms, cover generously with water, cover the pan and stew for one and one half hours. Be careful not to burn the meats—there should always be about 1 quart [1 liter] of liquid in the pan. Add the whole onion, parsnip, celeriac, peppers, peppercorns and bay leaf, and continue to cook until the meat looks almost mashed, about 30 minutes more. Remove the parsnip and celeriac, and add the crumbled hard rolls, the liver and 1 cup [¼ liter] of water. Cook for another 30 minutes. Let it cool.

Put the meat mixture through a food grinder three times, then add the nutmeg, eggs, melted butter and grated onion. Season with salt and pepper. Mix and put through the food grinder once more. Fry a spoonful of the mixture and taste it for seasoning.

Grease two round 2-quart [2-liter] baking dishes with lard and sprinkle with the bread crumbs. Fill the dishes with the meat mixture, pressing it down with a potato masher. Cover the dishes tightly and cook the terrines in a preheated 450° F. [230° C.] oven for one hour, taking care that they do not burn. Cool completely before serving.

IDA PLUCIŃSKA
KSIĄŻKA KUCHARSKA UDOSKONALONA

Rustic Terrine

Pâté Rustique

To make about 2½ pounds [1¼ kg.]

1 lb.	boneless pork, ground	½ kg.
1 lb.	boneless veal, lamb or beef, ground	½ kg.
2	eggs	2
1	onion, finely chopped	1
2 tbsp.	lard, melted	30 ml.
1¼ cups	dry white wine	300 ml.
	salt and pepper	
	mixed spices	
½ cup	gelatinous meat stock *(recipe, page 162)*	125 ml.

Mix the meats together, add the remaining ingredients and mix well. Pack the mixture into a buttered 5-cup [1¼-liter] terrine mold and cook it, uncovered, in a preheated 300° F. [150° C.] oven for two hours, or until the mixture has shrunk from the sides of the mold. When the terrine is cold, turn it out and decorate it as you wish.

TANTE MARGUERITE
LA CUISINE DE LA BONNE MÉNAGÈRE

Terrine of Ham, Pork and Veal

To make about 3 pounds [1½ kg.]

1 lb.	boneless ham, diced	½ kg.
1 lb.	boneless pork, ground	½ kg.
1 lb.	boneless veal, ground	½ kg.
1	garlic clove, chopped	1
6	juniper berries, crushed	6
½ tsp. each	dried thyme and marjoram leaves	2 ml. each
½ tsp.	ground mace	2 ml.
	salt and coarsely ground black pepper	
½ cup	white wine	125 ml.
2 tbsp.	brandy	30 ml.
¼ lb.	salt pork with the rind removed, blanched for 5 minutes, drained and cut into 2-inch [5-cm.] strips	125 g.
1 or 2	bay leaves	1 or 2

Mix the ham, pork and veal with the garlic, juniper berries, herbs and seasonings. Put the mixture into a bowl and pour over the wine and the brandy. Let the meats marinate for an hour or two. Fry a spoonful of the mixture and taste it for seasoning. Cover the bottom of a fairly shallow 6-cup [1½-liter] terrine mold with the strips of salt pork. Pack in the meat mixture, cover with more strips of salt pork and put a bay leaf or two in the center. Put the mold in a baking dish filled with water and cook in a preheated 300° F. [150° C.] oven for two and one half to three hours. The terrine is done when the mixture is firm and has shrunk from the sides of the mold. Let it cool.

Serve with toast and a salad.

ELIZABETH DAVID
CLASSICS: SUMMER COOKING

Veal, Pork and Chicken-Liver Terrine

Terrine aux Foies de Volailles

To make about 2½ pounds [1¼ kg.]

½ lb.	boneless veal loin, diced	¼ kg.
½ lb.	pork tenderloin, diced	¼ lb.
	salt and pepper	
	quatre épices	
3	shallots, chopped	3
2	garlic cloves, finely chopped	2
1 tbsp.	finely chopped fresh parsley	15 ml.
1 cup	Cognac	¼ liter
½ lb.	fresh pork belly, ground	¼ kg.
½ lb.	chicken livers, trimmed and ground	¼ kg.
¼ lb.	fresh pork fat, ground	125 g.
1	onion, finely chopped	1
½ cup	*crème fraîche* or heavy cream	125 ml.
1	egg	1
¼ lb.	pork caul, soaked and drained	125 g.

Combine the diced veal and pork with salt, pepper, a pinch of *quatre épices*, the shallots, garlic and parsley. Mix well, pour on the Cognac, refrigerate and let the meats marinate for 24 hours. Mix together the ground chicken livers, pork belly, pork fat and chopped onion; season with salt and pepper. Refrigerate the mixture.

The next day, combine the ground meat mixture with the marinated meat mixture and add the cream and the egg. Line a round 4-cup [1-liter] terrine with the pork caul, allowing it to hang over the edge. Pack in the meat mixture and fold over the edges of the caul. Cook the terrine in a water bath in a preheated 350° F. [180° C.] oven for two hours, or until the top is browned and the mixture is firm. Place a plate on the terrine, put a 4-pound [2-kg.] weight on the plate and let the terrine cool.

FRANÇOIS VOEGELING
LA GASTRONOMIE ALSACIENNE

Veal and Ham Mold

This loaf is probably a development of an earlier ham cake, traditional to Essex, that consisted of ground ham thickened with ale-soaked bread, the mixture being bound with eggs.

To make about 2 1/2 pounds [1 1/4 kg.]

1 lb.	boneless stew veal, coarsely chopped	1/2 kg.
1 lb.	boneless ham, coarsely chopped	1/2 kg.
1 tsp.	coarsely chopped fresh parsley	5 ml.
1 tsp.	grated lemon peel	5 ml.
1/4 tsp.	ground mace	1 ml.
	salt and pepper	
4	eggs, hard-boiled and sliced	4
1 1/4 cups	gelatinous meat stock (recipe, page 162)	300 ml.

Mix the veal and ham with the parsley, lemon peel, mace, and salt and pepper. Alternate layers of the meat mixture and the eggs in a greased 5-cup [1 1/4-liter] loaf pan or terrine. Fill it with stock, cover it with foil, and cook it in a water bath in a preheated 325° F. [160° C.] oven for two hours.

Let the loaf cool completely, then refrigerate it. Turn it out the following day and serve it cut into slices.

LIZZIE BOYD (EDITOR)
BRITISH COOKERY

Veal and Bacon Terrine

Terrine de Body

"Body" is a term used for veal in the Berry region of France. The quantity of white pepper called for in this recipe produces a very spicy terrine. The white pepper can be reduced, according to taste, to as little as 2 or 3 tablespoonfuls [30 or 45 ml.].

To make about 5 pounds [2 1/2 kg.]

2 lb.	bacon, very thinly sliced	1 kg.
2 lb.	veal scallops, very thinly sliced	1 kg.
2/3 cup	finely chopped onion	150 ml.
1 1/4 cups	finely chopped fresh parsley	300 ml.
2/3 cup	freshly ground white pepper	150 ml.
	salt and freshly ground black pepper	
1/2 cup	dry white wine	125 ml.
1	sprig thyme	1
1/2	bay leaf	1/2

Choose a rectangular 2 1/2-quart [2 1/2-liter] terrine or two smaller ones. Line the bottom and sides with slices of bacon placed lengthwise side by side. Put in a layer of veal scallops. Mix the onion, parsley and white pepper, and sprinkle in a layer of this mixture. Season to taste with salt and black pepper, taking into account the saltiness of the bacon.

Continue making layers of bacon, veal and seasonings until the terrine is full to the brim, finishing with bacon slices. Pour in the wine, and place the thyme and bay leaf on top. Cover the terrine. Cook it in a preheated 350° F. [180° C.] oven for about three hours for a large terrine or one and one half hours for smaller ones, or until the juices run clear.

Place a lightly weighted board on the meat while it cools. Refrigerate until it is very cold so that it slices nicely.

ACADÉMIE DES GASTRONOMES/ACADÉMIE CULINAIRE DE FRANCE
LA HAUTE CUISINE FRANÇAISE

Veal Pâté

To make about 3 pounds [1 1/2 kg.]

3 tbsp.	lard	45 ml.
2 lb.	boneless veal, cubed	1 kg.
1/2	onion, sliced	1/2
1 cup	water	1/4 liter
3	potatoes, peeled and quartered	3
3 tbsp.	butter	45 ml.
1/2 cup	flour	125 ml.
1/2 cup	sour cream	125 ml.
1	salt herring, soaked in several changes of water for 3 to 4 hours	1
	salt	
	black pepper or paprika	
	grated nutmeg	
2	eggs	2

Heat the lard in a skillet and brown the veal on all sides. Add the onion and the water, cover and simmer until the meat is tender. Cool. Remove the veal and press the onion and cooking liquid through a sieve. Meanwhile, boil the potatoes in water to cover until they are tender. Drain and cool them.

Melt the butter, add the flour and brown lightly, stirring constantly. Off the heat, stir in the sour cream and the sieved cooking liquid. Stirring constantly, bring to a boil and cook until this sauce is thick. Set aside.

Squeeze the water out of the herring, cut off the head and tail, and remove the skin and bones. Grind the herring, veal and potatoes together three times. Stir this mixture into the sauce and add salt, pepper or paprika, and nutmeg to taste. Add the eggs and mix thoroughly.

Pack the mixture into a greased 6-cup [1 1/2-liter] mold, pressing it down with a spoon. Cover the mold and place it in a saucepan with enough boiling water to come halfway up the sides. Cook over high heat for 45 minutes. Remove and uncover the mold.

When the terrine is slightly cooled, unmold it onto a round plate. Serve warm or cold.

ZOFIA CZERNY
POLISH COOKBOOK

Terrine of Veal and Pork

The ingredients for this dish can be varied—for instance, ham can be used instead of salt pork, more or less garlic can be used, and port or red wine can be substituted for white.

To make about 2½ pounds [1¼ kg.]

1 lb.	boneless veal, coarsely chopped	½ kg.
1 lb.	boneless pork, coarsely chopped	½ kg.
⅓ lb.	salt pork with the rind removed, blanched for 3 minutes, drained and coarsely chopped	150 g.
2	garlic cloves, chopped	2
½ tsp.	dried thyme leaves	2 ml.
	ground mace	
	salt and freshly ground black pepper	
½ cup	white wine	125 ml.
2½ cups	gelatinous meat stock (recipe, page 162), melted	625 ml.
1	bay leaf	1

Combine the meats, herbs, spices and wine. Fry a spoonful of the mixture and taste it for seasoning. Pack the mixture into a 6-cup [1½-liter] terrine, and add enough melted stock to come just level with the meat. Put the bay leaf on top, cover the terrine, and cook it in a water bath in a preheated 350° F. [180° C.] oven for two hours. When the terrine is cold, cover it with the rest of the melted stock and place it in the refrigerator to set the aspic.

ELIZABETH DAVID
CLASSICS: SUMMER COOKING

Paprika Veal Pâté

Paprikáspastétom

This is a scarlet pâté which can be turned out to serve. It comes from Budapest and it is delicious with rye bread.

To make about 2 pounds [1 kg.]

4 tbsp.	lard	60 ml.
1	onion, chopped	1
2 tsp.	sweet paprika	10 ml.
1½ lb.	boneless stew veal, diced	¾ kg.
½ tsp.	salt	2 ml.
2 tbsp.	water	30 ml.
1 tbsp.	puréed tomato	15 ml.
6	egg yolks	6
8 tbsp.	butter, softened	120 ml.

Heat the lard in a large skillet, add the onion, and cook it gently until it is soft and golden. Stir in the paprika and the

veal. Add the salt and the water, then cover and let it simmer gently, stirring from time to time and adding a little water occasionally. There should never be a lot of liquid.

After 30 minutes, stir in the puréed tomato. When the meat is tender, let it cool and put the whole thing, meat and gravy, through the fine disk of a food grinder. Beat the egg yolks and the butter together until smooth and creamy, and beat them into the cold ground meat, blending thoroughly. Pack the mixture into a 4-cup [1-liter] terrine. Refrigerate the pâté until you are ready to serve it.

SHEILA HUTCHINS
PÂTÉS AND TERRINES

Rigoletto Meat Loaf

Polpettone "Rigoletto"

To make about 1½ pounds [¾ kg.]

1 lb.	boneless veal, ground twice	½ kg.
3	chicken livers, trimmed and ground	3
¼ lb.	mortadella, chopped	125 g.
1¼ cups	freshly grated grana or Parmesan cheese	300 ml.
7	eggs, 5 lightly beaten, 2 hard-boiled and sliced	7
1 cup	basic white sauce (recipe, page 165)	¼ liter
	salt and pepper	
	grated nutmeg	
2 cups	gelatinous meat stock (recipe, page 162)	½ liter
1	sweet red pepper, halved, seeded, deribbed and cut into small pieces	1
2	sour gherkins, sliced	2

Mix together the meats, cheese, beaten eggs, white sauce, salt, pepper and a pinch of nutmeg. Pack the mixture into a buttered 6-cup [1½-liter] mold and place it on a rack in a pot. Pour in enough water to come halfway up the mold, cover the pot, bring the water to a boil and steam the loaf for one hour, or until it is firm and has shrunk from the sides of the mold. Let it cool in the water bath, then unmold it onto a plate. Refrigerate the loaf.

Wash the mold and refrigerate it until it is thoroughly chilled. Coat the inside of the mold with a thin layer of gelatinous meat stock. Chill it until it has set to an aspic, then arrange the pieces of red pepper and the slices of egg and gherkin on it. Add another layer of stock to hold the garnishes and chill until set. Return the meat loaf to the mold and pour in enough stock to fill the mold. Refrigerate until the aspic has set, then unmold the loaf to serve it.

CIA ERAMO
SEGRETI E NO DELLA CUCINA MANTOVANA

Terrine of Diced Mixed Meats

Terrine d'Albas

The technique of boning a rabbit is shown on pages 66-67.

To make about 9 pounds [4½ kg.]

2 to 3 lb.	rabbit, boned, the meat finely diced	1 to 1½ kg.
1 lb.	boneless lean veal, finely diced	½ kg.
1 lb.	boned pork loin or shoulder, finely diced	½ kg.
1 lb.	chicken livers, trimmed and finely diced	½ kg.
4 lb.	fresh pork fat, finely diced	2 kg.
4	eggs	4
6 tbsp.	salt	90 ml.
	pepper	
1 tbsp.	dried thyme leaves	15 ml.
1	bay leaf, crumbled	1
½ cup	Armagnac or other brandy	125 ml.

Knead the ingredients together until they are well combined. Pack the mixture into a 4½-quart [4½-liter] terrine and refrigerate it overnight. Place the terrine in a preheated 400° F. [200° C.] oven. After 30 minutes, reduce the heat to 350° F. [180° C.]. Cook for seven hours. Insert a skewer; if the juices run clear, the terrine is cooked. Serve cold.

HENRI PHILIPPON
CUISINE DU QUERCY ET DU PÉRIGORD

Terrine of Whatever You Like

Gâteau de Viande de Ce Que l'On Veut

To make about 4 pounds [2 kg.]

2 lb.	boneless lean beef, lamb or veal, or a mixture of these meats	1 kg.
¼ lb.	beef suet or marrow, chopped	125 g.
¼ lb.	ham	125 g.
	salt	
	mixed spices	
2 tsp.	chopped fresh parsley	10 ml.
2	scallions, finely chopped	2
1 cup	finely chopped fresh mushrooms	¼ liter
1 tsp.	powdered basil	5 ml.
4	egg yolks	4
¼ cup	*eau de vie* or other brandy	50 ml.
1¼ lb.	fresh pork fatback, 1 lb. [½ kg.] diced, the rest sliced into thick bards	600 g.

Chop or grind the meat with the beef suet and the ham. Season with salt, mixed spices, the parsley, scallions, mushrooms and basil. Add the egg yolks, *eau de vie* or other brandy, and the diced fatback; work the mixture well until it is thoroughly blended. Fry a spoonful of the mixture and taste it for seasoning.

Line a round 2-quart [2-liter] casserole with bards of fatback, pack in the meat mixture and cover with more bards. Cover the casserole with the lid and cook the terrine in a preheated 350° F. [180° C.] oven for four hours, reducing the heat to 250° F. [130° C.] after the first hour. Place a weighted board on top of the meat and let it cool.

To serve, turn the terrine out of the casserole onto a platter and scrape the covering of fat until it is uniformly white.

MENON
LES SOUPERS DE LA COUR

Country Terrine

Pâté de Campagne

To make about 5 pounds [2½ kg.]

2 lb.	boneless fatty pork, ground	1 kg.
1 lb.	boneless lean veal, ground	½ kg.
1 lb.	pork liver, trimmed and ground	½ kg.
3½ cups	fresh bread crumbs	875 ml.
1	large onion, finely chopped and sautéed in 2 tbsp. [30 ml.] butter until soft	1
3	garlic cloves, crushed to a paste with ½ tsp. [2 ml.] coarse salt	3
2 tbsp.	chopped fresh parsley	30 ml.
2 tsp.	mixed spices	10 ml.
1 tbsp.	mixed dry herbs	15 ml.
1 tbsp.	salt	15 ml.
5 or 6	eggs	5 or 6
½ cup	brandy	125 ml.
¼ lb.	pork caul, soaked and drained	125 g.
¼ lb.	fresh pork fatback, cut into long, thin strips	125 g.

Combine all of the ingredients except the caul and the strips of fatback. Mix thoroughly, using both hands. Fry a spoonful of the mixture and taste it for seasoning.

Line a 2½-quart [2½-liter] earthenware gratin dish with the caul, letting it hang over the edges. Pack in the mixture, mounding it up to form a dome. Press the strips of fat in a crisscross pattern over the surface and fold over the caul, molding it neatly.

Cook the terrine in a preheated 350° F. [180° C.] oven for one and one half hours, or until a skewer inserted in the center comes out hot.

PETITS PROPOS CULINAIRES

Whitby Polony

This cut into slices is delicious for breakfast. It is also much welcomed in Yorkshire as a sandwich filling.

To make about 2 pounds [1 kg.]

1 lb.	boneless lean beef, ground	½ kg.
½ lb.	boneless lean ham, ground	¼ kg.
4 cups	fresh bread crumbs	1 liter
	salt and pepper	
	ground mace	
	grated nutmeg	
	cayenne pepper	

Mix all the ingredients together, seeing that the seasoning is well distributed. Have a 6-cup [1½-liter] straight-sided stoneware jam jar well buttered, pack in the mixture, and cover the top firmly with two or three layers of parchment paper tied down securely. Put the jar into a saucepan of boiling water and steam it for three and one half hours, or until the mixture is firm to the touch. When cool, turn it out carefully.

MRS. ARTHUR WEBB
FARMHOUSE COOKERY

Veal and Ham Terrine

Ternera Fiambre

To make about 2½ pounds [1¼ kg.]

1 lb.	boneless veal, ground	½ kg.
½ lb.	veal liver, trimmed and ground	¼ kg.
½ lb.	boneless ham, one fourth ground, the rest sliced	¼ kg.
½ lb.	salt pork with the rind removed, blanched for 3 minutes, drained, one fourth ground, the rest sliced	¼ kg.
3	garlic cloves, finely chopped	3
1	onion, finely chopped	1
1 tbsp.	chopped fresh parsley	15 ml.
1 tsp.	salt	5 ml.
¼ tsp.	black pepper	1 ml.
½ tsp.	paprika	2 ml.
¼ tsp.	ground cinnamon	1 ml.
1	egg, beaten	1
⅓ cup	brandy	75 ml.
1	bay leaf	1

Mix together all of the ground meats. Add the garlic, onion, parsley, seasonings, spices, egg and brandy. Fry a spoonful

of the mixture and taste it for seasoning. Line a 6-cup [1½-liter] terrine with the slices of salt pork and fill it with the ground meat mixture, layering the ground meat with the slices of ham. Put the bay leaf on top. Stand the terrine in a pan of hot water, place it in a preheated 375° F. [190° C.] oven and cook for one to one and one half hours, or until the juices run clear. Weight it until cool, then chill it until the next day. To unmold, dip the terrine into hot water for a moment and turn it out onto a serving plate.

MARINA PEREYRA DE AZNAR AND NINA FROUD
THE HOME BOOK OF SPANISH COOKERY

Veal Cake

Serve this terrine with any cold sauce you like, or with vinegar, mustard and sugar.

To make about 3 pounds [1½ kg.]

4 lb.	veal breast, bones removed and reserved, meat cut into 3 pieces	2 kg.
	cayenne pepper	
	salt and white pepper	
	grated nutmeg	
	ground mace	
	ground cloves	
4 tbsp.	butter, thinly sliced	60 ml.
½ cup	finely chopped fresh parsley	125 ml.
2	salt anchovies, filleted, soaked in water for 30 minutes, drained, patted dry and finely chopped	2
4	eggs, hard-boiled and halved	4
½ lb.	lean slab bacon with the rind removed, sliced ½ inch [1 cm.] thick	¼ kg.

Season the veal with cayenne pepper, salt, white pepper, nutmeg, mace and cloves. Cover the bottom of a 6-cup [1½-liter] terrine mold with the thin slices of butter. Put in a piece of veal and sprinkle it with some of the chopped parsley and anchovies. Put in half of the egg halves, cover with bacon slices and repeat these layers, ending with the veal. Lay the veal bones on top to prevent the meat from drying out, cover the mold, and cook the terrine in a preheated 325° F. [160° C.] oven for four hours, or until the veal is very tender.

Remove the bones and lay a weight on the meat to press it and make it solid. Serve it cold.

LADY HARRIET ST. CLAIR (EDITOR)
DAINTY DISHES

Terrine of the House

Terrine Maison

The original version of this recipe calls for foie gras. Goose liver or duck liver may be used as a substitute.

To make about 4 pounds [2 kg.]

1 lb.	boneless lean veal, half cut into thin strips, half diced	½ kg.
1½ lb.	fresh pork belly with the rind removed, lean meat diced, fat chopped	¾ kg.
1	ham shank, bone removed, lean meat diced, fat chopped	1
⅔ lb.	chicken livers, trimmed and ground	300 g.
3 cups	dry white wine	¾ liter
½ cup	Cognac	125 ml.
2 tbsp.	salt	30 ml.
	pepper	
	grated nutmeg	
2	eggs	2
6 tbsp.	flour	90 ml.
¾ lb.	fresh pork fatback, sliced into bards	350 g.
¼ lb.	goose or duck livers, trimmed and sliced	125 g.
1	truffle, sliced	1
	melted lard	

Place the diced meats, chopped fat and chicken livers in a bowl and add the wine, Cognac and seasonings. Let the meats marinate for 24 hours. Knead the eggs and flour into the meats and the marinade. Fry a spoonful of the mixture and taste it for seasoning.

Line a 2½-quart [2½-liter] earthenware terrine mold with bards of fatback. Put in a layer of the meat mixture, a layer of veal strips, a layer of meat mixture, and so on, until the mold is half-full. Put in the sliced goose or duck liver and truffle, arranging them so that they will appear in the center of each slice. Continue the layers of meat mixture and veal strips until the mold is full. Cover the terrine with bards of fatback and cook it in a water bath in a preheated 300° F. [150° C.] oven for about three hours. It is done when a skewer inserted into the center comes out hot to the touch.

When the terrine is cool, cover the surface with a layer of melted lard; this will make it keep longer. Store the terrine in the refrigerator.

EUGÉNIE BRAZIER
LES SECRETS DE LA MÈRE BRAZIER

Terrine of Pork and Pork Liver

To make about 2½ pounds [1¼ kg.]

½ lb.	boneless pork shoulder, cubed	¼ kg.
½ lb.	pork liver, trimmed and cubed	¼ kg.
½ lb.	fatty salt pork, blanched for 3 minutes, drained and cubed	¼ kg.
½ cup	brandy	125 ml.
	salt and pepper	
	cayenne pepper	
1	garlic clove, lightly crushed	1
1	onion, chopped, or 6 shallots, chopped	1
2	sprigs thyme, 1 crumbled	2
2	bay leaves, 1 crumbled	2
1	slice firm-textured white bread, crust removed	1
1 tsp.	mixed spices	5 ml.
2	eggs	2
½ lb.	lean salt pork, blanched for 3 minutes and sliced into bards	¼ kg.

Place the pork, pork liver and cubed salt pork in a china bowl. Add the brandy, salt, pepper, cayenne, garlic, onion or shallots, and crumbled thyme and bay leaf. Mix together, cover the bowl with a cloth and a lid, and let the mixture marinate for several hours or until the next day.

Drain the meats. In a skillet, fry the cubes of salt pork until they have rendered their fat and look translucent; increase the heat and add the other marinated meats. Stiffen but do not brown them. Empty the contents of the skillet into the marinade bowl, including all liquid fat (it is important to use this fat in the mixture). Force all of the ingredients through the fine disk of a food grinder, finally passing the slice of bread through the machine to clear the juices (all is valuable). Add the mixed spices to this forcemeat and, with a wooden spoon, mix in the eggs thoroughly. Fry a spoonful of the forcemeat and taste it for seasoning.

Line a 4-cup [1-liter] terrine mold (a baking dish will do) with bards of salt pork, fill it with the forcemeat, and cover with the remaining bards of salt pork. Place the remaining bay leaf and the whole sprig of thyme on top. Cover the mold with a lid, stand it in a tray of water, and cook it in a preheated 350° F. [180° C.] oven for one and one half hours, or until the internal temperature reaches 160° F. [70° C.].

Remove the mold from the oven, let it stand for 30 minutes, then place a wooden board on the surface of the meat with a 1-pound [½-kg.] weight on top. Leave the terrine in the refrigerator until the following day.

Remove the wooden board and the thyme and bay leaf. Using a table knife, cut out slices from one end. Or unmold the terrine and slice it onto a dish.

STANLEY FORTIN
THE WORLD BOOK OF PORK DISHES

Terrine with Basil

La Terrine au Basilic

To make about 1½ pounds [¾ kg.]

½ lb.	veal liver, trimmed and cut into ¾-inch [2-cm.] cubes	¼ kg.
⅓ cup	marc or brandy	75 ml.
⅓ cup	olive oil	75 ml.
1 tsp.	dried thyme leaves	5 ml.
½ lb.	boneless lean pork, ground	¼ kg.
½ lb.	boneless veal, ground	¼ kg.
	salt and pepper	
2 cups	fresh basil leaves	½ liter
2	bay leaves	2

Combine the liver, marc or brandy, oil and thyme, and let the mixture marinate for at least two hours. Mix the ground meats and season them with salt and pepper.

Pack a ¾-inch [2-cm.] layer of the ground meats into a 3-cup [¾-liter] terrine mold. Add a layer of basil leaves, one of liver, another of basil, another of ground meats and so on, ending with the ground meats. Put the bay leaves on top and cover the mold.

Cook the terrine in a water bath in a preheated 400° F. [200° C.] oven for 45 minutes to one hour. Let the terrine cool, then place it in the refrigerator. Serve it cold with butter and black olives.

FLORENCE DE ANDREIS
LA CUISINE PROVENÇALE D'AUJOURD'HUI

Breton Terrine

Pâté Breton

To make about 3½ pounds [1¾ kg.]

1 lb.	boneless pork shoulder	½ kg.
1 lb.	pork liver, trimmed	½ kg.
1 lb.	fresh pork fat	½ kg.
4	onions	4
10	sprigs fresh parsley	10
½ lb.	fresh pork rind, half parboiled for 15 minutes, drained and finely chopped	¼ kg.
	salt and pepper	
1	egg	1
1	sprig thyme	1
1	bay leaf	1
¼ lb.	pork caul, soaked and drained	125 g.

Coarsely chop together the pork shoulder, pork liver, pork fat, onions and parsley. Mix in the chopped rind, season with

salt and pepper, and add the egg. Put the thyme and bay leaf into a shallow 2-quart [2-liter] baking dish. Put in the remaining pork rind, fat side down. Line the dish with the caul, letting it hang over the edges. Pack in the meat mixture, smooth the top and fold over the edges of the caul. Cook, uncovered, in a preheated 325° F. [160° C.] oven for two hours, or until the terrine is browned on top and has shrunk from the sides of the dish. Allow it to cool, then refrigerate the terrine for 24 hours before serving.

CÉLINE VENCE
ENCYCLOPÉDIE HACHETTE DE LA CUISINE RÉGIONALE

Beef Terrine from the Auvergne

Terrine de Boeuf Auvergnate

To make about 3 pounds [1½ kg.]

2	onions, finely chopped	2
2 tbsp.	butter	30 ml.
2 lb.	boneless beef chuck, cut into thin strips	1 kg.
	salt and freshly ground pepper	
⅔ lb.	boneless fatty pork, ground	300 g.
2	garlic cloves, finely chopped	2
2 tbsp.	chopped fresh parsley	30 ml.
2	eggs	2
	dried thyme leaves	
	quatre épices	
⅔ lb.	fresh pork rind	300 g.
½ lb.	fresh pork fatback, sliced into bards	¼ kg.
1 cup	red wine	¼ liter
2	bay leaves	2
	flour-and-water paste	

Sauté the onions in the butter for five minutes without letting them color. Season the beef strips with salt and pepper.

Mix the ground pork, sautéed onions, garlic, parsley and eggs. Season with salt, pepper, thyme and *quatre épices*.

Line a 6-cup [1½-liter] terrine with the pork rind, fat side down. Cover with a layer of fatback bards. Pack in a layer of the ground pork mixture, then a layer of the beef strips, and continue alternating these layers until the beef and the pork mixture have been used up. Pour on the red wine and cover the surface with bards of fat. Put the bay leaves on top and seal on the lid of the terrine with flour-and-water paste.

Place the terrine in a pan of boiling water and cook it in a preheated 250° F. [120° C.] oven for three and one half hours, adding more water to the pan if necessary. Remove the lid, weight the terrine and let it cool. Refrigerate it for 24 hours. To serve, unmold the terrine and remove the pork rind.

DOMINIQUE WEBER
LES BONNES RECETTES DES PROVINCES DE FRANCE

Sausage Balls from the Ardèche

Caillettes de l'Ardèche

These are eaten very hot, with mashed potatoes—or cold.

To make about 2½ pounds [1¼ kg.]

1 lb.	chard, parboiled for 5 minutes, drained and squeezed dry	½ kg.
¼ lb.	spinach, parboiled for 3 minutes, drained and squeezed dry	125 g.
1	celery rib, parboiled for 5 minutes and drained	1
⅓ lb.	pork liver, trimmed	150 g.
1 lb.	boneless fatty pork, ground	½ kg.
	salt and pepper	
	quatre épices	
	dried thyme leaves	
	dried basil	
¼ lb.	pork caul, soaked, drained and cut into 6-inch [15-cm.] squares	125 g.

Chop together all of the parboiled vegetables with the pork liver. Mix with the ground pork, season with salt, pepper, *quatre épices*, thyme and basil, and blend well. Fry a spoonful of the mixture and taste it for seasoning.

Form handful-sized balls of the mixture and wrap them in pieces of caul. Place them in a buttered baking dish and cook in a preheated 425° F. [220° C.] oven for 20 minutes, or until the internal temperature reaches 160° F. [80° C.].

EUGÉNIE BRAZIER
LES SECRETS DE LA MÈRE BRAZIER

Mrs. Moreton's Mixture

To make about 1 pound [½ kg.]

½ lb.	chicken livers, trimmed	¼ kg.
1	onion	1
½ lb.	boneless fatty pork, ground	¼ kg.
	salt and pepper	
1	garlic clove, crushed to a paste	1
2 or 3	sprigs fresh parsley, very finely chopped	2 or 3
1 tbsp.	sherry	15 ml.
6	slices lean bacon, 2 finely chopped	6
	rendered fat	

Grind the livers and onion and add them, juice and all, to the ground pork. Mix together. Add the salt and pepper, garlic, parsley and sherry. Work in the chopped bacon. Fry a spoonful of the mixture and taste it for seasoning. Grease a deep 4-

cup [1-liter] pan with rendered fat and line it with the bacon slices. Spoon in the liver mixture and cover it with thrice-folded, well-greased parchment paper. Cook the terrine in a water bath in a preheated 350° F. [180° C.] oven for about one and one half hours, or until a skewer inserted in the center of the terrine is hot to the touch when removed. Cool the terrine under a weight, and refrigerate it before serving.

JOYCE DOUGLAS
OLD DERBYSHIRE RECIPES AND CUSTOMS

Terrine of Mixed Meats and Chicken Livers

Pastel-Terrina de Carnes Variadas y Higaditos de Pollo

To make about 3 pounds [1½ kg.]

¾ lb.	boneless chicken breast, ground	350 g.
⅓ lb.	lean bacon, ground	150 g.
¾ lb.	boneless lean pork, ground	350 g.
½ lb.	chicken livers, trimmed and ground	¼ kg.
3	eggs, beaten	3
¼ cup	Cognac	50 ml.
½ cup	heavy cream, whipped	125 ml.
	salt and pepper	
10 oz.	lean salt pork with the rind removed, blanched for 3 minutes, drained and thinly sliced	300 g.
6	whole cloves	6
2	bay leaves	2
1	sprig thyme	1
	lettuce or watercress	

In a bowl, combine the ground chicken breast, bacon, pork and chicken livers. Add the eggs, Cognac and whipped cream. Season with salt and pepper, and mix well.

Line a 6-cup [1½-liter] terrine mold with some of the salt-pork slices. Pack in the meat mixture, pressing it down well. Stick the cloves into the remaining salt-pork slices and cover the meat with the slices. Arrange the bay leaves and the sprig of thyme on top.

Cover the terrine and place it in a water bath. Cook it in a preheated 325° F. [160° C.] oven for one and one half hours, or until the juices run clear. Turn off the oven, but leave the terrine in to cool. When it is tepid, remove it from the oven and weight it to cool completely, about three to four hours.

To serve the terrine, remove the bay leaves, thyme and cloves. Run a knife around the terrine and unmold it. Peel off the covering layer of salt pork. Cut the terrine into fairly thin slices and garnish with lettuce or watercress.

SIMONE ORTEGA
MIL OCHENTA RECETAS DE COCINA

Country Terrine with Hazelnuts

For a more finished look or if the terrine is not to be eaten soon, a thin layer of aspic can be poured over the surface. Another attractive preservation method, which will hold any terrine for 10 to 12 days, is to pour melted butter into the dish until it forms a solid protective layer over the meat. Chill, then coat the butter with a mixture of dried herbs. Cover and refrigerate until needed.

To make about 3½ pounds [1¾ kg.]

4	slices firm-textured white bread, crusts removed, soaked in water and squeezed dry	4
8 to 10	chicken livers, trimmed and finely chopped	8 to 10
⅓ lb.	salt pork with the rind removed, cut into small dice	150 g.
1	medium-sized onion, finely chopped	1
1	large garlic clove, crushed to a paste	1
1 lb.	boneless veal, ground	½ kg.
1 lb.	boneless chicken, ground (preferably dark meat)	½ kg.
¼ cup	chopped fresh parsley	50 ml.
	salt	
	freshly ground black pepper	
½ tsp.	dried thyme leaves	2 ml.
½ tsp.	dried savory leaves	2 ml.
2 tbsp.	Cognac	30 ml.
3	ground juniper berries	3
½ cup	hazelnuts, 3 large nuts reserved for garnish, the rest coarsely chopped	125 ml.
2	small juniper or hemlock sprigs	2

Crumble the soaked bread into a large mixing bowl and add the livers and all of the other ingredients except the garnish. Mingle everything well with your hands. Fry a spoonful of the mixture and taste it for seasoning.

Lightly butter a 7-cup [1¾-liter] terrine or soufflé dish and pack in the mixture. Cover the terrine lightly with foil and place it in a water bath. Cook it in a preheated 350° F. [180° C.] oven for one hour, or until the internal temperature reaches 160° F. [70° C.]. Remove the terrine and tip it slightly to drain off any liquids. Place a double thickness of foil on top and weight the terrine with a plate or a board and canned goods. When cool, place the weighted terrine in the refrigerator overnight. To garnish, arrange the three whole hazelnuts in a centered triangle and place the sprigs of piny green on either side.

JUDITH OLNEY
COMFORTING FOOD

Liver Spread

Leverpastei

To make about 1 pound [½ kg.]

½ lb.	pork liver, trimmed	¼ kg.
½ lb.	fresh pork belly with the rind removed	¼ kg.
1	onion	1
2 cups	water	½ liter
1 tsp.	salt	5 ml.
½ tsp.	freshly ground pepper	2 ml.
½ tsp.	grated nutmeg	2 ml.
¼ tsp.	ground cloves	1 ml.
	melted lard (optional)	

Simmer the liver, pork belly and onion in the water, with the salt, for one and one quarter hours. Drain the mixture, reserving the liquid.

Pass the warm meats and the onion through a food grinder three or four times. Add the pepper and spices and ⅔ cup [150 ml.] of the cooking liquid. Taste for salt.

Let the mixture cool in one large or several small containers, then refrigerate it if not serving it immediately. If you plan to keep the liver spread for more than two days, cover it with a layer of melted lard; it will then keep for about a week in the refrigerator.

RIA HOLLEMAN
PASTEI EN PÂTÉ

Italian Liver Terrine

Pasticcio di Fegato

To make about 1¾ pounds [875 g.]

3 tbsp.	butter	45 ml.
1 lb.	veal liver, trimmed and diced	½ kg.
1	bay leaf	1
½ lb.	chicken livers, trimmed	¼ kg.
	salt and pepper	
¼ cup	Marsala	50 ml.
4	slices firm-textured white bread, crusts removed	4
1 cup	freshly grated grana or Parmesan cheese	¼ liter
1	egg, lightly beaten	1
2	egg yolks, lightly beaten	2
	gelatinous meat stock *(recipe, page 162)*	

Melt the butter in a skillet. Add the veal liver and the bay leaf, and fry gently until the butter has been absorbed. Add the chicken livers, salt, pepper and Marsala. Cook gently for five minutes. Remove the livers and chop them fine. Remove and discard the bay leaf. Soak the bread in the gravy left in the skillet and mash it to a smooth paste. Add the bread paste to the liver and pass the mixture through a sieve or a food grinder. Add the cheese and eggs and mix well, adding a few spoonfuls of stock if the mixture is too stiff to blend well. Taste the mixture for seasoning.

Pack the mixture into a 5-cup [1¼-liter] mold lined with buttered parchment paper. Place the mold on a rack in a pot, pour in enough water to come halfway up the sides of the mold, cover the pot and steam the terrine for 45 minutes, or until it is firm.

Unmold the terrine and let it cool. Spoon over a coating of gelatinous stock. Refrigerate for a few hours to set the stock.

CIA ERAMO
SEGRETI E NO DELLA CUCINA MANTOVANA

Herbed Liver Terrine

Terrine d'Herbes aux Foies de Volailles ou de Gibier

To make about 3 pounds [1½ kg.]

1 lb.	chicken, game or rabbit livers, trimmed and chopped	½ kg.
⅓ lb.	ham, chopped	150 g.
⅓ lb.	bacon, chopped	150 g.
⅓ lb.	fresh pork belly, chopped	150 g.
1 lb.	spinach, stems removed, parboiled in salted water for 5 minutes, drained, squeezed dry and coarsely chopped	½ kg.
⅓ cup	fines herbes	75 ml.
½ tsp.	dried rosemary or thyme leaves	2 ml.
½	bay leaf, crumbled	½
1	garlic clove, crushed to a paste	1
1	onion, chopped	1
1	egg	1
	salt and pepper	
¼ tsp.	cayenne pepper	1 ml.
¼ tsp.	grated nutmeg	1 ml.
	quatre épices	
⅓ cup	Cognac	75 ml.
	fresh pork fatback, sliced into bards	
	flour-and-water paste	

In a large bowl, mix all of the meats, the spinach and the herbs with the garlic and onion. Moisten the mixture with the egg. Add all of the seasonings and the Cognac. Fry a spoonful of the mixture and taste it for seasoning.

Line a 5-cup [1¼-liter] terrine mold with bards of fatback. Pack the meat-and-herb mixture into the mold. Cover with thin bards of fatback. Put the lid on the mold; seal the edges with the flour-and-water paste.

Bring a shallow pan half-filled with water to a boil. Place the terrine in this water bath and cook it in a preheated 300° F. [150° C.] oven for about one and one half hours, or until the terrine reaches an internal temperature of 160° F. [70° C.]. Allow the terrine to cool and settle in the refrigerator overnight.

The dish may be served with salad and sour gherkins.

LOUISETTE BERTHOLLE
250 RECETTES DE SOLOGNE ET D'AILLEURS

Terrine of Chicken Livers

Terrine de Foies de Volailles

This terrine mixture, without the cream and Cognac, may be used as an element in more complex pâtés and terrines, such as Lovely Aurora's Pillow, demonstrated on pages 66-69. For the technique of removing marrow from bones, see page 28.

To make about 2½ pounds [1¼ kg.]

1 cup	gelatinous meat stock (recipe, page 162)	¼ liter
3	slices firm-textured stale white bread, crusts removed and crumbled	3
1	small garlic clove, crushed to a paste	1
1 lb.	chicken livers, trimmed	½ kg.
⅓ lb.	beef marrow	150 g.
	salt and pepper	
	cayenne pepper	
	mixed dried herbs	
3	eggs	3
½ cup	heavy cream	125 ml.
2 tbsp.	Cognac	30 ml.

Combine the stock and bread crumbs in a small saucepan and reduce, stirring with a wooden spoon, until the mixture becomes a firm paste. Mix the garlic into this panada. Combine the chicken livers, beef marrow, panada and seasonings. Put the mixture through a food grinder, then pass it through a fine-meshed sieve, a ladleful at a time, discarding fragments of tissue that remain in the sieve. Whisk in the eggs, cream and Cognac. Correct the seasoning if necessary.

Butter a 5-cup [1¼-liter] mold or terrine, line the bottom with buttered parchment paper and pour in the mixture. Immerse the terrine by two thirds in hot but not boiling water, cover it with foil and cook it in a preheated 350° F. [180° C.] oven for about one hour, or until the center is firm to the touch. Cool until tepid, then run a knife around the edge of the terrine and unmold it. Press plastic wrap around it to protect it from air. Serve the terrine well chilled.

RICHARD OLNEY
SIMPLE FRENCH FOOD

Liver Cheese

Leberpastete oder Leberkäse

To make about 2½ pounds [1¼ kg.]

1 lb.	pork or veal liver, trimmed	½ kg.
½ lb.	boneless pork loin	¼ kg.
14 oz.	fresh pork belly	425 g.
¼ lb.	salt anchovies, filleted, soaked in water for 30 minutes, drained and patted dry	125 g.
	salt and pepper	
1 tsp.	dried marjoram leaves	5 ml.
¼ cup	Madeira or Cognac	50 ml.
½ lb.	lean bacon or smoked tongue, thinly sliced	¼ kg.
	gelatinous meat stock *(recipe, page 162)*, chilled to set, and this aspic diced	

Pass the liver, pork, pork belly and anchovy fillets twice through a food grinder. Mix well with the pepper, salt if needed, marjoram, and Madeira or Cognac.

Line a piepan with bacon or tongue slices. Pack in the mixture and cover with the remaining slices of bacon or tongue. Cover the pan with foil and cook the pie in a water bath in a preheated 350° F. [180° C.] oven for one and a half to two hours, or until it is firm. After it has cooled, cut the pie into thin slices and decorate these with the diced aspic.

HENRIETTE DAVIDIS
PRAKTISCHES KOCHBUCH

Simple Liver Terrine

Le Papiton

To make about 2 pounds [1 kg.]

1 lb.	pork liver, trimmed and ground	½ kg.
1 lb.	boneless fatty pork, ground	½ kg.
4	slices firm-textured white bread, crusts removed, crumbled, soaked in stock *(recipe, page 162)* or water and squeezed dry	4
2 or 3	eggs	2 or 3
	salt and pepper	
	quatre épices	
	freshly grated nutmeg	
¼ cup	*eau de vie* or other brandy	50 ml.
¼ lb.	pork caul, soaked and drained	125 g.

Mix together all of the ingredients except the pork caul. Fry a spoonful of the mixture and taste it for seasoning. Line a 6-cup [1½-liter] terrine mold with the caul, fill it with the mixture and fold the edges of the caul over the top. Cover the mold and cook it for one and one half hours in a preheated 350° F. [180° C.] oven, reducing the heat to 325° F. [170° C.] after the first 30 minutes, and uncovering the mold after 30 minutes more to brown the top lightly. The terrine is done when a meat thermometer inserted into the center registers 160° F. [70° C.].

Refrigerate the terrine for two days before serving it, but do not keep it for longer than two weeks.

ZETTE GUINAUDEAU-FRANC
LES SECRETS DES FERMES EN PÉRIGORD NOIR

Terrine of Pork Liver

Terrine de Foies de Porc

To make about 6 pounds [3 kg.]

2 lb.	pork liver, trimmed and ground	1 kg.
3 lb.	boneless fatty pork, ground	1½ kg.
2 oz.	cooked beef tongue, chopped	60 g.
1	medium-sized onion, finely chopped	1
2 tbsp.	finely chopped shallots	30 ml.
	salt and pepper	
	mixed spices	
1 tsp.	ground thyme	5 ml.
1½ cups	flour	375 ml.
2 tbsp.	chopped truffles	30 ml.
3 tbsp.	pistachios, blanched, peeled and chopped	45 ml.
1 lb.	fresh pork fatback, one third diced, the rest sliced into bards	½ kg.
1	bay leaf	1

Work together the liver, fatty pork, tongue, onion, shallot, seasonings, flour, truffles and pistachios to obtain a compact paste, then divide the mixture into three parts. Fry a spoonful of this forcemeat and taste it for seasoning.

Line the inside of a 3-quart [3-liter] terrine mold with bards of fatback, place in it one of the parts of forcemeat, on it lay a bed of diced fatback, then another one of the parts of forcemeat, another layer of diced fatback, and on this the remaining part of forcemeat. The mold should be filled to 1 inch [2½ cm.] below the rim, then covered with bards of fatback; place the bay leaf on top and put on the lid. Stand the mold on a baking sheet, push it into a preheated 350° F. [180° C.] oven, and cook the terrine for one and a half hours, or until its internal temperature reaches 160° F. [70° C.].

When the terrine is cooked, remove the lid. Place on the terrine a round of wood the size of the inside of the mold. Weight the terrine lightly and let it thus cool for 12 hours.

CHARLES RANHOFER
THE EPICUREAN

Pork Liver Terrine

Pastel Terrina de Higado de Cerdo

To make about 2½ pounds [1¼ kg.]

1 lb.	pork liver, trimmed and coarsely ground	½ kg.
1 lb.	boneless pork with some fat, coarsely ground	½ kg.
	salt and pepper	
	mixed dried herbs	
2	eggs, beaten	2
¼ cup	Cognac	50 ml.
¾ lb.	sliced lean bacon	350 g.
	flour-and-water paste (optional)	

Combine the ground liver and pork in a bowl with the salt, pepper and a pinch of herbs. Add the eggs and the Cognac. Mix thoroughly.

Line a 4-cup [1-liter] terrine mold with some slices of bacon, and turn the meat mixture into the mold, pressing it down well. Cover with the remaining bacon and put on the lid. If the lid has an air hole for steam to escape, seal on the lid with the flour-and-water paste.

Place the terrine in a water bath and cook it in a preheated 300° F. [150° C.] oven for four hours. Let the terrine cool and refrigerate it for 48 hours before opening. Remove the top layer of bacon before slicing the terrine.

SIMONE ORTEGA
MIL OCHENTA RECETAS DE COCINA

Liver Terrine

Pâté de Foie

To make about 2 pounds [1 kg.]

1 lb.	chicken livers, trimmed, or ½ lb. [¼ kg.] chicken livers and ½ lb. veal liver, trimmed	½ kg.
1 lb.	boneless lean pork	½ kg.
1	small onion or shallot, chopped	1
2 tbsp.	chopped fresh parsley	30 ml.
2¼ tsp.	salt	11 ml.
2 tsp.	freshly ground pepper	10 ml.
¾ tsp.	ground ginger	4 ml.
¼ tsp.	ground cinnamon	1 ml.
3 tbsp.	brandy or 1 tbsp. [15 ml.] brandy and 1 tbsp. Madeira	45 ml.
6	slices lean bacon	6

Put the livers and the pork through the fine disk of a food grinder several times. Thoroughly mix all of the ingredients

except the bacon. Line a 4-cup [1-liter] loaf pan with the bacon slices, fill it with the meat mixture, and cook it in a preheated 350° F. [180° C.] oven for one and one half hours, or until the internal temperature reaches 160° F. [70° C.].

Remove the terrine from the oven and cool it under pressure (a brick wrapped in foil is perfect) until it is firm. Chill it thoroughly in the refrigerator for four to six hours. To serve the terrine, turn it out onto a serving plate and slice it.

MRS. ROBERT L. M. AHERN (EDITOR)
THE FINE ARTS COOKBOOK

Pork Liver Terrine from Périgord

Pâté de Froie de Porc

To make about 2½ pounds [1¼ kg.]

1 lb.	pork liver, trimmed and finely ground	½ kg.
1 lb.	fresh pork belly, finely ground	½ kg.
2	garlic cloves, chopped	2
3	shallots, chopped	3
¼ tsp. each	freshly grated nutmeg and ground cloves	1 ml. each
1 tsp.	salt	5 ml.
	freshly ground black pepper	
½ lb.	sliced bacon	¼ kg.
1	pig's foot, split	1
1	onion, sliced	1
1	carrot, sliced	1
1	bay leaf	1
1	sprig fresh parsley	1
1	sprig thyme	1
1	strip orange peel	1
½ cup	brandy	125 ml.
½ cup	dry white wine	125 ml.

Mix the ground liver and pork with the garlic, shallots, nutmeg and cloves, salt and pepper. Let the mixture stand, then fry a piece to test for flavor. Line a 2-quart [2-liter] terrine with the slices of bacon; loosely pile in the liver mixture. Arrange the split pig's foot, the onion and carrot, bay leaf, parsley, thyme and orange peel on top. Sprinkle with a little extra salt, pour the brandy and wine over the top and add a little water to come level with the top of the meat.

Cover the terrine with foil or a lid, and cook it for three to four hours in a preheated 300° F. [150° C.] oven. When the terrine has cooled, but before the aspic has set, remove the pig's foot, herbs and vegetables. This is a good way of surrounding a terrine with aspic made as it cooks and can be used with many other types of terrines.

SIMONE SEKERS
PÂTÉS, TERRINES AND POTTED MEATS

Veal Liver Terrine

Kalfsleverpâté

To make about 3 pounds [1 ½ kg.]

1 lb.	veal liver, trimmed	½ kg.
½ lb.	boneless lean veal	¼ kg.
1 lb.	fresh pork fatback, half cubed, half sliced into bards	½ kg.
1	large onion	1
3	salt anchovies, filleted, soaked in water for 30 minutes, drained and patted dry	3
30	brine-packed green peppercorns, drained	30
3 tbsp.	flour	45 ml.
1 ¼ cups	light cream	300 ml.
3	eggs, lightly beaten	3
1 tbsp.	salt	15 ml.
¼ tsp.	curry powder	1 ml.

Pass the liver, boneless veal, cubed fatback, onion, anchovies and half of the peppercorns through a food grinder three times. Add the flour, cream, eggs, salt and curry powder. Mix thoroughly. Let the mixture stand for at least 30 minutes. Add the remaining peppercorns. Fry a spoonful of the mixture and taste it for seasoning.

Line a 5-cup [1¼-liter] terrine mold with the bards of fatback. Press the liver mixture into the mold. Cover the terrine and cook it in a water bath in a preheated 325° F. [160° C.] oven for one and one half hours, or until the terrine is firm to the touch. Let it cool before slicing and serving it.

RIA HOLLEMAN
PASTEI EN PÂTÉ

Poor People's Liver Terrine

Le Pâté de Foie du Pauvre Monde

To make about 3 pounds [1 ½ kg.]

2 lb.	pork liver, trimmed and cut up	1 kg.
1 ½ lb.	fresh pork fat, cut up	¾ kg.
1	whole clove, ground	1
	freshly grated nutmeg	
	mixed spices	
	salt and pepper	
	lard, melted	

Pound together in a mortar all the ingredients except the lard or, better, put them through a food grinder. Fry a spoonful of the mixture and taste it for seasoning.

Place the mixture in a stoneware pot that is taller than it is wide, and put the pot in a pan of hot water set over medium heat. Cook, stirring, until the liver has changed from the color of the dregs of young red wine to the color of crushed strawberries. Force the hot mixture through a sieve with large holes to mix the fat thoroughly with the meat. Return the mixture to the pot and continue to stir and cook.

When the purée is a rosy beige, it is cooked. While still stirring, pour it into terrines or earthenware pots, filling them not quite to the top. Let them cool.

When the purée has set, cover it with a layer of melted lard. When this has set, cover the terrines with foil, then with their lids. These terrines will keep for a month, so long as they are refrigerated.

SUZANNE ROBAGLIA
MARGARIDOU

Danish-Style Liver Terrine

Danske Leverpastej

To make about 4 pounds [2 kg.]

3 lb.	pork or veal liver, trimmed and coarsely chopped	1 ½ kg.
½ lb.	fresh pork belly, coarsely chopped	¼ kg.
1	oil-packed flat anchovy fillet	1
2	onions, quartered	2
4	eggs	4
4 tbsp.	butter, melted	60 ml.
1 cup	flour, sifted	¼ liter
	salt and pepper	
	dried marjoram or thyme leaves	
1 cup	heavy cream, whipped	¼ liter
½ lb.	fresh pork fatback, sliced into bards	¼ kg.
1	cucumber, tomato or lemon, sliced	1

Put the liver, pork belly, anchovy and onions through the fine disk of a food grinder. Mix the ground ingredients together well, adding the eggs gradually. Add the melted butter by spoonfuls, alternately with the flour. Season the mixture with salt, pepper, and marjoram or thyme; fold in the whipped cream.

Line a large 2-quart [2-liter] square mold with the bards of fatback and add the liver mixture. Cover with parchment paper and cook in a water bath in a preheated 325° F. [160° C.] oven for one to one and one quarter hours, or until firm.

Let the terrine cool in its mold, then unmold it and put it on a plate right side up (the brown crust on top). Garnish with cucumber, tomato or lemon slices.

GRETE WILLINSKY
KULINARISCHE WELTREISE

Mixed Liver Terrine

Terrine Mazarguaise

To make about 2 ½ pounds [1 ¼ kg.]

1 lb.	chicken livers, trimmed and finely chopped	½ kg.
⅔ lb.	pork liver, trimmed and finely chopped	300 g.
⅔ lb.	fresh pork fat, finely chopped	300 g.
2	eggs, lightly beaten	2
3	slices firm-textured white bread, crusts removed, soaked in milk and squeezed dry	3
3 tbsp.	marc or brandy	45 ml.
	salt and pepper	
10	juniper berries, 4 crushed	10
¼ lb.	pork caul, soaked and drained	125 g.
1	bay leaf	1

Mix together the chopped livers and pork fat and add the eggs, bread and marc or brandy. Salt and pepper generously, for this dish should be quite highly seasoned. Mix in the juniper berries.

Line a 5-cup [1 ¼-liter] terrine mold with the pork caul, letting the edges of the caul hang over the sides. Pack in the meat mixture, put the bay leaf on top and fold over the edges of the caul.

Cook the terrine in a water bath in a preheated 375° F. [190° C.] oven for one and one half hours. Serve it cold.

FLORENCE DE ANDREIS
LA CUISINE PROVENÇALE D'AUJOURD'HUI

Baked Liver Terrine

Gebackene Leberpastete

To make about 1 ¼ pounds [600 g.]

⅓ cup	finely chopped onion	75 ml.
4 tbsp.	lard or rendered bacon fat	60 ml.
1 lb.	pork liver, trimmed and ground	½ kg.
2	salt anchovies, filleted, soaked in water for 30 minutes, drained, patted dry and chopped	2
2	eggs, lightly beaten	2
	salt	
	mixed spices	
2 tbsp.	dry bread crumbs	30 ml.

Sauté the onion in the lard or bacon fat until limp. Combine the onion with the ground liver, anchovies, eggs, salt and mixed spices, and 2 teaspoons [10 ml.] of the bread crumbs. Grease a 3-cup [¾-liter] ovenproof dish and sprinkle it with the remaining bread crumbs. Pour in the mixture. Cook the terrine in a preheated 300° F. [150° C.] oven for about 40 minutes, or until a skewer inserted into the center of the terrine is hot to the touch when removed. Serve hot or cold.

JOZA BŘÍZOVÁ AND MARYNA KLIMENTOVÁ
TSCHECHISCHE KÜCHE

Chicken Liver Terrine

To make about 2 ½ pounds [1 ¼ kg.]

1 ¼ lb.	chicken livers, trimmed	600 g.
½ cup	port	125 ml.
½ tsp.	dried thyme leaves	2 ml.
4	bay leaves, 2 crumbled	4
4	slices ham	4
¾ lb.	boneless fatty pork, ground	350 g.
3	slices firm-textured white bread, soaked in a little milk and squeezed dry	3
⅔ cup	dry white wine	150 ml.
½	garlic clove, finely chopped	½
	freshly ground black pepper	
½ lb.	bacon, or bacon and fresh pork fatback, thinly sliced	¼ kg.
2 tbsp.	lard, melted	30 ml.

Place the chicken livers in a bowl; add the port, thyme and the crumbled bay leaves. Let the livers marinate for at least two hours.

Put three quarters of the chicken livers through a food grinder with the ham, ground pork and bread. Stir in the wine to make a rather wet mixture. Add the garlic and pepper to taste. Mix well.

Line a 5-cup [1 ¼-liter] terrine with a few thin slices of bacon. For a more subtle flavor, ask the butcher for paper-thin strips of pork fatback. Then use thin strips of fatback alternately with thin slices of bacon to line the terrine.

Spread half of the liver-and-pork mixture in the bottom of the terrine; add the whole chicken livers and cover with the remaining liver-and-pork mixture.

Top with thin strips of bacon and two bay leaves. Cover the terrine and place it in a pan of boiling water. Cook it in a preheated 375° F. [190° C.] oven for one and one quarter to one and one half hours. Place a weight on the terrine—the excess juices will pour over the edges—and let it cool. When cold, coat it with a little melted lard. Chill the terrine in the refrigerator for two to three days before serving.

ROBERT CARRIER
THE CONNOISSEUR'S COOKBOOK

Chicken Liver Parfait
Parfait aux Foies de Volailles
To make about 3 pounds [1 ½ kg.]

2 lb.	chicken livers, trimmed	1 kg.
	ice water	
	salt and pepper	
¼ cup	Cognac	50 ml.
1 tbsp.	oil	15 ml.
1 ½ lb.	butter, softened	¾ kg.

Cover the chicken livers with ice water and let them soak for about two hours. Drain and pat them dry. Mix the livers with two pinches of salt, a small pinch of pepper, the Cognac and the oil. Place the mixture in a 5-cup [1¼-liter] terrine and let the livers marinate for two hours.

Cover the terrine, place it in a water bath and cook for about 40 minutes in a preheated 300° F. [150° C.] oven, or until the livers are firm but still pink in the middle. Let them cool, then drain the livers in a large sieve. Select about eight of the most perfect livers and set them aside.

Purée the remaining livers, then whisk in the butter, working the mixture until it is creamy. Correct the seasoning if necessary. Pack the mixture into the terrine, placing the reserved livers in the middle. Refrigerate for 24 hours. Serve sliced, with toast.

FÉLIX BENOIT AND HENRY CLOS JOUVE
LA CUISINE LYONNAISE

Danish Liver Terrine
Leverpostej
To make about 2 ½ pounds [1 ¼ kg.]

2 tbsp.	butter	30 ml.
2 tbsp.	flour	30 ml.
½ cup	milk	125 ml.
½ cup	heavy cream	125 ml.
1 lb.	pork or beef liver, trimmed and cubed	½ kg.
½ lb.	fresh pork fat, cubed	¼ kg.
1	small onion, coarsely chopped	1
3	oil-packed flat anchovy fillets	3
2	eggs, lightly beaten	2
1 ¼ tsp.	*quatre épices*	6 ml.
½ lb.	fresh pork fatback, sliced into bards	¼ kg.

In a small saucepan, melt the butter and stir in the flour. Remove from the heat and whisk in the milk and the cream. Return to the heat and bring to a boil, stirring constantly. Simmer for a few minutes, still stirring constantly, until the sauce is smooth and very thick. Let it cool.

Combine the liver, pork fat, onion and anchovies in a mixing bowl. Divide the meat mixture into three parts and purée it in a blender, one third at a time, moistening each batch with one third of the white sauce. Transfer each batch when smooth to a bowl. Add the eggs, salt and seasonings to the liver mixture. (The result will be very liquid.)

Line a 5-cup [1¼-liter] terrine mold with bards of fatback. Cover the bottom first and then press bards onto the sides and ends, cutting pieces to fit. Pour in the liver mixture. Do not put fatback on the top; it would sink in. Cover the terrine with heavy foil, sealing the edges well. Place it in a large shallow pan and pour in boiling water to come halfway up the sides of the mold. Set it in a preheated 350° F. [180° C.] oven and cook for one and three quarters hours.

Loosen the foil and let the terrine cool. When it has cooled to room temperature, cover and refrigerate it overnight. To unmold, run a knife around the edge of the mold, immerse it in hot water for a moment or two, and invert the liver terrine onto a platter or cutting board.

DOROTHY IVENS
PÂTÉS AND OTHER MARVELOUS MEAT LOAVES

Homemade Chicken Liver Terrine
Terrine Ménagère aux Foies de Volaille
To make about 2 ½ pounds [1 ¼ kg.]

1 lb.	chicken livers, trimmed, or, preferably, ¾ lb. [350 g.] chicken livers and ⅓ lb. [150 g.] chicken hearts, cleaned and halved	½ kg.
½ lb.	fresh pork belly, diced	¼ kg.
½ lb.	boneless fatty pork, ground	¼ kg.
½ lb.	fresh pork fatback, sliced into bards	¼ kg.
4	bay leaves	4
4	sprigs thyme	4
	Marinade	
½ cup	Armagnac	125 ml.
3 tbsp.	port	45 ml.
3 tbsp.	sherry	45 ml.
2 tsp.	chopped garlic	10 ml.
6 tbsp.	chopped fresh parsley	90 ml.
1 tsp.	dried thyme leaves	5 ml.
	freshly grated nutmeg	
1 tsp.	superfine sugar	5 ml.
1 tbsp.	salt	15 ml.
	freshly ground pepper	

Put the livers, hearts, if using, diced pork belly and ground pork in a bowl. Add the marinade ingredients, mix thoroughly with a fork and let the meats marinate overnight in the refrigerator.

Line a 5-cup [1¼-liter] terrine with fatback bards, then fill it almost to the brim with the marinated meats and the marinade liquid. Cover with the remaining bards of fatback, and top with overlapping bay leaves and thyme sprigs. Cook the terrine in a water bath in a preheated 425° F. [220° C.] oven for one and three quarters hours, uncovered. The top will be pleasantly browned.

Take the terrine out of the oven and out of the water bath, let it cool for three hours at room temperature and then refrigerate it overnight.

CAROLINE CONRAN (EDITOR)
MICHEL GUÉRARD'S CUISINE GOURMANDE

Danish Liver Pâté

Dansk Leverpostej

Liver pâté, homemade or bought, is extensively used for Danish open-faced sandwiches. As a first course, it is served slightly warm, accompanied by toast, with crisply fried lean bacon and fried mushrooms.

To make about 1½ pounds [¾ kg.]

10 oz.	pork liver, trimmed	300 g.
½ lb.	slab lean bacon or fresh pork belly with the rind removed	¼ kg.
½	medium-sized onion	½
7	oil-packed flat anchovy fillets, rinsed, patted dry and chopped	7
1 tsp.	salt	5 ml.
½ tsp.	pepper	2 ml.
½ tsp.	ground cloves	2 ml.
½ tsp.	ground allspice	2 ml.
2 tbsp.	butter	30 ml.
¼ cup	flour	50 ml.
1¼ cups	milk	300 ml.
1	egg, beaten	1
½ lb.	sliced bacon (optional)	¼ kg.

Grind the liver, slab bacon or pork belly, and onion twice. Add the anchovy fillets, blend well and add the seasonings.

Melt the butter in a saucepan, add the flour and cook gently over low heat for one minute, then gradually stir in the milk. Beating continuously, bring to a boil and cook for two to three minutes. Remove the pan from the heat and blend in the liver mixture. Add the egg.

Line a greased 4-cup [1-liter] loaf pan, if you wish, with slices of bacon. Pour in the liver mixture. Cover with foil or

greased parchment paper and place in a large roasting pan with approximately 1 inch [2½ cm.] of cold water. Place the pan in the center of a preheated 325° F. [160° C.] oven for one to one and one half hours. The liver pâté is cooked when a skewer comes away clean.

When the pâté is cooked, remove it from the oven and cool it with a heavy weight on top. Refrigerate it until it is cold before unmolding it.

PAULINE VIOLA AND KNUD RAVNKILDE
COOKING WITH A DANISH FLAVOUR

Chicken Liver Terrine with Black Peppercorns

Terrine de Foie de Volaille au Poivres Noirs

To make about 1¼ pounds [600 g.]

1 lb.	chicken livers, trimmed	½ kg.
2 tbsp.	Cognac	30 ml.
3 tbsp.	fresh tarragon leaves	45 ml.
2	large garlic cloves, finely chopped	2
	milk	
	grated nutmeg	
	salt	
1¼ cups	heavy cream	300 ml.
	coarsely crushed black peppercorns	

Marinate the livers in the Cognac for a couple of hours with the tarragon and the garlic. To make the livers pale in color, cover them with milk and refrigerate them overnight.

Purée the livers with nutmeg and salt in a blender or processor. Add the cream. Pour the mixture into a buttered 3-cup [¾-liter] terrine and top with a layer of crushed black peppercorns. Cover with foil and let the mixture sit for two hours. Cook the terrine in a water bath in a preheated 350° F. [180° C.] oven for one and one half hours. The water should just simmer gently; check it halfway through the cooking time and, if necessary, add some boiling water. The terrine is done when a skewer inserted into the center is hot to the touch when removed. Take out the terrine, cool it on a rack for two to three hours, then chill it in the refrigerator. Do not eat it for two days. It will keep for a week in the refrigerator.

SHEILA HUTCHINS
PÂTÉS AND TERRINES

Duck Liver Mousse
Mousse de Foies de Canard

This recipe is a creation of chef Charles Barrier of Tours.

To make about 7 pounds [3½ kg.]

2½ lb.	duck livers, trimmed	1¼ kg.
2½ lb.	fresh pork fatback with rind removed	1¼ kg.
3½ tbsp.	salt	52 ml.
½ tsp.	mixed spices	2 ml.
2 cups	*crème fraîche* or heavy cream	½ liter
15	egg yolks	15
⅔ cup	Cognac	150 ml.
1 cup	dried currants, soaked in warm water for 15 minutes and drained	¼ liter
1 cup	raisins, soaked in warm water for 15 minutes and drained	¼ liter

Grind or pound the livers and fatback with the seasonings to form a smooth paste. Add the cream, egg yolks, Cognac, currants and raisins. Turn the mixture into three shallow 5-cup [1¼-liter] terrine molds and cook them in a water bath in a preheated 325° F. [160° C.] oven for 20 to 25 minutes, or until the terrines are firm. Serve them cold the next day.

SIMONE MORAND
CUISINE ET GASTRONOMIE DU MAINE, DE LA TOURAINE ET DE L'ANJOU

Duck Liver Terrine with Currants and Raisins
Gâteau de Foies de Canard aux Raisins

To make about 2½ pounds [1¼ kg.]

1 lb.	duck livers, trimmed	½ kg.
¼ cup	Cognac	50 ml.
4 tsp.	salt	20 ml.
2 tsp.	freshly ground white pepper	10 ml.
2 tsp.	*quatre épices*	10 ml.
⅓ cup	dried currants	75 ml.
⅓ cup	raisins	75 ml.
¼ cup	white wine	50 ml.
⅓ cup	water	75 ml.
14 oz.	fresh pork belly with the rind removed, diced	425 g.
6	egg yolks	6
2 cups	heavy cream	½ liter

Place the livers in a bowl with the Cognac, salt, white pepper and *quatre épices*. In another bowl, mix the currants and raisins with the wine and water. Let both mixtures marinate for four hours. Grind the liver mixture with the diced pork belly as fine as possible. Add the egg yolks and cream and mix well. Sieve the mixture. It should be fairly liquid.

Pour the mixture into a buttered oval earthenware dish no more than 2½ inches [6 cm.] deep. Drain the currants and raisins and dry them well. Sprinkle them on the liver mixture, but do not stir them in lest they sink to the bottom.

Cover the dish and cook it in a water bath in a preheated 350° F. [180° C.] oven for 30 minutes, or until firm. Cool, then refrigerate it overnight. To serve, dip a tablespoon in hot water and scoop out three small balls of the terrine for each person. Accompany the terrine with hot toast.

PAUL-JACQUES LÉVÈQUE (EDITOR)
LES BONNES RECETTES DE LA CUISINE TOURANGELLE

Brain Pâté

The preparation of brains is demonstrated on pages 30-31. As a variation, let the cooked pâté cool slightly; then chill it. Coat it with aspic *(recipe, page 162)* flavored with sherry or Madeira. Garnish with chopped fresh parsley. Serve sliced and arranged on lettuce leaves, accompanied by sour gherkins, Dijon mustard and crusty French bread.

To make about 1½ pounds [¾ kg.]

½ cup	milk, scalded	125 ml.
⅓ cup	fresh bread crumbs	75 ml.
2	calf's brains, soaked in cold water for 1 hour, drained, membrane and red veins removed	2
4	eggs	4
1	garlic clove, finely chopped	1
3 tbsp.	chopped scallions	45 ml.
¼ tsp.	grated nutmeg	1 ml.
4 tbsp.	butter, softened	60 ml.
½ tsp.	salt	2 ml.
¼ tsp.	white pepper	1 ml.
	chopped fresh parsley	

Combine the milk and bread crumbs and blend well; let the mixture cool. Purée the brains and eggs in a blender; add the bread-crumb mixture and all of the remaining ingredients except the parsley. Mix well. Pour the mixture into a well-buttered 3-cup [¾-liter] baking dish or pan. Place in a large pan containing 1 inch [2½ cm.] of boiling water. Cook the pâté in a preheated 325° F. [160° C.] oven for 45 minutes, or until set (the sides will begin to shrink).

Let it cool for five minutes before unmolding it onto a serving platter. Garnish with chopped fresh parsley.

JANA ALLEN AND MARGARET GIN
INNARDS AND OTHER VARIETY MEATS

Terrine of Veal Sweetbreads
Terrine de Ris de Veau

To prepare the sweetbreads called for in this recipe, soak them for two hours in cold water, changing the water twice, drain, then blanch them for four minutes. Refresh and drain them, peel off their membranes and cool the sweetbreads under a weighted board.

A sweetbread terrine is accompanied to perfection by a sorrel mousse *(recipe, page 164)*.

To make about 3 pounds [1 ½ kg.]

¼ lb.	boneless lean veal, finely ground	125 g.
2 oz.	pork tenderloin, finely ground	60 g.
1 lb.	fresh pork fatback, one third finely diced, the rest sliced into bards	½ kg.
⅓ lb.	chicken livers, trimmed and chopped	150 g.
½ oz.	truffles or truffle peelings, chopped, juice reserved if using canned truffles	15 g.
	salt and pepper	
	freshly grated nutmeg	
	cayenne pepper	
2	carrots, finely chopped	2
1	celery rib, finely chopped	1
1	medium-sized onion, finely chopped	1
1 tsp.	mixed dried herbs	5 ml.
2 ½	bay leaves, ½ leaf finely crumbled	2 ½
2 tbsp.	butter	30 ml.
2 cups	gelatinous meat stock *(recipe, page 162)*	½ liter
1 ½ lb.	veal sweetbreads, soaked, drained, blanched, trimmed and weighted	¾ kg.
3	slices stale white bread, crumbled	3
2	eggs	2
⅓ cup	Madeira, sherry, port or Cognac	75 ml.
	melted lard (optional)	

Mix the veal, pork, diced fatback, chicken livers, truffles, salt, pepper, nutmeg and cayenne. Cover and leave at room temperature for several hours, or refrigerate overnight.

In a heavy pan over low heat, cook the carrots, celery, onion, mixed herbs, crumbled bay leaf and some salt in the butter for about 30 minutes, stirring from time to time; the vegetables should not brown. Melt the stock with the truffle juice, if using. Add the sweetbreads, pour in the stock, bring to a boil, cover and cook at a bare simmer for 45 minutes.

Transfer the sweetbreads to a plate. Strain the cooking liquid. Skim off any fat from the liquid, return it to a boil, set the pan on the side of the heat and simmer for 10 to 15 minutes, removing the fatty skin that forms on the surface. Stirring constantly, boil the liquid until it is thick and syr-upy and about ½ cup [125 ml.] remains. Add the crumbled bread and work the mixture to a firm, sticky paste.

Add this paste to the forcemeat with the eggs and Madeira, sherry, port or Cognac. Mix thoroughly with your hands. Fry a spoonful and taste it for seasoning. Line a 2-quart [2-liter] terrine mold (or two smaller molds) with bards of fatback and spread half of the forcemeat into the bottom. Press the sweetbreads into place in an even layer. Fill the mold with the remaining forcemeat, tap it to settle the contents, place the bay leaves on top and cover with fatback bards.

Cook the terrine in a water bath in a preheated 325° F. [160° C.] oven for about one and one quarter hours, or until a skewer inserted in the center is clean and hot to the touch when removed. Cool the terrine under a weight, then refrigerate it. If the terrine is to be kept for more than four to five days, pour melted lard over the surface before chilling it.

RICHARD OLNEY
SIMPLE FRENCH FOOD

Brain Cake
Gâteau de Cervelle

The technique of preparing brains is shown on pages 30-31.

To make about 1 ½ pounds [¾ kg.]

3 tbsp.	vegetable oil	45 ml.
1 ½ tbsp.	finely cut chives	22 ½ ml.
3 tbsp.	finely chopped fresh parsley	45 ml.
1	onion, finely chopped	1
2	calf's brains, soaked in water with 1 tsp. [5 ml.] vinegar for two hours, drained, membrane removed	2
¼ cup	dry vermouth or water	50 ml.
	chervil	
1 tsp.	salt	5 ml.
¼ tsp.	freshly ground white pepper	1 ml.
⅓ cup	pistachios, blanched, peeled and coarsely chopped	75 ml.
6	large eggs, lightly beaten	6

Pour the oil into a skillet, add the chives, parsley and onion, and sauté for five minutes. Blanch the brains in boiling water for five minutes, then remove, dry and add them to the skillet. Pour the vermouth or water into the pan, and simmer until all of the liquid evaporates. Cut the brains into cubes. Add the brains, the herbs from the skillet, a pinch of chervil, the salt, pepper and pistachios to the eggs. Pour this mixture into a buttered 5-cup [1¼-liter] soufflé dish, and cook it in a hot water bath in a preheated 350° F. [180° C.] oven for 30 minutes. Cool the cake for a few minutes, then unmold it onto a platter. Chill and serve it, cut into wedges.

MAYBELLE IRIBE AND BARBARA WILDER
PÂTÉS FOR KINGS AND COMMONERS

Traveler's Terrine

Pâté de Courraies

These are the proportions for a terrine large enough to fill the kind of baking dish used by restaurants. The quantities can be reduced—halved, for example—to make a smaller terrine.

To make about 10 pounds [5 kg.]

4 lb.	fresh pork fatback, coarsely chopped	2 kg.
2 lb.	pork liver, trimmed and coarsely chopped	1 kg.
2 lb.	boneless pork shoulder, coarsely chopped	1 kg.
½ lb.	pork heart, trimmed and coarsely chopped	¼ kg.
⅓ lb.	pork spleen, coarsely chopped	150 g.
5 or 6	pieces fresh pork rind, parboiled until tender and coarsely chopped	5 or 6
3	onions, chopped	3
1 tbsp.	chopped fresh parsley	15 ml.
4 tbsp.	salt	60 ml.
1 tsp.	freshly ground pepper	5 ml.
1 tsp.	mixed spices	5 ml.
1	large piece pork caul, soaked and drained	1

Combine all of the chopped meats with the onions and seasonings. Mix well. Fry a spoonful of the mixture and taste it for seasoning. Turn the mixture into a 5-quart [5-liter] baking dish and cover with the pork caul. Place in a preheated 475° F. [240° C.] oven for 10 minutes. Reduce the heat to 350° F. [180° C.], and cook for two and one half hours more, or until an internal temperature of 160° F. [70° C.] is reached.

LA CUISINE BRETONNE

Chicken Terrine

The technique of boning a bird is shown on pages 22-23.

To make about 2 pounds [1 kg.]

3 lb.	chicken, boned	1½ kg.
½ lb.	fresh pork belly	¼ kg.
1	shallot	1
1	garlic clove, crushed to a paste	1
½ tsp.	celery salt	2 ml.
½ tsp.	ground allspice	2 ml.
6	slices lean bacon	6

Slice the chicken breasts thin. Grind the rest with the pork belly, shallot, garlic and seasonings. Fry a spoonful of the

mixture and taste it for seasoning. Butter a 4-cup [1-liter] terrine mold or casserole, and put three slices of bacon on the bottom. On top of these, put a layer of the ground meats, then a layer of chicken slices and then the remaining bacon slices. Continue to fill the mold with alternate layers of the ground meats and chicken slices, finishing with the ground meats.

Place the mold in a water bath and cook it in a preheated 325° F. [160° C.] oven for one and one half to two hours, or until the terrine is firm and has shrunk from the sides of the mold. Pour off the excess fat and weight the top as the terrine cools. Serve it cold, in the mold.

MISS READ
MISS READ'S COUNTRY COOKING

Sweetbread and Crayfish Terrine

This unusual combination of ingredients provides a balance between the creaminess of the sweetbreads and the resilient texture and unctuous flavor of the crayfish. If crayfish are unavailable, you can substitute an equal weight of medium-sized shrimp and their shells.

To make about 3 pounds [1 ½ kg.]

6 to 8	paper-thin slices fresh pork fatback	6 to 8
1	pair veal sweetbreads, soaked in cold water for 2 hours, trimmed of gristle and fat	1
1 cup	dry white wine	¼ liter
1	small carrot	1
1	medium-sized onion, quartered	1
1	bunch fresh parsley	1
1	celery rib	1
¼ tsp.	dried tarragon leaves	1 ml.
1 tbsp.	coarse salt	15 ml.
½ tsp.	freshly cracked black pepper	2 ml.
½ lb.	live crayfish, cooked and shelled, the shells chopped and reserved	¼ kg.
1 ¼ lb.	boneless lean veal	600 g.
½ cup	chicken fat	125 ml.
¼ tsp.	freshly ground white pepper	1 ml.

Line a 7-cup [1¾-liter] rectangular terrine mold with the fatback, letting the excess hang over the edges. Chill.

Place the sweetbreads in a nonreactive saucepan with cold water to cover, and add the wine, carrot, onion, parsley, celery, tarragon, 1½ teaspoons [7 ml.] of the salt and the black pepper. Slowly bring to a boil; cover and reduce the heat to a simmer. Cook for 30 minutes. With a slotted spoon, remove the sweetbreads to a dish. Peel off the membranes and let the sweetbreads cool.

Add the crayfish shells to the sweetbread cooking liquid. Cook slowly, uncovered, for 45 minutes. Strain the liquid into a small pan and cook over high heat until reduced to ¼ cup [50 ml.]. Let cool slightly.

Put the veal and chicken fat through the fine disk of a food grinder. Season with the remaining 1½ teaspoons [7 ml.] of salt and the white pepper. Stir in the crayfish. Break the sweetbreads gently apart into ½-inch [1-cm.] pieces. Add to the veal-and-crayfish mixture. Stir in the reduced liquid.

Spoon the mixture into the prepared mold and tap it against the work surface to settle it. Smooth the top and bring the excess fatback up to cover the top, adding more if needed. Cover the top with foil, sealing tightly.

Place the terrine in a water bath in a preheated 350° F. [180° C.] oven and cook it for one hour. Let the terrine cool to room temperature; refrigerate it overnight. To serve, cut the terrine into ½-inch [1-cm.] slices.

TOM MARGITTAI AND PAUL KOVI
THE FOUR SEASONS

Pork and Spinach Loaf

Caillette Valentinoise

To make about 4 pounds [2 kg.]

4 lb.	pig's head, fat and lean	2 kg.
	salt and pepper	
3	garlic cloves	3
½ lb.	spinach	¼ kg.
1	small Savoy cabbage, quartered and cored	1
1 lb.	pork liver, trimmed	½ kg.
1 lb.	boneless pork shoulder	½ kg.
1	sprig fresh parsley	1
1	egg	1
	freshly grated nutmeg	
¼ lb.	pork caul, blanched for ½ minute and drained	125 g.
2 tbsp.	butter	30 ml.
1	thin slice fresh pork fatback, 1 inch [2½ cm.] square	1
1	small branch dried sage	1

Place the pig's head in a pot, cover it with water and add salt, pepper and one garlic clove. Bring it to a boil and simmer until the meat is tender, about two hours. Remove the meat from the cooking liquid and discard the bones.

Cook the spinach and cabbage in the cooking liquid until they are tender—about 15 minutes for the cabbage and five minutes for the spinach. Drain each, pressing to extract excess liquid. Reserve the cooking liquid.

Chop together the cooked meat and vegetables with the liver and pork shoulder. Chop the two remaining garlic

cloves with the parsley and add them to the mixture. Add the egg and season with salt, pepper and grated nutmeg. Mix well. Spread out the pork caul in a large dish; put in the meat mixture, mounding it up, and wrap the edges of the caul around it to enclose it completely.

Pour 2 cups [½ liter] of the reserved cooking liquid into a baking dish. Put in the butter and place the wrapped meat mixture in the baking dish so that the folded edges of the caul are underneath. In the middle, place the square of pork fat, secured with the branch of sage. Place in a preheated 375° F. [190° C.] oven and cook, uncovered, for one hour. Baste regularly with the juices and the remaining cooking liquid after the first 30 minutes; make sure that the loaf does not dry out. It may be eaten either hot or cold.

PAUL BOUILLARD
LA CUISINE AU COIN DU FEU

Bresse Cake

Gâteau Bressan

The technique of preparing brains is shown on pages 30-31.

To make about 1 ½ pounds [¾ kg.]

¼ lb.	fresh pork fatback, finely chopped	125 g.
½ lb.	chicken livers, trimmed and chopped	¼ kg.
2	sheep's brains, soaked in water with 1 tsp. [5 ml.] vinegar for 2 hours, drained, membrane and red veins removed	2
	salt and pepper	
1	slice firm-textured dry white bread, crust removed, boiled in milk and drained	1
5	eggs	5
	tomato sauce (recipe, page 166), enriched with heavy cream	

In a mortar, pound the fatback with the livers and brains to form a very smooth paste. Add salt, pepper and the bread. Mix thoroughly and, one by one, add the eggs.

Line the bottom of a 3-cup [¾-liter] mold with buttered parchment paper, butter the sides and pour in your mixture. Stand the mold in a pan of cold water. Put on a lid and cook it in a preheated 250° F. [130° C.] oven for about three and one half hours. Turn the cake out onto a serving dish and remove the paper. Serve with enriched tomato sauce.

X. M. BOULESTIN AND A. H. ADAIR
SAVOURIES AND HORS-D'OEUVRE

Chartres Chicken Terrine

Terrine de Volaille à la Chartres

A duck terrine may be made following the same method.

To make about 6 pounds [3 kg.]

4	boneless chicken breasts, skinned and halved lengthwise	4
¼ cup	Cognac	50 ml.
½ cup	Madeira	125 ml.
1 lb.	fresh pork fatback, sliced into bards	½ kg.
½ lb.	boneless ham, cut into thick strips	¼ kg.
2 oz.	truffles, poached in Madeira and diced	60 g.
	gelatinous meat stock (recipe, page 162)	
Forcemeat		
1 lb.	boneless chicken meat, ground	½ kg.
½ lb.	boneless lean veal, ground	¼ kg.
½ lb.	boneless lean pork, ground	¼ kg.
1¾ lb.	fresh pork fatback, ground	875 g.
	salt and pepper	
	mixed spices	
4	eggs	4

Marinate the chicken breasts in the Cognac and Madeira for two hours.

For the forcemeat, work all of the ingredients together and press them through a sieve. Drain the chicken breasts and mix the marinade into the forcemeat. Fry a spoonful of the mixture and taste it for seasoning.

Line a 4-quart [4-liter] terrine mold with fatback bards, letting them hang over the edges. Pack in a layer of forcemeat, then put in one of the halved chicken breasts. Surround the breast with ham and truffles. Cover it with forcemeat. Repeat these layers until all of the ingredients are used up. Fold the fatback bards over the top of the terrine, adding more bards if necessary to cover.

Cover the mold tightly, place it in a water bath and cook the terrine in a preheated 350° F. [180° C.] oven for two hours, or until a meat thermometer inserted into the center registers 160° F. [70° C.]. Place a weighted board on the terrine, let it cool and then place it in the refrigerator for 12 hours. Coat the top with gelatinous stock and chill until it sets to an aspic.

ÉDOUARD NIGNON (EDITOR)
LE LIVRE DE CUISINE DE L'OUEST-ÉCLAIR

Chicken and Ham Pâté

Pâté de Poulet et Jambon

To make about 2 ½ pounds [1 ¼ kg.]

¾ lb.	whole boneless chicken breast, skinned, tendons and cartilage removed, one fourth cut into chunks, the rest cut into long strips	350 g.
¼ lb.	prosciutto or Westphalian ham, cut into strips	125 g.
½ lb.	boneless lightly smoked ham or Canadian bacon, one half cut into strips, the rest cut into chunks	¼ kg.
1 tsp.	ground allspice	5 ml.
½ tsp.	dried thyme leaves	2 ml.
¼ tsp.	cayenne pepper	1 ml.
	salt and pepper	
1	medium-sized onion, sliced	1
2	garlic cloves	2
½ cup	Madeira or port	125 ml.
¼ cup	dry white wine	50 ml.
¼ cup	brandy	50 ml.
2	bay leaves	2
1	slice firm-textured white bread	1
1 lb.	boneless fatty pork, ground	½ kg.
1	egg, beaten	1
1 tbsp.	oil	15 ml.

Place the chicken chunks and strips in one small, deep dish. Combine the hams in another. Sprinkle half of the allspice plus the thyme, cayenne and pepper over the two dishes. Sprinkle salt on the chicken. Scatter the onion slices over the two dishes; tuck a garlic clove into each one. Pour ¼ cup [50 ml.] of the Madeira or port over the chicken and pour the wine over the hams; divide the brandy between the two dishes. Turn the meats with your hands so that all the surfaces are moistened. Tuck a bay leaf in each dish, cover, and refrigerate overnight, turning the meats occasionally.

Remove the bay leaves and reserve them. Lift out the chunks of ham, chicken, onion and garlic, and strain the marinades. Set the meat strips aside. Put the meat chunks, the onion, garlic and then the bread through a food grinder. Combine all of the ground ingredients in a large bowl with the ground pork.

Pour the marinade into a small, nonreactive skillet and reduce it by half over high heat. Pour it over the ground meats and add the remaining allspice, ½ teaspoon [2 ml.] of pepper and 1 teaspoon [5 ml.] of salt. Mix the meats and seasoning well by kneading them with your hands. Pour over the beaten egg and mix again. Fry a spoonful of this mixture and taste it for seasoning.

Select a 6-cup [1½-liter] terrine and oil it heavily. Layer in one third of the forcemeat and pat it smooth. Place alternating rows of chicken and ham strips over the forcemeat, laying them lengthwise in the dish. Cover the strips with another third of the forcemeat and another layer of strips, and finally the rest of the forcemeat. Smooth the top. Lightly press the reserved bay leaves onto the top and sprinkle on the remaining Madeira. Spread the oil over the surface.

Cover the terrine tightly with foil, place a cover on the foil and set it in a water bath. Cook the terrine in a preheated 350° F. [180° C.] oven for one and one half hours, or until the terrine reaches an internal temperature of 160° F. [70° C.]. Remove it from the oven and let it cool. Weight the top of the terrine and refrigerate it for at least two days. (The weights can be removed after 24 hours.) To serve, cut directly from the terrine and serve it with crusty bread and pickles.

CAROL CUTLER
THE SIX-MINUTE SOUFFLÉ AND OTHER CULINARY DELIGHTS

Chicken and Lemon Terrine

Terrine de Poulet au Citron

The technique of boning a bird is shown on pages 22-23.

To make about 4 pounds [2 kg.]

4 lb.	chicken, boned, the liver reserved	2 kg.
¾ lb.	fresh pork belly with the rind removed	350 g.
½ lb.	boneless lean veal	¼ kg.
2	eggs	2
2 tbsp.	brandy	30 ml.
	salt and freshly ground pepper	
	ground cloves, cinnamon and nutmeg	
1	lemon, peel and white pith removed, segments skinned and coarsely chopped, seeds removed	1
10	slices lean bacon	10

Cut the breast and leg meat of the chicken into thick slices. Grind the remaining chicken with the reserved liver, pork belly and veal. Beat the eggs with the brandy, plenty of salt and pepper and a pinch of each of the spices. Blend this well into the ground meats. Fry a spoonful of this mixture and taste it for seasoning. Blend in the chopped lemon.

Line a 2-quart [2-liter] terrine with bacon slices. Press in half of the ground meat mixture, lay on the slices of chicken and cover with the remaining ground mixture. Lay any remaining bacon slices over the top. Cover the terrine with a double layer of foil, stand it in a water bath and cook it in a preheated 350° F. [180° C.] oven for two and one half to three hours. When cooked, the terrine should have shrunk from the sides of the dish and the juices should run clear. Refrigerate it overnight before serving.

HELGE RUBINSTEIN
FRENCH COOKERY

Polish Goose Terrine

Pasztet z Drobiu

To make about 4 pounds [2 kg.]

6 to 7 lb.	goose, quartered, with giblets reserved	3 to 3½ kg.
¼	small celeriac	¼
1	carrot	1
1	parsnip	1
2 oz.	fresh pork fatback	60 g.
	salt and pepper	
½ tsp.	paprika	2 ml.
½	bay leaf	½
7 cups	water	1¾ liters
10 oz.	veal liver, trimmed and sliced	300 g.
1 cup	chopped fresh mushrooms, or ⅓ oz. [10 g.] dried mushrooms, soaked in warm water for 30 minutes, drained and chopped	¼ liter
½	medium-sized onion, sliced	½
2	large hard rolls	2
3	eggs	3
2	egg yolks	2
¼ tsp.	grated nutmeg	1 ml.
¼ tsp.	ground ginger	1 ml.

Put the goose and the goose neck, heart and gizzard, the celeriac, carrot, parsnip, fatback, pepper, paprika, bay leaf and water in a pot. Cover and simmer for about two hours, removing the fatback after 30 minutes and adding salt after one hour. Let the mixture cool. Bone the goose and thinly slice the fatback. Strain the stock. Put the goose liver, veal liver, mushrooms and onion in a pan. Bring ½ cup [125 ml.] of the stock to a boil and add it to the pan. Cover and simmer for 10 minutes. Remove the goose liver and set it aside.

Soak the rolls in a little cool stock. Put them through a food grinder with the goose meat and the veal-liver mixture. Grind a second time, using a fine disk. Mix with the eggs, egg yolks, salt, pepper, nutmeg and ginger. Beat this forcemeat until it is fluffy. Fry a spoonful and taste it for seasoning.

Line a 2-quart [2-liter] baking dish with the slices of fatback. Dice the goose liver, add it to the forcemeat and fill the dish with this mixture, tapping it down to eliminate air pockets. Put the dish on a rack in a large pot with enough water to come halfway up the sides of the dish. Cover, bring to a boil, and steam it for one and one half hours, or until the terrine shrinks from the dish. Alternatively, cook it in a water bath in a preheated 350° F. [180° C.] oven. When the terrine is tepid, unmold it onto a platter. Serve warm or cold.

HELENA HAWLICZKOWA
KUCHNIA POLSKA

Turkey Terrine

Terrine de Dinde

The technique of boning a bird through the back is demonstrated on pages 79-81. If a small turkey is not obtainable, substitute a large chicken.

To prepare a goose terrine, substitute a small goose for the turkey and cover the cooked terrine with rendered goose fat. The carcass of either bird may be used for stock.

To make about 4 pounds [2 kg.]

4 lb.	turkey, boned through the back	2 kg.
½ lb.	boneless lean veal	¼ kg.
1 lb.	fresh pork belly with the rind removed	½ kg.
	salt and pepper	
	mixed spices	
1 cup	gelatinous meat stock (recipe, page 162)	¼ liter
½ lb.	fresh pork fatback, half cut into lardons, half sliced into bards	¼ kg.
1	large bay leaf	1
	rendered chicken fat or lard	

Remove the thigh and leg meat from the turkey skin, discarding any sinews. Leave the breast meat attached to the skin. Combine the thigh and leg meat with the veal and pork belly; season with salt and mixed spices, and grind. Pound in a mortar to obtain a smooth forcemeat. Fry a spoonful of this mixture and taste it for seasoning. Mix in the stock and set the forcemeat aside.

Season the lardons with salt and pepper and use them to lard the breast meat.

Press a thick layer of forcemeat into the bottom of a round 2-quart [2-liter] terrine mold about 6½ inches [16 cm.] deep. Sprinkle the turkey breast with salt and mixed spices and spread it with a layer of forcemeat. Form the turkey gently into a ball, with the skin outside. Press the turkey into the bed of forcemeat in the mold. Cover the turkey with the remaining forcemeat, packing it down the sides. Sprinkle with salt, cover with bards of fatback and place the bay leaf on top. Put the lid on the mold.

Cook the terrine in a water bath in a preheated 325° F. [160° C.] oven for three hours, or until the juices run clear when it is pricked with a trussing needle. When the terrine has cooled, cover the surface with melted chicken fat or lard.

JULES GOUFFÉ
LE LIVRE DE CUISINE

Duck Terrines

This recipe produces two different terrines: the simple presentation, containing diced duck meat, shown on pages 22-25 and the layered one demonstrated on pages 26-27. The technique of boning a bird is demonstrated on pages 22-23.

The breast meat may be marinated overnight in ⅓ cup [75 ml.] of dry white wine, 1 tablespoon [15 ml.] of olive oil, a pinch of dried herbs, a crumbled bay leaf, salt and pepper.

To make about 5 pounds [2½ kg.]

two 4 to 5 lb.	ducks, boned, breast of one sliced, breast of the other diced, remaining meat and livers chopped, carcasses reserved	two 2 to 2½ kg.
1½ lb.	fresh pork fatback, ⅔ lb. [300 g.] finely diced, the rest sliced into bards, rind reserved	¾ kg.
1	large garlic clove, crushed to a paste	1
½ cup	dry bread crumbs	125 ml.
½ lb.	boneless lean veal, ground	¼ kg.
½ lb.	boneless ham, diced	¼ kg.
4	chicken livers, trimmed and ground	4
⅓ cup	pistachios, blanched, peeled and coarsely chopped	75 ml.
2	eggs	2
¼ cup	Cognac	50 ml.
1 tsp.	mixed dried herbs	5 ml.
3	whole cloves, heads only, ground	3
	ground allspice	
	grated nutmeg	
	cayenne pepper	
	salt and freshly ground pepper	
	bay leaves	
	melted lard (optional)	
Duck stock		
2	reserved duck carcasses	2
	reserved fatback rind	
4 cups	water	1 liter
1	onion, sliced	1
1	carrot, sliced	1
1	bouquet garni, with 1 celery rib	1
	salt	

For the stock, break or cut up the duck carcasses and add them, with the rind, to the water. Bring slowly to a boil, skim, and add all of the other ingredients. Simmer, half-covered, for two and one half to three hours. Strain the liquid, let it settle, skim off the fat, bring it back to a boil and simmer—set to the side of the heat so that a skin forms on one side and can be drawn off with a spoon. Repeat the skimming several times, then increase the heat and, stirring, boil to reduce the liquid rapidly. When the quantity is reduced by half, transfer the stock to a small saucepan and continue to boil until it is thick, syrupy and reduced to ½ cup [125 ml.].

Mix the garlic with the bread crumbs, pour in the stock and work to a thick, sticky paste. Add the chopped duck meat and livers, the diced fatback, veal, ham, chicken livers, pistachios, eggs, Cognac, herbs, spices, salt and pepper. Mix thoroughly with your hands. Fry a spoonful of this forcemeat and taste it for seasoning. Add the diced duck breast to half of the forcemeat and incorporate well.

Line the sides and bottoms of two 6-cup [1½-liter] terrine molds with bards of fatback. Fill one mold with the forcemeat that includes the diced duck. In the other mold, layer the remaining forcemeat with the sliced duck breast, beginning and ending with forcemeat. Tap the molds against a table to settle their contents. Place one or two bay leaves on the top of each terrine, gently press a bard of fatback over all, cover, and cook in a water bath in a preheated 350° F. [180° C.] oven for about one and three quarters hours. The terrines are done when the centers feel firm and the juices run clear.

Remove the lids and place weighted boards on the terrines. Allow them to cool completely—several hours or overnight—before removing the weights. Unless the terrines are to be eaten within two to three days, pour a layer of melted lard over the surface of each, replace the lids and refrigerate. The flavor will improve if they are left for at least three to four days and, protected by the layer of lard, they may be kept, uncut, for a couple of weeks.

PETITS PROPOS CULINAIRES

Goose Terrine
La Terrine d'Oie
To make about 3 pounds [1½ kg.]

1 lb.	boneless goose meat, all fat removed	½ kg.
1½ lb.	fresh pork fatback, ½ lb. [¼ kg.] sliced into bards	¾ kg.
2	onions	2
1	shallot	1
	fines herbes	
1 cup	*eau de vie* or other brandy	¼ liter
2	eggs, beaten	2
	salt and pepper	
1 tbsp.	dried thyme leaves	15 ml.
1	bay leaf, crumbled	1

Set aside several nice slices of goose and grind the rest with the unsliced fatback, onions, shallot and fines herbes. Add the *eau de vie* or other brandy and mix well. Work in the beaten eggs. Season this forcemeat with salt and pepper. Fry a spoonful and taste it for seasoning.

Place a large bard of fatback in the bottom of a 6-cup [1½-liter] terrine mold and pack in half of the forcemeat. Cover with the slices of goose and season with salt and pepper. Add the remaining forcemeat. Cut the remaining bards of fatback into strips and arrange them on top of the forcemeat in a lattice pattern. Sprinkle with the thyme and bay leaf.

Cover the terrine and cook it in a preheated 300° F. [150° C.] oven for two and one half to three hours, or until a skewer inserted in the center feels hot when removed.

SIMONE MORAND
CUISINE ET GASTRONOMIE DU MAINE, DE LA TOURAINE ET DE L'ANJOU

Turkey Terrine with Olives
Terrine de Dinde aux Olives
To make about 2½ pounds [1¼ kg.]

1	onion, chopped	1
1	garlic clove, chopped	1
3 tbsp.	chopped fresh parsley	45 ml.
2	eggs	2
2 tbsp.	milk	30 ml.
2 tbsp.	Cognac	30 ml.
2 cups	fresh bread crumbs	½ liter
	salt and pepper	
	quatre épices	
1 lb.	boneless turkey breast, one third chopped, the rest cut into thin strips	½ kg.
1 lb.	boneless fatty pork, ground	½ kg.
½ lb.	fresh pork fatback, sliced into bards	¼ kg.
1 cup	Mediterranean-style black olives, pitted and quartered	¼ liter
1	sprig thyme	1
1	bay leaf	1

In a blender, purée the onion, garlic and parsley with the eggs, milk, Cognac, bread crumbs, salt and pepper, and a pinch of *quatre épices*. Transfer this mixture to a bowl and combine it with the chopped turkey and the ground pork.

Line a 6-cup [1½-liter] terrine with bards of fatback. Put in half of the meat mixture, then place the turkey strips and olive pieces on top. Cover with the remaining meat mixture. Place a few small fatback bards on top, with the thyme and bay leaf. Cover the terrine and cook it in a water bath in a preheated 350° F. [180° C.] oven—replenishing the hot water if necessary—for one and one half hours, or until the juices run clear. Chill the terrine overnight before serving.

JACQUELINE GÉRARD
BONNES RECETTES D'AUTREFOIS

Duck Loaf

Try turkey meat done this way but substitute lemon peel for the orange. A little celery salt helps, too.

To make about 1 ½ pounds [¾ kg.]

1 cup	ground cooked duck meat	¼ liter
1 cup	ground lean ham	¼ liter
2 cups	fresh bread crumbs	½ liter
¾ cup	finely chopped fresh mushrooms	175 ml.
1	onion, finely chopped	1
1 tsp.	grated orange peel	5 ml.
1 tsp.	dried marjoram leaves	5 ml.
2	eggs	2
1 cup	milk	¼ liter
	salt and pepper	

Blend together all of the ingredients except the eggs, milk, and salt and pepper. When well mixed, beat the eggs into the milk, season, and blend with the rest of the ingredients.

Pack the mixture into a greased 4-cup [1-liter] loaf pan and cook, uncovered, in a preheated 325° F. [160° C.] oven for about one hour, or until the loaf is firm and the top is browned. It will begin to come away from the sides of the pan when done. The loaf is equally good hot or cold.

MISS READ
MISS READ'S COUNTRY COOKING

Ballotine of Duck

The technique of boning a bird through the back is demonstrated on pages 79-81.

To make about 4 pounds [2 kg.]

4 to 5 lb.	duck, boned through the back, liver reserved	2 to 2½ kg.
	salt and pepper	
½ cup each	dried apricots and apples, soaked in ½ cup [125 ml.] sherry vinegar for 4 hours	125 ml. each
¾ cup	sliced fresh mushrooms	175 ml.
1 tbsp.	butter	15 ml.
1½ lb.	boneless fatty pork, ground	¾ kg.
1	garlic clove, finely chopped	1
2 cups	fresh bread crumbs	½ liter
¼ cup	brandy	50 ml.
	mixed dried herbs	

Season the flesh of the duck lightly with salt and pepper. Spread the fruits over the duck, tucking some fruit pieces

into the leg and wing cavities. Sauté the mushrooms briefly in the butter and let them cool. Combine the ground pork, garlic, bread crumbs, brandy and herbs. Spread the pork mixture on the duck, arrange a row of mushroom slices down the middle and place the duck liver on top. Re-form the duck, wrapping the skin around the stuffing and pressing the duck back into shape. Place the stuffed duck in a mold just large enough to hold it. Cook in a 300° F. [150° C.] oven for three hours. Turn off the heat and let the terrine cool in the oven.

PETITS PROPOS CULINAIRES

Duck Terrine with Mushrooms

La Terrine de Canard aux Champignons

The technique of boning a bird is shown on pages 22-23. Larding is demonstrated on page 74.

To make about 3½ pounds [1¾ kg.]

4 lb.	duck, boned, the meat cut into pieces, the liver, heart and bones reserved	2 kg.
1	onion, chopped	1
2 tbsp.	eau de vie or other brandy	30 ml.
⅓ cup	white wine	75 ml.
¾ cup	water	175 ml.
1 lb.	fresh pork fatback, half cut into lardons, half sliced into bards	½ kg.
	finely chopped fresh parsley	
½ lb.	boneless fatty pork, ground	¼ kg.
½ lb.	mushrooms	¼ kg.
1 tbsp.	oil	15 ml.
1	garlic clove, crushed to a paste	1
	salt and pepper	

Place the duck bones in a nonreactive saucepan with the onion, *eau de vie* or other brandy, wine and water. Bring to a boil, cover and simmer for two hours. Strain this stock.

Roll the fatback lardons in the parsley and use them to lard the pieces of duck. Chop the trimmings of meat scraped from the bones with the liver and heart. Mix with the ground pork. Sauté the mushrooms in the oil with the garlic; drain and chop them. Add the mushrooms to the meat mixture and season with salt and pepper. Moisten this forcemeat with a little stock. Fry a spoonful and taste it for seasoning.

Line a 6-cup [1½-liter] terrine mold with fatback bards. Put in a layer of forcemeat, a layer of duck pieces and so on, until the mold is full. Cover with fatback bards. Pour in the remaining stock. Cover the terrine and cook it in a water bath in a preheated 325° F. [160° C.] oven for two and a half hours, or until it reaches an internal temperature of 160° F. [70° C.]. Cool it, then chill it for 24 hours before serving.

SIMONE MORAND
CUISINE ET GASTRONOMIE DU MAINE, DE LA TOURAINE ET DE L'ANJOU

Duck Terrine from Rouen

Terrine de Canard à la Rouennaise

The technique of boning a bird is shown on pages 22-23.

To make about 3 pounds [1 ½ kg.]

4 to 5 lb.	duck, boned, the bones and breasts reserved, the remaining meat and liver finely chopped	2 to 2½ kg.
8	thin slices fresh pork fatback, 2 cut into strips	8
1	truffle, cut into strips	1
½ cup	Cognac	125 ml.
½ cup	Madeira	125 ml.
	salt and pepper	
½ lb.	boneless lean pork, finely chopped	¼ kg.
2	carrots, sliced	2
1	onion, thickly sliced	1
2 cups	white wine	½ liter
2 cups	water	½ liter
1	bay leaf	1
1	sprig thyme	1

Place the duck breasts and the strips of fatback and truffle in a bowl. Add the Cognac, Madeira, salt and pepper and marinate for at least three hours. Drain off the marinade and thinly slice the duck breasts. Mix the chopped duck and duck liver with the pork, and season with salt and pepper. Line a 6-cup [1½-liter] terrine with slices of fatback. Put in half of the chopped meats, then a layer of duck slices, fatback strips and truffle strips. Cover with the remaining chopped meats, then with a second layer of duck slices and fatback and truffle strips. Cover the terrine with the remaining fatback, and cook it in a water bath in a preheated 350° F. [180° C.] oven for two hours.

Meanwhile, place the duck bones in a nonreactive saucepan with the carrots, onion, white wine, water, bay leaf, thyme, salt and pepper. Bring to a boil, reduce the heat, simmer for 45 minutes, then strain the stock and refrigerate it. When chilled, remove any fat that has solidified on top.

Refrigerate the terrine for 24 hours. At the end of this time, wipe the top to remove any solidified fat. Heat the duck stock, pour it over the terrine and refrigerate until the stock sets to an aspic.

MARIE BISSON
LA CUISINE NORMANDE

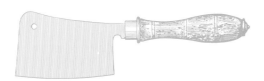

Layered Duck Terrine

Terrine de Caneton Le Chambertin

The technique of boning a bird is shown on pages 22-23.

The following recipe is from Le Chambertin restaurant in New York City.

To make about 5 pounds [2½ kg.]

5 to 6 lb.	duck, boned, the breast skin and liver reserved, breast meat sliced and the remaining meat ground	2½ to 3 kg.
¼ lb.	boneless lean ham, diced	125 g.
5	slices fatty bacon, diced	5
1¼ tsp.	dried thyme leaves	6 ml.
1¾ tsp.	salt	9 ml.
	freshly ground black pepper	
¼ cup	Madeira	50 ml.
¼ lb.	boneless veal, ground	125 g.
¼ lb.	boneless lean pork, ground	125 g.
½ lb.	fresh pork fat, ground	¼ kg.
2	eggs, beaten	2
½ tsp.	ground allspice	2 ml.
¼ cup	marc or Cognac	50 ml.
1 tbsp.	butter	15 ml.
1 lb.	fresh pork fatback, sliced into bards	½ kg.

Place the breast meat of the duck in a bowl with the diced ham and bacon, ¼ teaspoon [1 ml.] each of thyme and salt, ⅛ teaspoon [½ ml.] of pepper and the Madeira. Let this mixture marinate for at least two hours, stirring occasionally.

Mix the ground meats, eggs, the remaining seasonings, and the marc or Cognac. Dice the duck liver, sauté it in the butter and add it to the ground mixture. Drain and reserve the duck breast. Add the ham, bacon and marinade to the ground mixture. Fry a spoonful and taste it for seasoning.

Line a 2-quart [2-liter] loaf pan with bards of fatback. Pack in half of the meat mixture and spread the breast pieces on top. Cover with the rest of the meat mixture and the breast skin. Cover the pan with foil, place in a water bath, and cook in a preheated 400° F. [200° C.] oven for one and one quarter hours, or until the loaf shrinks away from the sides of the pan and the fat runs clear when the loaf is pricked.

Remove from the oven, loosen the foil, and place a brick or a smaller, weighted loaf pan on the loaf. When cool, refrigerate the loaf overnight with the weight still in place.

To unmold, remove the duck skin from the top. Run a knife around the edge, dip the pan briefly in hot water and turn out the loaf onto a platter. Remove any solidified fat, but leave the jellied meat juices. Serve in slices.

DOROTHY IVENS
PÂTÉS AND OTHER MARVELOUS MEAT LOAVES

Duck and Orange Terrine

La Terrine de Canard à l'Orange

The technique of boning a bird is shown on pages 22-23.

To prepare the sweetbreads called for in this recipe, soak them for two hours in a bowl of cold water, changing the water once or twice, drain, then blanch them for four minutes. Refresh and drain them, peel off their membranes and cool the sweetbreads under a weighted board.

To make about 4 pounds [2 kg.]

4 lb.	duck, boned, the meat finely diced, the bones reserved	2 kg.
4 cups	white wine	1 liter
1	onion, sliced	1
1	carrot, sliced	1
	salt and pepper	
10 oz.	boneless lean pork, finely diced	300 g.
1¾ lb.	boneless fatty pork, finely diced	850 g.
¼ lb.	veal sweetbreads, soaked, drained, blanched, trimmed, weighted and chopped	125 g.
1	orange, the peel grated, the white pith removed and the flesh sliced	1

Place the duck meat in a bowl with the wine, onion and carrot. Season with salt and pepper, cover, and let the meat marinate in the refrigerator for 24 hours.

Drain the duck meat, reserving the marinade, and mix the meat with the diced pork. Fill a 2-quart [2-liter] terrine with layers of this meat mixture, sprinkling each layer with chopped sweetbreads and grated orange peel. Cover the terrine and cook it in a preheated 350° F. [180° C.] oven for one and one half hours.

Meanwhile, place the duck bones in a saucepan with the marinade and cook them for about one hour, or until you obtain a well-reduced stock. Strain the stock.

Let the terrine cool slightly, remove any fat and wipe the top clean. Decorate the top with slices of orange, and pour on the stock. Chill the terrine until the stock has set to an aspic. Before serving, remove any fat that has risen to the top.

RAYMOND THUILIER AND MICHEL LEMONNIER
LES RECETTES DE BAUMANIÈRE

Duck Terrine

Pâté de Canard

The duck for this terrine may either be boned through the neck to make a pouch, as demonstrated on pages 32-33, or boned through the back, as shown on pages 79-81. To fill the pouch, the forcemeat should be combined with the other fill-ing ingredients; boning through the back permits a layered presentation. The duck legs may be boned or left intact.

To make about 3½ pounds [1¾ kg.]

4 to 5 lb.	duck, boned, meat finely chopped or ground, liver reserved	2 to 2½ kg.
2 lb.	boneless pork, finely chopped or ground	1 kg.
5 tbsp.	brandy or Madeira	75 ml.
	salt and pepper	
	quatre épices or mixed spices	
1	large egg	1
¼ lb.	poultry livers, trimmed	125 g.
2	truffles, sliced (optional)	2
½ lb.	fresh pork fatback, sliced into bards	¼ kg.

Combine the duck meat and pork with the brandy or Madeira and seasonings. Let this forcemeat marinate for two hours. Bind it with the egg. Fry a spoonful and taste for seasoning. Lay the duck skin flesh side up, and put half the forcemeat in the middle in a flat layer. Lay on it the duck liver, poultry livers and truffles, if using. Then put on the remaining forcemeat. Pat this filling into a nice shape to enclose the livers, then wrap the skin around and sew it into shape. Press the duck gently into a buttered 2-quart [2-liter] terrine. Cover with fatback and foil. Cook in a preheated 350° F. [180° C.] oven for one and a half hours. Serve cold.

JANE GRIGSON
THE ART OF MAKING SAUSAGES, PÂTÉS AND OTHER CHARCUTERIE

Duck and Hazelnut Terrine

Terrine de Canard aux Noisettes

The technique of boning a bird is shown on pages 22-23.

To make about 4½ pounds [2¼ kg.]

5 lb.	duck, boned, the breast and leg meat sliced, the remaining meat ground	2½ kg.
½ lb.	boneless pork blade roast, diced	¼ kg.
½ lb.	boneless veal shoulder, diced	¼ kg.
½ lb.	lean fresh pork belly, rind removed, diced	¼ kg.
2	eggs	2
1 cup	salted hazelnuts	¼ liter
	quatre épices	
	salt and pepper	
½ lb.	fresh pork fatback, sliced into bards	¼ kg.
2	bay leaves	2
	flour-and-water paste	

Put the ground duck meat through a food grinder with the pork, veal and pork belly. Add the eggs, hazelnuts, *quatre épices*, salt and pepper to the ground meats and mix very well. Fry a spoonful of the mixture and taste it for seasoning.

Line a 2½-quart [2½-liter] terrine with bards of fatback, letting them hang over the edges. Place a bay leaf at the bottom of the terrine and pack in layers of forcemeat and duck slices, beginning and ending with forcemeat. Place the remaining bay leaf on top and cover the meat with the over-hanging fatback bards.

Cover the terrine with a lid and seal it with flour-and-water paste. Cook it in a water bath in a preheated 340° F. [175° C.] oven for two and one half hours. Cool the terrine and refrigerate it for 24 hours before serving.

BERNARD AND CHRISTINE CHARRETTON
LES BONNES RECETTES DU CHASSEUR

Spanish Hare Terrine

Pâté de Liebre

To bone the hare, follow the technique used for rabbit shown on pages 66-67.

This recipe can also be used for rabbit.

To make about 4 pounds [2 kg.]

5 to 6 lb.	hare, boned and sliced, bones crushed	2½ to 3 kg.
1	calf's foot	1
1	large onion, sliced	1
2	carrots, sliced	2
1¼ cups	dry white wine	300 ml.
1¼ cups	water	300 ml.
10	thin slices lean bacon	10
½ lb.	boneless lean pork, ground	¼ kg.
½ lb.	boneless veal, ground	¼ kg.
3 oz.	boneless ham, ground	90 g.
1 tsp.	salt	5 ml.
½ tsp.	pepper	2 ml.

Place the hare bones in a nonreactive pot with the calf's foot, onion, carrots, wine and water. Simmer for about one and one half hours, or until the meat from the calf's foot falls away from the bones.

Remove and bone the calf's foot. Strain the stock and keep it warm. Line a 2-quart [2-liter] terrine with slices of bacon. Finely chop the meat from the calf's foot and mix it with the ground pork, veal and ham. Make alternate layers of sliced hare and ground meat, seasoning each layer with salt and pepper.

Pour in the stock, cover with the remaining bacon and stand the terrine in a pan of boiling water. Cook in a preheated 400° F. [200° C.] oven for one and one half hours. Let it cool before serving it.

MARINA PEREYRA DE AZNAR AND NINA FROUD
THE HOME BOOK OF SPANISH COOKERY

Rabbit Cake

Gâteau de Lapin

The technique of boning a rabbit is shown on pages 66-67.

If you use a wild rabbit, it is not necessary to marinate it; a domestic rabbit should be marinated. After boning and slicing a domestic rabbit, marinate the pieces for two hours in 1 cup [¼ liter] of white wine, ¼ cup [50 ml.] of Cognac, six bay leaves, four sprigs of thyme, four whole cloves, a pinch of grated nutmeg, a few sprigs of fresh parsley, a sliced onion, salt and pepper and, if you wish, two quartered garlic cloves.

To make about 2 pounds [1 kg.]

4 lb.	rabbit, boned, the leg and saddle meat sliced, the remaining meat ground with the liver, and the bones broken up	2 kg.
½	calf's foot, cut into pieces	½
	salt and pepper	
¼ lb.	fresh pork fat, ground	125 g.
2 tbsp.	chopped fresh parsley	30 ml.
3	scallions, chopped	3
2	shallots, chopped	2
1 tbsp.	dried thyme leaves	15 ml.
	mixed spices	
2	eggs	2
½ lb.	fresh pork fatback, sliced into bards	¼ kg.
⅓ cup	brandy	75 ml.
	fresh parsley sprigs	

Place the rabbit bones in a saucepan with the calf's foot. Season lightly with salt, cover with water and simmer very gently for two hours. Strain this stock and continue to simmer it until it is reduced by one half.

Meanwhile, combine the ground rabbit meat with the pork fat, parsley, scallions, shallots, thyme, salt and pepper, mixed spices and eggs. Knead the mixture to form a smooth forcemeat. Fry a spoonful of the mixture; taste for seasoning.

Butter a 4-cup [1-liter] terrine. Line it with bards of fat-back, make a layer of rabbit slices, cover with forcemeat, and continue these layers until the terrine is full, ending with rabbit slices. Cover with bards of fatback. Put the lid on the terrine and cook it in a preheated 250° F. [120° C.] oven for four hours.

After the terrine has baked for two hours, slowly pour in the reduced stock, which should be slightly syrupy. Half an hour before the end of the cooking time, sprinkle on the brandy. Do not forget to replace the lid.

Let the terrine cool completely and then refrigerate it overnight. The next day, unmold it onto a serving platter and surround it with sprigs of fresh parsley to serve.

BENJAMIN RENAUDET
60 RECETTES POUR PRÉPARER LE LAPIN DOMESTIQUE

Rabbit Rillettes

Rillettes de Lapin

The technique of boning a rabbit is shown on pages 66-67.

To make about 4 pounds [2 kg.]

3 to 4 lb.	rabbit, boned and coarsely chopped	1 ½ to 2 kg.
2 lb.	boneless pork loin, coarsely chopped	1 kg.
1 lb.	fresh pork fat, chopped	½ kg.
2 cups	water	½ liter
1 cup	white wine	¼ liter
1	sprig thyme	1
1	bay leaf	1
	salt and pepper	

Place all of the ingredients in a large, nonreactive saucepan. Bring to a boil, reduce the heat to low, cover, and simmer for three hours, stirring occasionally. Let the meats cool. Pack the mixture into stoneware pots. Cover the pots with parchment paper and store them in the refrigerator.

MARIE BISSON
LA CUISINE NORMANDE

Terrine of Sliced Rabbit

Pâté de Lapin

The technique of boning a rabbit is shown on pages 66-67.

To make about 2 pounds [1 kg.]

3 to 4 lb.	rabbit, boned, meat sliced	1 ½ to 2 kg.
⅓ lb.	fresh pork fatback, sliced into bards	150 g.
	salt and pepper	
2 to 3 tbsp.	Cognac	30 to 45 ml.
6 oz.	veal liver, trimmed and thinly sliced	175 g.
1 ½ cups	gelatinous meat stock (recipe, page 162), melted	375 ml.
2	truffles, sliced (optional)	2

Put the sliced rabbit and the fatback bards in a bowl with the salt, pepper and Cognac. Marinate them for one to two hours. Meanwhile, blanch the veal liver in 1 cup [¼ liter] of the stock for four minutes. Drain the liver; discard the stock.

In a 4-cup [1-liter] rectangular terrine, arrange a closely packed layer of the marinated rabbit slices. Cover with a thin layer of fatback bards, add a few truffle slices if you have them, then a layer of liver slices. Continue these layers until the terrine is well filled. Press the meats down with your hand and cover the terrine with a lid or buttered parchment paper.

Cook the terrine in a preheated 350° F. [180° C.] oven for two hours, or until the juices run clear. Cool it until tepid, then pour in the remaining ½ cup [125 ml.] of stock. Refrigerate the terrine overnight. The next day, remove any fat that has risen to the surface.

TANTE MARGUERITE
LA CUISINE DE LA BONNE MÉNAGÈRE

Rabbit Terrine with Prunes

Le Pâté de Lapin aux Pruneaux

The technique of boning a rabbit is shown on pages 66-67.

To make about 4 pounds [2 kg.]

4 ½ lb.	rabbit, boned	2 ¼ kg.
15	dried prunes, pitted	15
1 cup	red wine	¼ liter
½ lb.	boneless fatty pork, ground	¼ kg.
1	egg	1
	salt and pepper	
	quatre épices	
¼ lb.	fresh pork fatback, sliced into bards	125 g.
1	sprig thyme	1
½	bay leaf	½
½ cup	marc or other brandy	125 ml.

Marinade

2 cups	red wine	½ liter
½ cup	marc or other brandy	125 ml.
2 tbsp.	walnut oil	30 ml.
1	onion, sliced	1
1	carrot, sliced	1
1	garlic clove, lightly crushed	1
1	clove	1
½ tsp. each	dried thyme and tarragon leaves	2 ml. each
1	bay leaf	1
½ tsp.	peppercorns, whole or coarsely cracked	2 ml.

Combine all of the marinade ingredients and put in the rabbit. Cover and marinate overnight in the refrigerator. Separately, marinate the prunes in the red wine.

The next day, remove the rabbit from the marinade and set aside six or eight nice slices of meat. Grind the remaining rabbit meat and mix it with the ground pork and the egg. Season lightly with salt, pepper and *quatre épices*. Fry a spoonful of the forcemeat and taste for seasoning.

Line a 2-quart [2-liter] terrine with bards of fatback. Put in a layer of forcemeat, half of the rabbit slices and all of the prunes. Make another layer of slices and cover them with the remaining forcemeat. Cover with bards of fatback. Put the thyme, tarragon and bay leaf on top and pour over the brandy, pressing the meat down into the terrine. Cover it and cook it in a water bath in a preheated 375° F. [190° C.] oven for about one hour, or until the internal temperature reaches 160° F: [70° C.].

When the terrine is done, uncover it and let it rest for several minutes. Place a weighted plate on top of the meat and refrigerate it for 24 hours before serving.

SIMONE MORAND
CUISINE ET GASTRONOMIE DU MAINE, DE LA TOURAINE ET DE L'ANJOU

Rabbit and Vegetable Terrine

Recette du Gâteau de Lapin

The technique of boning a rabbit is shown on pages 66-67.

To make about 1 ½ pounds [¾ kg.]

1	rabbit hindquarter (saddle and thighs), boned and thickly sliced, bones reserved	1
4 cups	white wine	1 liter
	salt	
1	onion, chopped	1
1	sprig thyme	1
1 ¼ cups	coarsely chopped fresh mushrooms	300 ml.
1 ¼ cups	heavy cream	300 ml.
2	carrots, thinly sliced and parboiled for 3 minutes	2
½ cup	freshly shelled peas, parboiled for 3 minutes	125 ml.

Put the rabbit meat in a nonreactive saucepan with the wine, a bit of salt, the onion and thyme. Add the rabbit bones, bring to a boil and simmer for about one hour. (It is the aspic obtained by cooking the bones that ensures the firmness of the terrine.) Remove the rabbit slices and set them aside. Strain off the rabbit cooking liquid and boil to reduce it to about ⅔ cup [150 ml.].

Meanwhile, cook the chopped mushrooms in the cream for 20 minutes. Purée the mushroom mixture in a blender and combine it with the reduced rabbit stock.

Make a layer of carrots in the bottom of an oiled 3-cup [¾-liter] terrine, cover with a layer of mushroom cream, then with a layer of rabbit slices and a layer of peas. Continue making layers of carrots, mushroom cream, rabbit and peas until all of the ingredients are used up. Refrigerate the terrine for at least six hours before unmolding it to serve.

RAYMOND THUILIER AND MICHEL LEMONNIER
LES RECETTES DE BAUMANIÈRE

Madeleine Cannot's Rabbit Terrine

Pâté de Lapin de Madeleine Cannot

The technique of boning a rabbit is shown on pages 66-67.

To make about 2 ½ pounds [1 ¼ kg.]

2 lb.	rabbit, boned and ground, the bones and the liver, if available, reserved	1 kg.
2 lb.	veal hindshank, halved	1 kg.
4 cups	white wine	1 liter
½ lb.	fresh pork rind	¼ kg.
1	bouquet garni	1
2	carrots, cut into pieces	2
1	large onion	1
½ tsp.	quatre épices	2 ml.
1	whole clove	1
	peppercorns	
	salt and pepper	
1 lb.	fresh pork belly, ground	½ kg.
½ tsp.	freshly grated nutmeg	2 ml.
2	eggs, beaten	2
2	shallots, chopped	2
¼ cup	Cognac or Calvados	50 ml.
1	bay leaf	1

Place the rabbit bones in a nonreactive stockpot with the veal hindshank and pork rind, and bring to a boil. Skim, then reduce the heat to low and add the wine, bouquet garni, carrots, onion, *quatre épices*, clove, a few peppercorns and 1 tablespoon [15 ml.] of salt. Simmer, uncovered, for two hours. Strain the stock.

Mix the rabbit and pork belly, and season with the nutmeg, salt and pepper. Add the eggs and shallots and mix well. Fry a spoonful of the mixture and taste for seasoning.

Put half of the meat into a 6-cup [1½-liter] terrine mold. Put in the rabbit liver, if using, and cover with the remaining meat. Pack firmly and smooth the top. Combine half of the stock with the Cognac or Calvados and pour the mixture over the meat. Place the bay leaf on top and put on the lid. Cook the terrine in a water bath in a preheated 325° F. [160° C.] oven for two hours, or until the juices run clear. About 15 minutes before the end of the cooking time, remove the lid to brown the top lightly.

Cool the terrine until lukewarm, then pour in the rest of the stock. Refrigerate the terrine and serve it the following day with a green salad.

ANNE VERNON
111 RECETTES POUR LE LAPIN

Rabbit Terrine with Beer

Pâté Bourgeois au Lapin

To make about 3 pounds [1 ½ kg.]

2 lb.	boneless rabbit meat, coarsely chopped	1 kg.
1 ¼ cups	beer or light ale	300 ml.
1 lb.	fresh pork belly with the rind removed, coarsely chopped	½ kg.
3	bay leaves	3
½ tsp.	dried thyme leaves	2 ml.
1 tsp.	chopped fresh parsley	5 ml.
	salt and pepper	
14	thin slices lean bacon	14

Put the rabbit in a bowl with the beer or ale. Add the chopped pork belly and all of the herbs and seasonings. Cover and let the meats marinate overnight in the refrigerator.

Grind the rabbit and the pork separately. Fry a spoonful of each mixture and taste for seasoning. Line a 6-cup [1½-liter] ovenproof dish with the sliced bacon, then pack the ground meats into the dish in alternating layers. Pour in the beer marinade. Cover with foil and a lid, and cook the terrine in a preheated 300° F. [150° C.] oven for two and one half to three hours, or until the terrine reaches an internal temperature of 160° F. [70° C.]. Cool.

SHEILA HUTCHINS
PÂTÉS AND TERRINES

Hare Terrine with Ham and Pork

Pâté de Lièvre

To bone the hare, follow the technique used for rabbit shown on pages 66-67.

To make about 5 pounds [2½ kg.]

4 to 5 lb.	hare or rabbit, boned, giblets reserved	2 to 2½ kg.
1¾ lb.	boneless pork, ground	875 g.
¼ tsp.	dried thyme leaves	1 ml.
¼ tsp.	freshly grated nutmeg	1 ml.
1	bay leaf, crumbled	1
	salt and pepper	
½ cup	Cognac	125 ml.
1 lb.	boneless ham, sliced and cut into wide strips	½ kg.
1 lb.	fresh pork fatback, sliced into strips	½ kg.

Cut the tender part of the back of the hare (the saddle) into strips and reserve. Put the rest of the hare meat, including the giblets, through a food grinder. Mix with the ground pork. Add the seasonings, including plenty of salt and pepper, and half of the Cognac. Let this mixture rest for an hour.

Place the strips of ham and hare in a bowl. Season; cover with the remaining Cognac. Let stand for one hour.

Fry a spoonful of the forcemeat and taste it for seasoning. Line a 2½-quart [2½-liter] porcelain or earthenware casserole with strips of pork fatback. Fill it with 1 inch [2½ cm.] of the forcemeat. Then add a layer of ham strips and hare strips. Repeat these layers (fatback, forcemeat, ham and hare strips) until the casserole is full. Top with fatback strips, which should completely cover the last layer.

Cover the casserole. Place it in a water bath and cook it in a preheated 350° F. [180° C.] oven for one and one quarter hours. Serve it cold for a first course or buffet.

The terrine keeps very well in a cool place so long as the top layer of fat is undisturbed.

JULIETTE ELKON
A BELGIAN COOKBOOK

Layered Hare Terrine

Le Pâté de Lièvre

To bone the hare, follow the technique used for rabbit shown on pages 66-67.

To make about 3 pounds [1 ½ kg.]

3 to 4 lb.	hare, boned, the liver reserved	1 ½ to 2 kg.
1 lb.	boneless fatty pork, ground	½ kg.
	salt and pepper	
1 lb.	fresh pork fatback, sliced into bards	½ kg.
¼ cup	Cognac, Armagnac or marc	50 ml.
2	sprigs thyme	2
2	sprigs rosemary	2
1	bay leaf	1
2	sprigs fresh parsley	2
6	juniper berries, lightly crushed	6
	flour-and-water paste	
	melted lard (optional)	

Thickly slice the meat from the thighs and saddle of the hare. Finely chop the remaining hare meat and the liver, and mix it with the ground pork. Season with salt and pepper. Fry a spoonful of the mixture and taste it for seasoning. Line a 2-quart [2-liter] terrine mold with fatback bards, letting them hang over the sides. Put in a layer of forcemeat, then a layer of hare slices. Partly cover with fatback bards; salt and pepper lightly. Repeat these layers until all the meat has been used, ending with the forcemeat. Sprinkle with the Cognac, Armagnac or marc. Fold the bards over to cover the meat. Place all the herbs on top. The mold should be three quarters full. Seal on the lid with the flour-and-water paste.

Place the mold in a water bath and cook it in a preheated 350° F. [150° C.] oven for three hours. Let it rest for 12 hours, then uncover the mold and remove the herbs. To keep the terrine for several weeks, pour a thick layer of melted lard over the top. In any case, refrigerate the terrine for five to six days before serving.

ZETTE GUINAUDEAU-FRANC
LES SECRETS DES FERMES EN PÉRIGORD NOIR

Grandmother's Rabbit Terrine

Terrine de Lapereau Mère-Grand

To make about 4 pounds [2 kg.]

¼ lb.	fresh pork rind	125 g.
2 lb.	rabbit, cut into serving pieces	1 kg.
1 lb.	boneless veal, cut into finger-sized pieces	½ kg.
1 lb.	boneless pork, cut into finger-sized pieces	½ kg.
1	calf's foot, boned and cut into strips	1
½ lb.	fresh pork fat, cut into strips	¼ kg.
½ lb.	boneless fatty pork, ground	¼ kg.
3	carrots, thinly sliced	3
2	onions, thinly sliced	2
	salt and pepper	
1	bay leaf, crumbled	1
1	sprig thyme	1
2	whole cloves, crushed	2
	grated nutmeg	
3 cups	white wine	¾ liter
1	large bard of fresh pork fatback	1
	flour-and-water paste	

Line a 7-cup [1¾-liter] terrine mold with the pork rind, fat side down. Cover with a layer of the rabbit, veal, pork, calf's-foot pieces and pork-fat strips. Cover the meats with a ½-inch [1-cm.] layer of ground pork. Add a layer of carrot and onion slices; season with salt and pepper. Mix the herbs and spices, and sprinkle some of the mixture over the meats. Repeat these layers until the mold is full. Do not pack down the layers; the terrine will swell during cooking. Slowly pour in the wine. Cover the terrine with the bard of fatback, and seal on the lid with flour-and-water paste.

Cook the terrine in a preheated 300° F. [150° C.] oven for two hours, or until its internal temperature reaches 160° F. [70° C.]. Cool the terrine, then store it in the refrigerator until the next day.

MYRETTE TIANO
LES GIBIERS

Hare Terrine

Hazepâté

To make about 4 pounds [2 kg.]

2½ lb.	legs or quarters of hare, membranes and bones removed	1¼ kg.
10 oz.	boneless lean pork	300 g.
10 oz.	pork liver, trimmed	300 g.
10 oz.	fresh pork belly	300 g.
5	slices lean bacon	5
6 tbsp.	Madeira	90 ml.
1 tbsp.	unflavored powdered gelatin, softened in 2 tbsp. [30 ml.] water	15 ml.
2 tbsp.	flour	30 ml.
2	eggs, lightly beaten	2
1 tbsp.	salt	15 ml.
1 tsp.	freshly ground pepper	5 ml.
	cayenne pepper	
⅓ lb.	fresh pork fatback, sliced into bards	150 g.
Marinade		
1 cup	red wine	¼ liter
1	onion, finely chopped	1
1	garlic clove, lightly crushed	1
1	bay leaf	1
5	juniper berries, coarsely crushed	5
½ tsp.	dried thyme leaves	2 ml.
½ tsp.	dried marjoram leaves	2 ml.

Cut several nice pieces of hare meat into thin strips. Combine all of the marinade ingredients, put in the strips of hare, cover, and marinate in the refrigerator for at least 24 hours.

Remove the hare strips from the marinade, strain the liquid, and discard the bay leaf and juniper berries. To make the forcemeat, combine the remaining hare meat, the lean pork, liver, pork belly, bacon, and the onion and herbs from the marinade. Pass the mixture through a food grinder. Add the marinade liquid, the Madeira, softened gelatin, flour, eggs, salt, black pepper and a pinch of cayenne pepper. Mix thoroughly and let the mixture rest for 30 minutes. Fry a spoonful of the forcemeat and taste it for seasoning.

Line a 2-quart [2-liter] terrine with fatback bards. Put in a layer of forcemeat, then a layer of hare strips until the terrine is full, finishing with the forcemeat. Cover with fatback bards. Put a lid on the terrine and cook it in a water bath in a preheated 325° F. [160° C.] oven for two hours, or until the juices run clear. Weight the terrine while it cools.

RIA HOLLEMAN
PASTEI EN PÂTÉ

A Simple Hare Terrine
Lièvre en Terrine

To bone the hare, follow the technique used for rabbit shown on pages 66-67.

To make about 4 pounds [2 kg.]

4 to 5 lb.	hare, boned and finely chopped	2 to 2½ kg.
1 lb.	boneless lean veal, finely chopped	½ kg.
1 lb.	boneless pork, finely chopped	½ kg.
3	scallions, chopped	3
1	bay leaf, crumbled	1
1 tsp.	dried thyme leaves	5 ml.
½ tsp.	ground cloves	2 ml.
2 tbsp.	chopped fresh parsley	30 ml.
	salt and pepper	
¾ lb.	fresh pork fatback, sliced into bards	350 g.
3 tbsp.	eau de vie or other brandy	45 ml.

Mix all the ingredients except the fatback bards and the brandy. Fry a little of the mixture and taste it for seasoning.

Line a 2¼-quart [2¼-liter] terrine with fatback bards, put in the meat mixture and cover it with the remaining bards. Sprinkle with the brandy. Place the terrine in a pre-heated 325° F. [160° C.] oven and cook for four to five hours, or until an internal temperature of 160° F. [70° C.] is reached. Weight the terrine until it has cooled completely.

A.-B. DE PÉRIGORD
LE TRÉSOR DE LA CUISINIÈRE ET DE LA MAÎTRESSE DE MAISON

Beaufort Hare Terrine
Pâté de Lièvre à la Beaufort

To bone the hare, follow the technique used for rabbit shown on pages 66-67.

To make about 8 pounds [4 kg.]

5 lb.	hare, boned, the meat cut into small slices, the bones and trimmings reserved	2½ kg.
½ lb.	chicken hearts and gizzards (optional)	¼ kg.
4 cups	gelatinous meat stock (recipe, page 162)	1 liter
¾ lb.	fresh pork fatback, sliced into bards	350 g.
1 lb.	basic forcemeat (recipe, page 163)	½ kg.
1 lb.	boneless smoked ham, cut into strips	½ kg.
2 lb.	boneless pork loin, cut into strips	1 kg.
¼ lb.	truffles, sliced	125 g.

In a pan, place the hare bones and trimmings, the chicken giblets, if using, and the stock. Simmer uncovered for two to three hours, or until you have a very rich, well-reduced stock. Strain the stock and set it aside.

Cover the bottom of a 4-quart [4-liter] terrine mold with bards of fatback. Layer the forcemeat, hare slices, ham strips and pork strips, distributing the truffles evenly among the layers. Repeat until all of these ingredients are used. Cover the meats with bards of fatback and put the lid on the mold.

Cook the terrine in a water bath in a preheated 325° F. [160° C.] oven for two and one half hours, basting it often with stock. The terrine is done when it has shrunk from the sides of the mold.

Replace the lid with a piece of parchment paper and weight the terrine until it has cooled completely.

TANTE MARGUERITE
LA CUISINE DE LA BONNE MÉNAGÈRE

Small Hare Terrines, Saint Hubert
Petites Terrines de Lièvre Saint-Hubert

The cepes called for in this recipe are edible wild mushrooms; they are available dried at specialty food markets.

To make about 2 pounds [1 kg.]

½ lb.	boneless fatty pork, ground	¼ kg.
1 lb.	boneless hare, finely chopped	½ kg.
¼ lb.	fresh pork fat, finely chopped	125 g.
1 oz.	dried cepes, soaked in warm water for 30 minutes, drained, stems cut off and finely chopped	30 g.
1	truffle, finely chopped	1
	salt and pepper	
	mixed spices	
⅓ cup	Cognac	75 ml.
½ cup	Madeira	125 ml.
2	eggs	2
18	small round slices fresh pork fatback	18
	melted lard	

Combine the ground pork, chopped hare, pork fat, cepes and truffle. Season with salt, pepper and spices; work in the Cognac, Madeira and the eggs. Fry a spoonful of the mixture and taste it for seasoning. Fill 18 individual ¼-cup [50-ml.] porcelain baking dishes with this mixture. Cover each with a round of fatback and place the terrines in a water bath. Cook them in a preheated 325° F. [160° C.] oven for one hour, or until firm.

Press each terrine lightly and tilt it to pour off some of the cooking juices; pour a little melted lard over the top of each one and let it cool.

To serve, arrange the terrines on a napkin on a platter.

LÉON ISNARD
LA CUISINE FRANÇAISE ET AFRICAINE

Long-Keeping Game Terrine

Terrine de Gibier de Longue Conservation

The original version of this recipe calls for the hare's blood to bind the terrine and the liver to flavor it; both are drawn from the animal when it is eviscerated, and both must be used at once. In this version of the terrine, an egg is substituted for the blood, and chicken livers replace the hare liver. To bone the hare, follow the technique shown for rabbit on pages 66-67.

To make about 4 pounds [2 kg.]

4 lb.	hare, boned	2 kg.
1½ lb.	fresh pork belly, ground	¾ kg.
	salt and pepper	
1	garlic clove, chopped	1
2	shallots, chopped	2
1	onion, chopped	1
¼ cup	finely chopped fresh parsley	50 ml.
	mixed spices	
¼ cup	Cognac	50 ml.
1	egg	1
4	chicken livers, trimmed	4
1 lb.	fresh pork fatback, half sliced into bards, half cut into strips	½ kg.
	flour-and-water paste	
4 tbsp.	lard, melted	60 ml.
Marinade		
1¼ cups	red wine	300 ml.
1	bouquet garni	1
1	onion, sliced	1
1 tsp.	peppercorns	15 ml.

Combine all of the marinade ingredients, put in the hare meat, cover, and let it marinate in the refrigerator for two to three days. Drain the meat and cut it into strips.

Combine the ground pork belly with a little salt and pepper, the garlic, shallots, onion, parsley, spices, Cognac and egg. Mix this forcemeat well. Pass the livers through a sieve and add them to the pork forcemeat. Fry a spoonful of the forcemeat and taste it for seasoning.

Line a 2-quart [2-liter] terrine with bards of fatback. Place a layer of the forcemeat on the bottom, then a layer of the hare meat and fatback strips. Continue layering in this manner until the terrine is full. Cover it with the remaining fatback bards.

Place a lid on the terrine and seal it with a little flour-and-water paste. Cook in a preheated 350° F. [180° C.] oven for about two hours, or until the internal temperature reaches 160° F. [70° C.]. Uncover the terrine, place a weight-ed board on the meat and let it cool completely. Cover it with the melted lard; when this has set, cover the terrine with foil and store it in the refrigerator.

LE CORDON BLEU

Hare Terrine from Orléans

Farce de Lièvre Haché de l'Orléanais

To bone the hare, follow the technique used for rabbit shown on pages 66-67.

To make about 4 pounds [2 kg.]

5 lb.	hare, boned and coarsely chopped, bones broken	2½ kg.
1 lb.	boneless veal shoulder, coarsely chopped	½ kg.
1 lb.	boneless pork loin, coarsely chopped	½ kg.
⅓ lb.	beef suet, coarsely chopped	150 g.
2	garlic cloves, finely chopped	2
2 tbsp.	finely cut chives	30 ml.
¼ cup	finely chopped fresh parsley	50 ml.
1	sprig thyme, leaves only	1
¼	bay leaf, crumbled	¼
1	whole clove, crushed	1
	salt and pepper	
1 lb.	fresh pork fatback, half sliced into bards, half diced	½ kg.
½ cup	Armagnac or other brandy	125 ml.
	flour-and-water paste	
1 cup	white wine	¼ liter

Combine the chopped meats and beef suet with the herbs and seasonings. Line a 2-quart [2-liter] terrine mold with the bards of fatback, letting them hang over the edges. Put in half of the meat mixture, cover with the diced fatback and add the rest of the meat. Pour in the Armagnac or other brandy and cover with the overhanging bards. Seal a lid on the mold with flour-and-water paste. Set the mold in a water bath, and cook the terrine in a preheated 300° F. [150° C.] oven for four hours, or until the mixture is firm and the juices are clear.

Meanwhile, combine the hare bones with the wine in a nonreactive saucepan. Cover and simmer until only ⅔ cup [150 ml.] of liquid is left. Strain this stock.

When the terrine is cooked, remove it from the oven, let it cool until tepid, then break the paste seal. Remove the lid and cut off the top covering of barding fat. Pour the stock into the mold. Replace the lid and let the terrine cool completely. Refrigerate it for 24 hours before unmolding and slicing it.

CÉLINE VENCE
ENCYCLOPÉDIE HACHETTE DE LA CUISINE RÉGIONALE

Hare Cake in Aspic

To bone the hare, follow the technique shown on pages 66-67.

To make about 5 pounds [2½ kg.]

5 to 6 lb.	hare, boned and ground	2½ to 3 kg.
1½ lb.	boneless veal, ground	¾ kg.
1¼ cups	chopped fresh mushrooms	300 ml.
3	shallots, chopped	3
1 tsp. each	dried thyme and marjoram, crumbled	5 ml. each
1 tbsp.	chopped fresh parsley	15 ml.
	salt and pepper	
3	eggs, lightly beaten	3
½ lb.	salt pork with the rind removed, blanched for 3 minutes, drained and diced	¼ kg.
3 or 4	sour gherkins, diced	3 or 4
10	slices lean bacon	10
4 cups	gelatinous meat stock (recipe, page 162)	1 liter
3 tbsp.	strained fresh lemon juice	45 ml.

Pound the hare and veal together to make a smooth forcemeat. Add the mushrooms, shallots, herbs, salt and pepper, eggs, salt pork and gherkins. Fry a spoonful and taste for seasoning. Line a 2-quart [2-liter] mold with the slices of bacon and fill it with the meat mixture. Cover and cook it in a preheated 325° F. [160° C.] oven for one and one half hours, or until the juices run clear. Let it cool, then turn out the hare cake into a deep dish. Combine the stock and lemon juice, pour them over the hare cake and chill to set this aspic.

F. COLLINGWOOD AND J. WOOLAMS
THE UNIVERSAL COOK

Hare Mousse

To make about 1½ pounds [¾ kg.]

½ lb.	boneless lean hare, diced	¼ kg.
2 tbsp.	chopped ham	30 ml.
1	thick slice onion, chopped	1
4 tbsp.	butter	60 ml.
	salt and pepper	
2½ cups	gelatinous meat stock (recipe, page 162)	625 ml.
2 cups	basic white sauce (recipe, page 165), cooled	½ liter
6	egg yolks	6

Lightly fry the hare, ham and onion in the butter. Season with salt and pepper. When the butter is nearly absorbed, pour in ⅔ cup [150 ml.] of the stock, cover and cook slowly for 30 minutes, or until the hare is tender and most of the stock has been absorbed.

Pound the cooked mixture in a mortar, then purée it through a sieve. Mix the cold white sauce with the egg yolks, then add the sieved meat and mix well. Pour the mixture into a 4-cup [1-liter] mold lined with greased parchment paper. Cook it in a water bath in a preheated 350° F. [180° C.] oven for one hour, or until the mixture has set. Chill the remaining stock to set it to an aspic. Serve the mousse chilled, garnished with chopped or diced aspic.

Alternatively, coat the mousse with aspic: Line a mold slightly larger than the one used for cooking the mousse with melted aspic; chill it to set. Place the unmolded mousse on the layer of aspic, fill the gaps around the sides with more liquid aspic and chill it to set. Unmold the mousse just before serving.

PELLEGRINO ARTUSI
LA SCIENZA IN CUCINA E L'ARTE DI MANGIAR BENE

Hare Cake

Gâteau de Lièvre

To bone the hares and the rabbits, follow the technique demonstrated on pages 66-67. The technique of boning a bird is demonstrated on pages 22-23.

To make about 7 pounds [3½ kg.]

two 4 to 5 lb.	hares, boned, the saddle meat diced	two 2 to 2½ kg.
½ lb.	boneless lean mutton or lamb	¼ kg.
two 2 to 3 lb.	rabbits, boned	two 1 to 1½ kg.
1	old partridge, boned	1
½ lb.	boneless lean pork	¼ kg.
½ lb.	beef suet or marrow	¼ kg.
	salt and pepper	
	mixed spices	
	fines herbes	
2	garlic cloves, finely chopped	2
2	truffles, diced	2
1 lb.	fresh pork fatback, half diced, half sliced into bards	½ kg.
½ lb.	boneless ham, diced	¼ kg.
⅓ cup	pistachios, blanched and peeled	75 ml.
4	eggs	4

Chop together the hare meat (except the diced saddles), mutton or lamb, rabbits, partridge, pork, and suet or marrow. Season the meats with salt and pepper, mixed spices, fines herbes and chopped garlic. Mix in the diced hare meat, truffles, diced fatback, ham, blanched pistachios and eggs. Fry a spoonful of the mixture and taste it for seasoning.

Line a round 4-quart [4-liter] terrine with bards of fatback, pack in the meat mixture and cover it with the remaining bards. Cook the cake, covered, in a preheated 300° F. [150° C.] oven for two to three hours, or until the internal temperature reaches 160° F. [70° C.].

Serve the cake cold, whole or sliced.

MARIN
LES DONS DE COMUS

━━━━━━━━━━●◆●━━━━━━━━━

Wild Duck Terrine
Terrine de Canard

The technique of boning a bird through the back is demonstrated on pages 79-81.

Pheasant and other game birds may be treated similarly.

To make about 2 pounds [1 kg.]

4 lb.	wild duck, preferably a mallard, boned through the back with the wings and drumsticks left intact	2 kg.
¾ lb.	fresh pork fatback, one third cut into strips, the rest sliced into bards	350 g.
2 oz.	lean ham, cut into strips	60 g.
2 oz.	corned beef tongue, cut into strips	60 g.
2 oz.	truffles, cut into small strips	60 g.
⅓ cup	pistachios, blanched and peeled	75 ml.
	salt	
	mixed spices	
½ cup	Cognac	125 ml.
¼ lb.	boneless lean veal, coarsely chopped	125 ml.
½ lb.	fresh pork fat, coarsely chopped	¼ kg.
3	eggs	3

Spread out the duck and cut all of the meat away, being careful not to pierce the skin. Cut the breast meat into strips and combine them with the strips of pork fatback, ham and tongue, the truffles, pistachios, salt, mixed spices and ¼ cup [50 ml.] of the Cognac. Let the meats marinate for at least one hour.

Make a forcemeat by finely grinding the remaining duck meat with the chopped veal and pork fat. Work in salt, mixed spices, the eggs and the remaining Cognac to make a smooth mixture. Fry a spoonful of it and taste it for seasoning.

Spread a layer of forcemeat on the inner surface of the duck skin, then arrange a layer of the marinated meats, truffles and pistachios. Repeat these layers until all of the ingredients are used up. Bring the edges of the duck skin over the stuffing and sew them together to return the duck to its original shape. Wrap the duck in the bards of pork fat-

back. Place the duck in a terrine mold just large enough to hold it, put on the lid and set the mold in a water bath. Cook the terrine in a preheated 375° F. [190° C.] oven for about one and one half hours. The duck is completely cooked when the melted fat surrounding it is clear. Cool the terrine slightly, weight it and refrigerate it for 24 hours.

This terrine is most often served directly from the mold, but it may be unmolded, scraped free of fat, decorated with truffle or hard-boiled egg white and glazed with an aspic made with the duck bones.

PAUL BOCUSE AND LOUIS PERRIER
LE GIBIER

Pheasant Terrine with Almonds
Terrine de Faisan

The technique of boning a bird is shown on pages 22-23.

To make about 4 pounds [2 kg.]

two 3½ lb.	pheasants, boned	two 1¾ kg.
½ lb.	fresh pork belly with the rind removed	¼ kg.
	salt and pepper	
	freshly grated nutmeg	
2	shallots, finely chopped	2
⅔ cup	almonds, blanched, peeled and coarsely chopped	150 ml.
1	egg, beaten	1
6	poultry livers, trimmed and thinly sliced	6
2	pieces barding fat	2

Grind the pheasant meat with the pork belly. Season with salt and pepper. Add the nutmeg, shallots, almonds and the beaten egg. Fry a spoonful of this forcemeat and taste it for seasoning.

Line a 2-quart [2-liter] terrine with one of the pieces of barding fat. Layer the forcemeat and the thinly sliced livers in the terrine, beginning and ending with the forcemeat. Season each layer with salt and pepper. Cover the meats with the second piece of barding fat. Cover the terrine and cook it in a water bath in a preheated 350° F. [180° C.] oven for one and one half hours, or until an internal temperature of 160° F. [70° C.] is reached. Serve the terrine cold on the following day.

BERNARD AND CHRISTINE CHARRETTON
LES BONNES RECETTES DU CHASSEUR

Pheasant Pie or Tureen

This recipe is adapted from Sweets and Supper Dishes à la Mode by Mrs. Harriet de Salis, published in 1898. The technique of boning a bird through the back is demonstrated on pages 79-81.

To make about 3 pounds [1½ kg.]

two 3 lb.	pheasants, boned through the back, the bones reserved	two 1½ kg.
	salt and pepper	
1	onion, chopped	1
1 lb.	basic forcemeat (recipe, page 163)	½ kg.
2	truffles, chopped	2
2 cups	gelatinous meat stock (recipe, page 162), pheasant bones added	½ liter
2 tbsp.	butter	30 ml.
1	bay leaf	1
	Oyster forcemeat	
12	shucked live oysters, coarsely chopped, the liquor strained	12
1 cup	fine dry bread crumbs	¼ liter
3 tbsp.	butter, diced	45 ml.
½ tsp.	grated lemon peel	2 ml.
	grated nutmeg	
	cayenne pepper	
	salt	
2 tsp.	chopped fresh parsley	10 ml.
1	egg yolk	1

To make the oyster forcemeat, mix all of the ingredients very well together, adding a little of the oyster liquor. Taste for seasoning. Lay the pheasants on a cloth, breasts downward. Season the interiors with a little salt and pepper and chopped onion. Fill the interiors of the birds with the oyster forcemeat. Roll the birds over together to make one large sausage shape.

Combine the basic forcemeat with the truffles. Line a 2-quart [2-liter] terrine with this truffle forcemeat and put in the stuffed pheasants. Cover them with the rest of the forcemeat. Pour in a little stock and on top place the butter and bay leaf. Cover the terrine with a well-fitting piece of parchment paper or foil, and a lid. Stand the terrine in a water bath and cook it in a preheated 350° F. [180° C.] oven for about one and one half hours, or until the internal temperature reaches 160° F. [70° C.]. When the terrine is cooked, pour in another ⅔ cup [150 ml.] of the stock and let it cool. Chill the terrine and the remaining stock. To serve, chop the jellied stock and use it to decorate the top of the terrine.

SHEILA HUTCHINS
ENGLISH RECIPES AND OTHERS FROM SCOTLAND, WALES AND IRELAND

Marinated Venison Terrine

Reepâté

To make about 3 pounds [1½ kg.]

1 lb.	boneless venison	½ kg.
1¼ lb.	salt pork with the rind removed, blanched for 3 minutes, one third thinly sliced	600 g.
½ lb.	venison or veal liver, trimmed	¼ kg.
1	onion	1
1	shallot	1
1	egg, lightly beaten	1
2 tbsp.	flour	30 ml.
1 tbsp.	salt	15 ml.
1 tsp.	freshly ground pepper	5 ml.
1 tsp.	dried thyme leaves	5 ml.
½ tsp.	ground bay leaf	2 ml.
1 tsp.	ground savory	5 ml.
½ tsp.	ground cloves	2 ml.
1	thick slice firm-textured white bread	1
1½ cups	thinly sliced button mushrooms, cooked until soft in 2 tbsp. [30 ml.] butter with 1 tsp. [5 ml.] fresh lemon juice	375 ml.
	Marinade	
1	carrot, finely chopped	1
1	shallot, finely chopped	1
1 tbsp.	olive oil	15 ml.
1 cup	red wine	¼ liter
¼ cup	red wine vinegar	50 ml.
½ tsp.	salt	2 ml.
	freshly ground pepper	
1	sprig fresh parsley	1
1	bay leaf	1
1	sprig thyme	1
5	sage leaves	5

To prepare the marinade, lightly fry the carrot and shallot in the oil. Add the remaining ingredients and simmer gently for 10 minutes. Let it cool, put in the venison, cover it and marinate it in the refrigerator for 24 hours.

Drain the venison, reserving the liquid, and pass it twice through a food grinder with the unsliced salt pork, the liver, onion and shallot. Add the egg, flour, salt, pepper, herbs and cloves. Soak the bread in the marinade and add it to the mixture. Let the mixture rest for 30 minutes, then add the mushrooms. Fry a spoonful and taste for seasoning.

Line a 6-cup [1½-liter] terrine mold with slices of salt pork. Pack the venison mixture into the mold and cover it with slices of salt pork. Put on the lid and cook the terrine in a water bath in a preheated 325° F. [160° C.] oven for one and one half hours, or until it reaches an internal temperature of 160° F. [70° C.]. Let the terrine cool.

RIA HOLLEMAN
PASTEI EN PÂTÉ

—————————————◆—————————————

Terrine of Venison

To make about 5 pounds [2½ kg.]

2 tbsp.	butter	30 ml.
2 cups	sliced fresh mushrooms	½ liter
1	McIntosh apple, peeled, cored and cut into eighths	1
½ lb.	celeriac, cut into ¼-inch [6-mm.] cubes	¼ kg.
1 lb.	boneless venison, ⅔ lb. [300 g.] cut into chunks, the rest cut into ¼-inch [6-mm.] cubes	½ kg.
14 oz.	fresh pork fat, 12 oz. [325 g.] cut into chunks, the rest cut into ¼-inch [6-mm.] cubes	425 g.
½ lb.	pork butt, cut into chunks	¼ kg.
1½ cups	red wine	375 ml.
1 tbsp.	brine-packed green peppercorns, drained and crushed	15 ml.
4	bay leaves	4
2	garlic cloves, crushed to a paste	2
6	shallots, finely chopped	6
¼ tsp.	celery seeds	1 ml.
½ cup	Calvados	125 ml.
2	eggs	2
⅓ cup	pistachios, blanched and peeled	75 ml.
2	truffles, cut into ¼-inch [6-mm.] cubes	2
¼ lb.	boneless ham, cut into ¼-inch [6-mm.] cubes	125 g.
2 tbsp.	coarse salt	30 ml.
½ tsp.	freshly ground black pepper	2 ml.
6 to 8	paper-thin fresh pork fatback slices	6 to 8

In a 10-inch [25-cm.] skillet, melt the butter. Add the mushrooms, apple and celeriac. Cook until softened but not brown; cool. Stir in the chunks of venison, pork fat and pork butt. Put the mixture through the fine disk of a food grinder.

In a nonreactive saucepan, mix the red wine, green peppercorns, one of the bay leaves, the garlic, shallots and celery seeds, and heat through. Heat the Calvados in a small pan.

Ignite it; while it flames, pour it over the wine mixture. Shake the pan until the flames die. Cook the mixture over high heat until only 2 tablespoons [30 ml.] of liquid remain. Remove and discard the bay leaf. Let cool, then stir the contents of the saucepan into the ground meat mixture. Stir in the cubed venison and pork fat, the eggs, pistachios, truffles and ham. Season with salt and pepper. Mix until well blended. Fry a spoonful of the mixture and taste it for seasoning.

Line a 2-quart [2-liter] terrine with the fatback slices, their edges slightly overlapping. Spoon the mixture into the terrine. Smooth out the top. Rap the terrine against the counter a few times to eliminate any air bubbles. Lay three bay leaves across the top. Cover with a double thickness of foil. Cook the terrine in a water bath in a preheated 350° F. [180° C.] oven for one and one quarter hours.

Cool the terrine and then refrigerate it. For full flavor to develop, wait two to three days before serving. Serve sliced, directly from the terrine.

TOM MARGITTAI AND PAUL KOVI
THE FOUR SEASONS

—————————————◆—————————————

Venison Terrine

Wildpastete

The terrine is spicier if two salt anchovies, filleted, soaked, drained and finely chopped, and 1 tablespoon [15 ml.] of chopped capers are stirred into the mixture.

To make about 2 pounds [1 kg.]

1 lb.	boneless venison, diced	½ kg.
1	venison or pork liver, trimmed and puréed	1
18	thin slices bacon	18
1	onion, chopped	1
1	hard roll, soaked in water and squeezed dry	1
	salt and pepper	
3	juniper berries, crushed	3
1 tsp.	dried thyme leaves	5 ml.
2 tbsp.	red wine	30 ml.
2	egg yolks	2
	fresh bread crumbs (optional)	

In a steamer basket or a colander set over 1¼ inches [3 cm.] of boiling water, steam the venison, six slices of bacon and the onion in a tightly covered pan for 25 minutes. Pass the mixture through a food grinder twice and add the liver, roll, salt, pepper, juniper berries, thyme, wine and egg yolks. If needed, add bread crumbs to absorb any excess liquid. Blend the mixture well. Fry a spoonful and taste it for seasoning.

Line a 5-cup [1¼-liter] terrine with the remaining bacon, then fill it with the mixture. Cover the terrine and cook it in a water bath in a preheated 350° F. [180° C.] oven for one and one half hours. The terrine may be served either hot or cold.

JOZA BŘÍZOVÁ AND MARYNA KLIMENTOVÁ
TSCHECHISCHE KÜCHE

Venison Pâté

To make about 3 pounds [1 ½ kg.]

1 lb.	salt pork with the rind removed, finely chopped	½ kg.
2 lb.	boneless lean venison, very finely chopped	1 kg.
1 cup	chopped fresh mushrooms	¼ liter
2 tbsp.	butter	30 ml.
1	egg	1
1 cup	fresh bread crumbs	¼ liter
½ tsp.	pepper	2 ml.
¼ tsp.	ground mace	1 ml.
¼ tsp.	ground allspice	1 ml.
1 tbsp.	brandy	15 ml.
1 tbsp.	Madeira	15 ml.
½ cup	fine dry bread crumbs	125 ml.
2	thin slices bacon	2
	watercress	
	gelatinous meat stock *(recipe, page 162)* (optional)	

Cover the salt pork with tepid water and let it stand for four to five minutes; drain it. In a mixing bowl, combine the venison and the drained salt pork. In a skillet, sauté the mushrooms in the butter over low heat for four to five minutes. Add them to the venison mixture. Beat the egg in a bowl and add the fresh bread crumbs, the spices, brandy and Madeira; blend well. Add this mixture to the meat mixture and work it all together thoroughly with your hands. Fry a spoonful of this mixture and taste it for seasoning.

Form the mixture into a cylindrical loaf and dredge it in the dry bread crumbs. Place the loaf in a greased roasting pan. Lay the two slices of bacon on top. Bake in a preheated 325° F. [160° C.] oven for two hours. After the first half hour, add a little water to the pan from time to time to prevent the loaf from scorching, and baste it at 20-minute intervals with the pan juices. When the loaf is done—its juices will run clear when the loaf is pierced with a knife tip—transfer it to a platter to cool, then refrigerate it. Serve it with a garnish of watercress or, if desired, coated with aspic.

MORTON G. CLARK
FRENCH-AMERICAN COOKING FROM NEW ORLEANS TO QUEBEC

Vegetable Terrines

Vegetable Terrine

Terrine Verte

To make about 4 pounds [2 kg.]

10 oz.	fresh young sorrel, shredded	300 g.
10 tbsp.	butter, softened	150 ml.
3	slices stale firm-textured white bread, crusts removed, soaked in hot water and squeezed dry	3
3	garlic cloves, crushed to a paste	3
1 lb.	spinach, parboiled for 3 minutes, drained, squeezed dry and chopped	½ kg.
1 lb.	Swiss chard, stemmed, parboiled for 3 minutes, drained, squeezed dry and chopped	½ kg.
½ lb.	green beans, trimmed, cut into strips and parboiled for 8 minutes	¼ kg.
3	carrots, diced and parboiled for 10 minutes	3
1 cup	dried Great Northern or navy beans, soaked overnight, drained, boiled in water for 1 ½ hours, or until tender, drained and puréed	¼ liter
¾ cup	elbow macaroni, cooked *al dente* and drained	175 ml.
½ tsp. each	finely chopped fresh, or crumbled dried, savory and marjoram leaves	2 ml. each
	salt and pepper	
	cayenne pepper	
3	eggs	3

Duxelles

1	large onion, finely chopped	1
2 tbsp.	butter	30 ml.
½ lb.	fresh mushrooms, finely chopped	¼ kg.
	salt and pepper	
¼ cup	chopped fresh parsley	50 ml.
1 tsp.	strained fresh lemon juice	5 ml.

For the *duxelles*, cook the chopped onion gently in the butter for 20 minutes or so, without permitting it to color. Add the mushrooms, turning the heat high and tossing and stirring until the mushrooms' moisture has evaporated. Season, add the parsley, and cook for a couple of minutes over low heat. Stir in the lemon juice.

Stew the sorrel in 2 tablespoons [30 ml.] of the butter, stirring it occasionally, for 10 minutes, or until all of the excess moisture has evaporated and the sorrel is reduced almost to a purée.

Mix the bread paste thoroughly with the garlic. Combine the *duxelles,* the sorrel and the bread paste with the remaining ingredients in a large mixing bowl, mix thoroughly with your hands and turn the mixture into a buttered 2-quart [2-liter] terrine mold. Tap the mold several times against a folded towel to settle the contents. Cover and cook in a water bath in a preheated 350° F. [180° C.] oven for about one and one half hours. Cool the terrine under a weight and refrigerate it for a day before serving.

RICHARD OLNEY
SIMPLE FRENCH FOOD

Dol Terrine

Pâté de Dol

This vegetable terrine from the town of Dol in Brittany is said to have the taste of hare.

To make about 3 pounds [1 ½ kg.]

1 lb.	dried red kidney beans, soaked overnight and drained	½ kg.
1	carrot	1
2	onions, each stuck with 2 whole cloves	2
2	garlic cloves	2
1	bouquet garni	1
	salt and pepper	
	mixed spices	
1	egg	1
1 cup	red wine	¼ liter
¼ lb.	fresh pork fatback, half finely chopped, half sliced into bards	125 g.
½ lb.	boneless fatty pork, ground	¼ kg.

Place the beans in a saucepan with the carrot, onions, garlic and bouquet garni. Just cover with water, bring to a boil, cover, and simmer for two and one half hours, or until the beans are very tender, adding more boiling water, if necessary, to keep the beans covered. Remove the onions and bouquet garni.

Drain, then sieve the bean mixture to form a thick, dry purée. Add the salt, pepper and mixed spices; moisten the purée with the egg and wine. Work the finely chopped fatback into the ground pork. Mix the meats with the bean purée until thoroughly blended.

Pack the mixture into a 6-cup [1½-liter] terrine mold and cover with the bards of fatback. Cook the terrine in a preheated 400° F. [200° C.] oven for 45 minutes, or until a skewer inserted into the center of the terrine comes out clean. Allow it to cool before eating.

LA CUISINE BRETONNE

Anton Mosimann's Covent Garden Vegetable Terrine

The author of this recipe, chef at the Dorchester Grill in London, suggests serving it with tomato vinaigrette (recipe, page 165). For easier unmolding, the bottom of the terrine mold may be lined with parchment paper.

To make about 2 pounds [1 kg.]

2 cups	forcemeat mousseline (recipe, page 164), made with chicken	½ liter
¼ lb.	watercress, stems removed, parboiled for 3 minutes and puréed	125 g.
2 oz.	fresh morels, halved, or ½ oz. [15 g.] dried morels, soaked in warm water for 30 minutes and drained	60 g.
¼ lb.	green beans, parboiled for 8 to 10 minutes, drained and cooled	125 g.
6	artichoke bottoms, parboiled for 25 minutes, drained, cooled and sliced	6
2	large carrots, cut into julienne, parboiled for 5 to 10 minutes and cooled	2
2 oz.	sugar or snow peas, parboiled for 3 minutes and drained (optional)	60 g.
2 oz.	broccoli florets, parboiled for 6 minutes, drained and cooled (optional)	60 g.
2 oz.	small zucchini, parboiled for 5 minutes, drained, cooled and halved lengthwise (optional)	60 g.

Mix one quarter of the chicken forcemeat mousseline with the watercress purée. Butter a 5-cup [1¼-liter] terrine mold and pack the watercress mixture into the bottom. Make successive layers of the vegetables (one variety to a layer), separating each layer of vegetable with a layer of the chicken mousseline.

Cover the mold with a lid or a piece of buttered parchment paper. Cook the terrine in a water bath in a preheated 300° F. [150° C.] oven for 25 to 30 minutes, or until firm to the touch. Cool the terrine. Refrigerate it for a minimum of eight hours. Unmold and slice as needed.

NAOMI BARRY
INTERNATIONAL HERALD TRIBUNE

Chicken and Vegetable Terrine

This terrine can be made up to five days in advance.

To make about 2 pounds [1 kg.]

3 tbsp.	finely chopped shallots	45 ml.
2 tbsp.	butter	30 ml.
1 lb.	chicken breasts, boned, skinned and cubed	½ kg.
½ cup	oil	125 ml.
¼ cup	champagne vinegar or white wine vinegar	50 ml.
1½ tsp.	salt	7 ml.
¼ tsp.	freshly ground black pepper	1 ml.
1	egg	1
4 to 5	carrots, cut into julienne, parboiled for 5 minutes, drained and refreshed	4 to 5
1 lb.	green beans, parboiled for 5 to 7 minutes, drained and refreshed	½ kg.
1 cup	ripe oil-packed Mediterranean-style black olives	¼ liter
	tomato vinaigrette (recipe, page 165)	

Sauté the shallots in the butter over medium heat until soft but not brown. Let them cool.

Place the chicken in a food processor with the oil, vinegar, salt, pepper, egg and shallots. Process until very smooth. Alternatively, pass the chicken through the medium disk of a food grinder, pound it in a mortar with the other ingredients and pass the mixture through a fine-meshed sieve. This will be the binder.

Place equal amounts of the chicken binder in three bowls. Cut the carrots to the length of the beans. Add the carrots to one bowl, the beans to another, and leave the third bowl plain. Using your hands, mix the vegetables into the binder, making sure that they are completely coated.

Butter an 8-by-4-inch [20-by-10-cm.] loaf pan. Put in enough of the plain chicken binder to coat the bottom. Add a layer of carrot mixture, keeping the carrots in as straight a line as possible. Next add a layer of bean mixture, keeping the beans as straight as possible. Using a spatula, layer some plain chicken binder on top of the beans—just enough to barely coat them—and place a row of black olives down the center. Being careful not to disturb the carrots or beans, push the olives into the bottom layers of vegetables so that the mixture stays flat. Coat this layer of olives with a paper-thin layer of chicken binder. Then repeat the carrot, bean, and chicken-binder layers. Cover the top with buttered parchment paper, pressing the paper directly on top of the terrine. Tap the pan on the counter a few times to eliminate air bubbles. Place it in a water bath and cook it in a preheated 350° F. [180° C.] oven for one hour, or until firm.

Let the terrine cool for one hour. Drain off any water that has collected on the surface. Run a knife between the terrine and the pan, and unmold the terrine onto a board. Pat it dry with paper towels. Wrap the terrine in plastic wrap, then in foil, and refrigerate it for three hours or overnight.

Place a serving of tomato vinaigrette on each chilled plate. Place two or three thin slices of the terrine in a pretty pattern on top of the sauce and serve.

MICHÈLE URVATER AND DAVID LIEDERMAN
COOKING THE NOUVELLE CUISINE IN AMERICA

Zucchini Terrine

La Terrine de Courgettes du Restaurant "La Ligne" à Paris

Serve this terrine with a sauce of heavy cream, yogurt, *fromage blanc* and herbs (the same as those used in the terrine), whipped together until light.

To make about 6 pounds [3 kg.]

4 lb.	zucchini, thinly sliced	2 kg.
3	medium-sized onions, thinly sliced	3
3 tbsp.	olive oil	45 ml.
3½ cups	fresh bread crumbs, soaked in milk and squeezed dry	750 ml.
6	eggs, beaten	6
	salt and pepper	
2½ tsp.	freshly grated nutmeg	12 ml.
1 cup	finely chopped fresh tarragon leaves	¼ liter
1 cup	chopped fresh mint leaves	¼ liter
14 oz.	sorrel (about 4 cups [1 liter])	425 g.
2 tsp.	butter	10 ml.

Cook the zucchini and the onions in the olive oil over low heat until they are very soft. Crush the mixture with a fork. Add the softened bread crumbs to the zucchini mixture and blend well. Beat in the eggs, salt and pepper, nutmeg, tarragon and mint. Stew the sorrel in the butter until it has melted to a purée.

Generously butter a 7-cup [1¾-liter] terrine and put in half of the zucchini mixture. Spread the sorrel in a layer on top, then cover with the rest of the zucchini mixture. Cover and cook the terrine in a water bath in a preheated 325° F. [160° C.] oven for one to one and one half hours, or until the terrine is just firm. Uncover the terrine, turn off the oven and leave the terrine in the cooling oven to dry out a little. When the terrine is completely cool, refrigerate it. Unmold it the next day and serve cut into slices.

ODETTE REIGE
LES TERRINES DE VIANDES, DE COQUILLAGES ET POISSONS, DE LÉGUMES

Vegetable Terrine Olympe
Terrine de Legumes "Olympe"

Preserved grapevine leaves are available in Middle Eastern food stores, gourmet shops and some supermarkets. This terrine may be served with tomato vinaigrette (recipe, page 165) or with avocado vinaigrette, as shown on page 41.

To make about 3 pounds [1½ kg.]

6	medium-to large-sized artichokes	6
½	lemon	½
1 tbsp.	butter	15 ml.
	salt	
1 lb.	boneless ham, finely diced and chilled	½ kg.
6 tbsp.	strained fresh lemon juice	90 ml.
¼ tsp.	freshly ground pepper	1 ml.
2	egg whites	2
1 cup	peanut oil	¼ liter
8	preserved grapevine leaves, rinsed and drained	8
10 oz.	small young carrots, parboiled for 8 minutes and chilled	300 g.
½ lb.	young green beans, parboiled for 5 minutes and chilled	¼ kg.
10 oz.	freshly shelled peas, parboiled for 3 minutes and chilled	300 g.

Trim the tops and bottoms of the artichokes and rub them with the lemon to prevent them from darkening. Melt the butter in a casserole large enough to hold the artichokes side by side. Add the artichokes, cover the casserole, and cook over low heat for 10 minutes to bring out their flavor. Then add salt and add enough water to immerse the artichokes completely. To protect their color, cover them with a sheet of wax paper cut to fit the shape of the casserole. Cover the casserole, bring the water to a simmer, and cook slowly for 20 to 30 minutes, depending on the size of the artichokes. Let them cool in the liquid, then drain them. Remove all of the leaves and the chokes, and trim the bottoms so that they are smooth and even. Chill them thoroughly in the refrigerator.

Chill the container of a food processor or blender. Put in the ham, lemon juice, and salt and pepper; blend briefly, then add the egg whites. When the whites are well blended, incorporate the oil a little at a time. Though the oil has to be added slowly, the whole operation should be completed as quickly as possible so that the filling does not become warm. If necessary, return the container to the freezer.

Choose a nonmetallic, 2-quart [2-liter] terrine mold and line the bottom and sides with grapevine leaves. Spread a thin bed of ham filling over the bottom of the mold and arrange neat rows of carrots over it. Add another layer of filling, then the green beans, packing them together in one layer and reserving a few for garnishing.

Spread more filling over the beans, then arrange the artichoke bottoms, cut in half so as to fit together as closely as possible. Add more filling, followed by the peas in an even layer. Finish with the remainder of the ham filling. Fold the grapevine leaves over the top of the terrine and cover it with a sheet of buttered wax paper. Set the terrine in a pan of boiling water and cook it for 30 minutes.

Cool the terrine in the pan of water and chill it for at least eight hours, or preferably overnight, before unmolding. To serve, cut the terrine into slices ¾ inch [2 cm.] thick.

JEAN & PIERRE TROISGROS
THE NOUVELLE CUISINE OF JEAN & PIERRE TROISGROS

Layered Chick-Pea Terrine
Granata di Ceci

The author suggests that the filling for this terrine may be any meat, poultry or fish stew of your choice, garnished with sliced hard-boiled eggs, cooked mushrooms or thinly sliced truffles. To make the stew, cooked meat, poultry or fish may be diced and combined with a velouté sauce (recipe, page 165).

To make about 4 pounds [2 kg.]

1½ lb.	dried chick-peas, soaked overnight, boiled until tender and drained	¾ kg.
4	thick slices firm-textured white bread, crusts removed, soaked in milk and squeezed dry	4
10 oz.	Parmesan, *provola* or *caciocavallo* cheese, grated (about 3⅓ cups [825 ml.])	300 g.
6	egg yolks	6
	salt and pepper	
¼ cup	chopped fresh parsley	50 ml.
1 lb.	mixed vegetables (celery, carrots, artichoke bottoms, zucchini, etc.), diced or sliced, and parboiled	½ kg.
1½ cups	meat stew	375 ml.

Pound the cooked chick-peas with the soaked bread and press the mixture through a sieve. Add the grated cheese, egg yolks, salt, pepper and chopped parsley, and mix well.

Butter a 2-quart [2-liter] terrine mold and arrange a decorative layer of vegetables on the bottom. Add a layer of the chick-pea mixture. Continue to make layers of vegetables and chick-peas, adding the meat stew in one layer in the center. When the mold is full, cover it tightly. Place it in a water bath in a preheated 350° F. [180° C.] oven, or place it on a rack in a large covered pan containing enough boiling water to come halfway up the sides of the mold and set it over low heat. Cook the terrine for two hours, or until firm.

Let the terrine rest for 10 minutes, then unmold it onto a serving dish and serve it hot.

IPPOLITO CAVALCANTI, DUCA DI BUONVICINO
CUCINA TEORICO-PRATICA

Fish and Shellfish Terrines

Salmon Terrine with Truffles and Pistachios

Terrine de Saumon aux Truffes et aux Pistaches

The author suggests that this dish may be garnished with lettuce leaves and quarters of lemon, and served with green mayonnaise *(recipe, page 164)* or a vinaigrette enriched with herbs *(recipe, page 165)*.

To make about 4 pounds [2 kg.]

2 lb.	salmon fillets, skinned	1 kg.
½ cup	port	125 ml.
1 cup	Cognac	¼ liter
	salt and pepper	
1 lb.	pike, halibut, cod or sole fillets, skinned and puréed	½ kg.
	grated nutmeg	
½ lb.	butter, softened	¼ kg.
2	eggs	2
4	egg yolks	4
½ lb.	fresh pork fatback, sliced into bards	¼ kg.
⅓ cup	pistachios, blanched and peeled	75 ml.
2	truffles, peeled and cut into matchsticks	2
	flour-and-water paste	
Panada		
3½ tbsp.	butter	52 ml.
1¼ cups	water	300 ml.
2 tsp.	salt	10 ml.
1 cup	flour	¼ liter

Marinate the salmon in the port, Cognac, salt and pepper.

To make the panada, bring the butter and water to a boil. Stir until the butter melts, then pour in the salt and flour. Beat until the mixture is smooth and pulls away from the sides of the pan. Turn out onto a buttered plate, spread the mixture evenly, cover with buttered paper and let it cool.

Season the puréed fish with salt, pepper and nutmeg. Mix it with the cooled panada, beating vigorously with a wooden spoon. Beat in the butter and, one at a time, beat in the eggs and egg yolks. Then force this fish forcemeat through the finest disk of a food mill. Chill.

Meanwhile drain the salmon and reserve the marinade. Line a 2-quart [2-liter] terrine with overlapping bards of fatback, leaving plenty of overhang all around. Spread on a layer of fish forcemeat, then the salmon in one layer. Sprinkle with the pistachios and truffles. Cover with the remaining fish forcemeat and fold the bards of fatback over to cover. Place a last bard of fatback on top and pour the marinade over it. Set on the lid and seal it with flour-and-water paste.

Place the terrine on a rack set in a large pot. Pour in hot water to come two thirds of the way up the terrine. Cover the pot and bring the water to a boil. Reduce the heat to low and cook the terrine slowly for two hours. From time to time, check the water level; add boiling water if necessary. Let the terrine cool, then refrigerate it for at least 24 hours.

Unmold the terrine and remove all traces of fat and grease. Slice the terrine, and return the slices to the mold or arrange them on a platter.

LOUISETTE BERTHOLLE
SECRETS OF THE GREAT FRENCH RESTAURANTS

Salmon Terrine with Green Mousse

La Terrine de Saumon à la Mousse Verdurette

The author suggests serving this terrine with a green mayonnaise *(recipe, page 164)*, made with lemon juice.

To make about 3 pounds [1 ½ kg.]

14 oz.	salmon fillets, skinned and ground	425 g.
¼ cup	*crème fraîche* or heavy cream	50 ml.
6	eggs	6
½ tsp.	paprika	2 ml.
	salt and pepper	
1 lb.	freshly shelled young peas, parboiled for 4 minutes and drained	½ kg.
¼ cup	very finely chopped sorrel	50 ml.
1 cup	very finely chopped fresh parsley	¼ liter
2 tbsp.	very finely cut chives	30 ml.

Place the salmon in a bowl with half of the cream, three eggs, the paprika, salt and pepper. Beat well.

Purée the peas in a food mill or a food processor. Add the sorrel, parsley, chives and the remaining cream. Season with salt and pepper. Beat well to form a smooth mousse, and gradually incorporate the three remaining eggs.

Butter a 6-cup [1½-liter] terrine. Put in half of the salmon mixture, cover with the pea mousse and add the rest of the salmon. Cover the terrine with foil, place it in a water bath and cook in a preheated 350° F. [180° C.] oven for one hour. Let the terrine cool, then refrigerate it.

ODETTE REIGE
LES TERRINES DE VIANDE, DE COQUILLAGES ET POISSONS, DE LÉGUMES

Flounder in a Green Coat

Bot in 't Groen

If you wish, you may decorate the terrine after turning it out by brushing on a layer of fish aspic (recipe, page 163), making crosswise rows of chopped parsley and chopped hard-boiled egg whites and yolks, and covering the garnish with another layer of fish aspic.

To make about 2½ pounds [1¼ kg.]

2½ lb.	flounder fillets, skinned, half finely chopped, half cut into strips	1¼ kg.
¼ cup	heavy cream	50 ml.
3	egg yolks	3
½ cup	velouté sauce (recipe, page 165), made with fish stock	125 ml.
	salt and pepper	
9 oz.	butter, ½ lb. [¼ kg.] diced and softened	275 g.
1 cup	spinach, parboiled for 3 minutes, drained, squeezed dry and chopped	¼ liter
¼ cup	finely chopped shallots	50 ml.
¼ cup	dry white wine	50 ml.
¼ tsp.	chopped fresh tarragon	1 ml.

Combine the chopped fish with the cream, egg yolks, velouté sauce, salt and pepper. Purée the mixture in a blender or a food processor until smooth. Add the softened butter and purée for 10 to 15 seconds more. Fold in the chopped spinach. Taste the mixture for seasoning.

Sauté the shallots in the remaining butter until softened. Add the fish strips, wine and tarragon; season with salt and pepper. Cook for two minutes, or until the fish is just firm. Transfer the fish to a bowl, reduce the cooking juices over high heat to 3 tablespoons [45 ml.], and pour over the fish.

Butter a 6-cup [1½-liter] terrine mold and put in half of the spinach mixture. Lay the fish strips in lengthwise and fill the mold with the remaining mixture. Tap the mold on the table to remove any air bubbles, cover with parchment paper and foil, and place it in a water bath. Cook the terrine in a preheated 300° F. [150° C.] oven for one hour, or until the mixture is set and has shrunk from the sides of the dish. Weight the terrine, let it cool and refrigerate it overnight. Turn it out to serve.

HUGH JANS
VRIJ NEDERLAND

Terrine of Salmon with Eggs and Almonds

To make about 3 pounds [1½ kg.]

½ lb.	salmon fillets, skinned	¼ kg.
½ lb.	trout or bluefish fillets, skinned	¼ kg.
7	eggs, 5 hard-boiled	7
1⅔ cups	heavy cream, chilled	400 ml.
1 tsp.	salt	5 ml.
	pepper	
1 cup	very finely chopped mixed fresh herbs (parsley, chives and lemon thyme, if available)	¼ liter
½ cup	almonds, blanched and peeled	125 ml.

Purée the fish and the two raw eggs together in a blender or a food processor, or pound them together with a pestle in a heavy bowl. Press the purée through a sieve to strain out any connective membranous filaments. Place the purée in a small bowl, cover it with plastic wrap and refrigerate it for at least one and one half hours.

Stir 1 cup [¼ liter] of the chilled cream into the purée to lighten the mixture. Season well. Whip the remaining cream until loosely thickened but not firm, and fold it into the purée. Transfer approximately one third of the mixture to a small bowl and stir in the mixed herbs. Add the almonds to the larger portion of the mixture. Generously butter a 6-cup [1½-liter] terrine mold. Cut a piece of parchment paper or brown paper to fit the bottom of the mold, set the paper in place and butter it.

Frost the sides and bottom of the mold with the green purée, reserving some to top the terrine. Smooth in half of the almond-enriched purée. Lay the hard-boiled eggs in a row down the middle and cover with the remaining almond purée. Smooth the remaining green purée over the top.

To settle its contents, give the mold a good tap on a towel-covered counter. Cover lightly with foil and place the terrine in a water bath. Cook it in a preheated 350° F. [180° C.] oven for one hour. Let the terrine cool to room temperature. Tip the mold to drain off any juices, then cover the terrine with two layers of heavy foil and weight it with three 1-pound [½-kg.] cans. Refrigerate for 12 to 24 hours.

To serve, run a knife around the edge of the mold, dip the bottom briefly in hot water and turn out the terrine. Peel off the paper. Serve with lemon wedges, mayonnaise, thin toast and unsalted butter.

JUDITH OLNEY
SUMMER FOOD

Hot Striped-Bass Pâtés with Asparagus Tips

To make about 2 pounds [1 kg.]

1 lb.	striped-bass fillets, skinned	½ kg.
¼ cup	dry white wine	50 ml.
2 tsp.	finely chopped shallots	10 ml.
1 tsp.	chopped fresh tarragon leaves	5 ml.
2	egg whites	2
	salt and pepper	
1¼ cups	milk, made with nonfat dry milk and water	300 ml.
	melted butter	
12	asparagus tips, parboiled for 3 or 4 minutes	12
3	medium-sized fresh mushrooms, the stems trimmed and the caps quartered	3
1 tsp.	olive oil	5 ml.
3 tbsp.	nonfat dry milk	45 ml.
1 cup	fish stock (recipe, page 163)	¼ liter
1 tbsp.	fromage blanc	15 ml.
1 tsp.	crème fraîche	5 ml.
4	small sprigs tarragon	4

Put the bass fillets in an oval dish that will hold them compactly in one layer; pour on the wine, spread 1 teaspoon [5 ml.] of the chopped shallots and the tarragon leaves over the fillets, and let them marinate for two hours. Drain the fillets and reserve the marinade. Cut ½ pound [¼ kg.] of the fillets into ½-inch [1-cm.] dice. Put the diced fish into a blender and add the egg whites and salt and pepper. Blend for two minutes. Then, and not before, add the milk, and blend again for two or three minutes.

Cut the remaining fish into ¼-inch [6-mm.] dice or a little smaller. With a pastry brush, very lightly butter four 1-cup [¼-liter] terrines or soufflé molds. Fill them halfway with the puréed fish mixture, add one quarter of the diced fish and three asparagus tips to each one, then add the remainder of the purée. Cover the terrines with lids or with foil, and cook them in a water bath in a preheated 425° F. [220° C.] oven for 15 minutes.

Before putting the terrines in the oven, start the sauce. In a heavy-bottomed, nonreactive saucepan, heat the remaining shallots and the mushrooms in the olive oil without letting them color. Add the reserved wine marinade and simmer it to evaporate the alcohol. Dissolve the nonfat dry milk in the fish stock, and add this to the saucepan. Simmer the sauce, covered, over low heat for 15 minutes, then add the *fromage blanc* and the *crème fraîche,* and beat well. Keep the sauce warm.

To serve, unmold the terrines and pour off any excess liquid. Transfer them to heated plates, cover with the sauce, and decorate each serving with a small sprig of tarragon.

MICHEL GUÉRARD
MICHEL GUÉRARD'S CUSINE MINCEUR

Scallop Terrine

La Terrine de Coquilles Saint-Jacques des "Copains"

To prepare live mussels for this recipe, scrub them thoroughly and remove all traces of beard. Steam them in a covered saucepan until they have opened. Remove the mussels from the open shells, discarding any that remain closed.

To make about 4 pounds [2 kg.]

12	sea scallops	12
2	shallots, chopped	2
8 tbsp.	butter, 6 tbsp. [90 ml.] softened	120 ml.
⅓ cup	Cognac or Armagnac	75 ml.
1 lb.	pike fillets, skinned and ground	½ kg.
3	eggs, the yolks separated from the whites, the whites stiffly beaten	3
1 tbsp.	fines herbes	15 ml.
	salt and pepper	
	quatre épices	
2 cups	fresh white bread crumbs, soaked in milk and squeezed dry	½ liter
3 tbsp.	crème fraîche or heavy cream	45 ml.
¼ lb.	pork caul, soaked and drained	125 g.
¼ lb.	cooked shelled shrimp	125 g.
20	live mussels, cooked and shelled	20

Lightly sauté the scallops and the shallots in 2 tablespoons [30 ml.] of the butter. Add half of the Cognac or Armagnac and ignite it. When the flame dies, set the scallops aside.

Combine the ground pike with the egg yolks and fines herbes. Work the mixture until it is smooth, season it with salt and pepper, and add a pinch of *quatre épices* and the remaining Cognac or Armagnac. Combine the bread crumbs with the softened butter, and incorporate this panada into the pike forcemeat and chill it for one hour. Slowly work in the cream, then the egg whites, and chill the mixture for 30 minutes more.

Line a 2-quart [2-liter] terrine with the pork caul. Spread the bottom with a layer of the pike forcemeat, then make a layer of scallops, shrimp and mussels. Continue these layers, ending with forcemeat. Place the terrine in a water bath and cook it in a preheated 350° F. [180° C.] oven for one to one and one half hours, or until the mixture is firm to the touch. Refrigerate it and serve cold the following day.

ODETTE REIGE
LES TERRINES DE VIANDES, DE COQUILLAGES ET POISSONS, DE LÉGUMES

Dutch Eel Terrine

Palingpâté

The technique of skinning an eel is shown on pages 58-59.

To make about 2 pounds [1 kg.]

2 lb.	live eel, skinned, boned and cut into 3-inch [17-cm.] pieces	1 kg.
1¼ cups	fish stock (recipe, page 163)	300 ml.
3	garlic cloves, finely chopped	3
2 tbsp.	olive oil	30 ml.
1 cup	finely chopped fresh parsley	¼ liter
	salt and pepper	
1½ tbsp.	strained fresh lemon juice	22½ ml.
1	small head lettuce, shredded	1

Marinade

1¼ cups	dry white wine	300 ml.
1	carrot, finely chopped	1
1	onion, finely chopped	1
¼ cup	chopped fresh parsley	50 ml.
3 tbsp.	strained fresh lemon juice	45 ml.
2	garlic cloves, lightly crushed	2
½ tsp.	dried thyme leaves	2 ml.
1	bay leaf, crumbled	1

Ravigote sauce

1	garlic clove, crushed to a paste	1
3 tbsp.	wine vinegar	45 ml.
3 tbsp.	Dijon mustard	45 ml.
1 cup	olive oil	¼ liter
3	eggs, hard-boiled and finely chopped	3
⅓ cup	chopped onion	75 ml.
¼ cup	chopped sour gherkins	50 ml.
2 tbsp.	chopped fresh parsley	30 ml.
½ tbsp.	strained fresh lemon juice	7 ml.
	salt and pepper	

Combine all of the marinade ingredients, add the eel and marinate it for two hours, turning the pieces frequently. Transfer the eel and its marinade to a nonreactive saucepan and add the fish stock. Bring it to a simmer and poach the eel for 45 minutes.

Remove the eel with a slotted spoon and bone it. Strain the cooking liquid and boil it until it has reduced to 1¾ cups [425 ml.]. Cool and degrease it thoroughly. Sauté the finely chopped garlic in the olive oil until golden. Add the parsley.

Oil a 5-cup [1¼-liter] terrine mold and put in one third of the eel. Season and cover it with one third of the parsley mixture. Repeat these layers two more times. Season the reduced cooking liquid with salt, pepper and lemon juice, and pour it into the mold. Cover the contents of the mold with foil, then with a piece of cardboard that fits in the mold. Weight the cardboard and chill the terrine for three hours, or until the aspic has set. Turn it out onto a serving dish.

To make the ravigote sauce, mix the garlic, vinegar and mustard. Slowly add the olive oil, then stir in the chopped eggs, onion, gherkins and parsley. Season with the lemon juice, salt and pepper. Decorate the serving dish with shredded lettuce and serve the terrine with the sauce.

HUGH JANS
VRIJ NEDERLAND

Fisherman's Terrine

Terrine du Pêcheur

Serve this terrine with a watercress mousse *(recipe, page 164)* or with a *sauce antiboise*, made by combining mayonnaise with chopped raw mushrooms in lemon juice, garlic, shallots, fines herbes and diced peeled-and-seeded tomatoes.

To make about 2 pounds [1 kg.]

7 oz.	perch fillets, skinned and finely ground	200 g.
7 oz.	pike fillets, skinned and finely ground	200 g.
7 oz.	eel fillets, skinned and finely ground	200 g.
2	eggs	2
2 tbsp.	Cognac	30 ml.
1⅔ cups	*crème fraîche* or heavy cream, chilled	400 ml.
6	sea scallops, diced	6
1 cup	finely chopped fresh mushrooms	¼ liter
1 cup	finely chopped fresh parsley	¼ liter
⅔ cup	finely cut chives	150 ml.
2 tbsp.	chopped fresh tarragon leaves	30 ml.
1	truffle, finely diced, 2 tbsp. [30 ml.] juice reserved if truffle is canned	1
2 tbsp.	pistachios, blanched, peeled and chopped	30 ml.
	salt and pepper	

Mix together all of the ground fish. Work in the eggs and Cognac, chill thoroughly, and work in the cream little by little. Add all of the remaining ingredients and correct the seasoning. Turn the mixture into a buttered 6-cup [1½-liter] terrine, cover, and cook it in a water bath in a preheated 250° F. [120° C.] oven for one and one half hours, or until it is firm to the touch. Let the terrine cool and refrigerate it.

PAUL-JACQUES LÉVÈQUE (EDITOR)
LES BONNES RECETTES DE LA CUISINE TOURANGELLE

Terrine of Eel with White Wine

Terrine d'Anguilles au Vin de Tursan

This terrine may be served with the watercress mousse demonstrated on page 15. The technique of skinning an eel is shown on pages 58-59.

To make the terrine even more rich and moist, you can line the dish with strips of pork fatback, then cover them with fine rounds of lemon peel, before coating the terrine with the forcemeat. You may substitute for the eel fillets the same weight of carp or mullet fillets.

To make about 3 pounds [1½ kg.]

2	large live eels, skinned and boned, or 1 lb. [½ kg.] eel fillets, skinned	2
½ lb.	butter, 14 tbsp. [210 ml.] softened	¼ kg.
¾ lb.	small button mushrooms, diced	350 g.
1½ tbsp.	chopped fresh parsley	22½ ml.
1 tbsp.	chopped shallots	15 ml.
	salt and pepper	
¾ lb.	salmon or whiting fillets, skinned	350 g.
2	eggs	2
1 tsp. each	chopped fresh chervil, tarragon and chives	5 ml. each
	cayenne pepper	
	powdered saffron	

Marinade

1 cup	dry white wine, preferably Tursan	¼ liter
	salt and freshly ground pepper	
3 tbsp.	Armagnac (optional)	45 ml.
1 tbsp. each	chopped fresh chervil, tarragon and chives	15 ml. each

Put the eel fillets into a deep, heatproof earthenware dish and add the marinade ingredients. Let it marinate overnight in the refrigerator.

Put the dish containing the eels and marinade over low heat until the liquid bubbles gently. Cover with a piece of foil and cook for 20 minutes. Take the foil off and let the eels cool in their marinade. Their flesh will have shrunk somewhat during the cooking.

Heat 2 tablespoons [30 ml.] of the butter in a skillet and add the diced mushrooms. Sauté them for five minutes. Add 1 tablespoon [15 ml.] of the parsley, the shallots, salt and pepper, and continue cooking for another two minutes. Put the mixture on a plate to cool.

Put the salmon or whiting, 2 teaspoons [10 ml.] of salt and some pepper into the chilled bowl of a blender. Blend for 30 to 40 seconds to obtain a smooth purée. Add the eggs, one by one, and blend for another 20 seconds. Add the softened butter, the remaining parsley, the chopped herbs and a pinch each of cayenne and saffron, and blend for a further 30 seconds, until the mixture is smooth. Transfer this forcemeat to a bowl and blend in the cooled mushroom mixture.

Drain the eel fillets and cut them in half lengthwise. Spread the inside of a 6-cup [1½-liter] terrine with a ½-inch [1-cm.] layer of forcemeat. Then fill the terrine by alternating layers of eel fillets and the remaining forcemeat, ending with a layer of forcemeat. Cover with a piece of foil, which will act as a lid, and place the terrine in a water bath. Cook it for three hours in a preheated 275° F. [140° C.] oven. Let the terrine cool for several hours at room temperature and then place it in the refrigerator overnight.

Serve the terrine as it is, without unmolding it.

CAROLINE CONRAN (EDITOR)
MICHEL GUÉRARD'S CUISINE GOURMANDE

Cod Pâté

To make about 1½ pounds [¾ kg.]

2 cups	fish stock (recipe, page 163)	½ liter
¼	small celeriac	¼
5	sprigs fresh parsley	5
1	large onion, chopped	1
	salt	
1 lb.	cod steak, skinned and sprinkled with vinegar	½ kg.
3 oz.	fresh pork fatback, chopped	90 g.
⅔ cup	crumbled stale bread	150 ml.
2 tbsp.	beaten egg	30 ml.
1½ tsp.	potato starch	7 ml.
	ground ginger	
	grated nutmeg	
	paprika	
2 tbsp.	dry bread crumbs	30 ml.

Simmer the stock with the celeriac, parsley and half of the chopped onion for 10 minutes. Strain the stock into another pot and reserve the vegetables. Season the stock with salt and poach the fish in the stock for 10 minutes, or until it flakes easily. Drain the fish and remove any bones.

Cook the fatback in a skillet over low heat until it has melted, add the remaining chopped onion and sauté, without browning, until the onion is limp. Soak the crumbled bread in the fish stock and squeeze it. Grind together the fish, bread, sautéed onion and the vegetables from the stock. Add the egg and the potato starch to the mixture, knead well, and season to taste with salt, ginger, nutmeg and paprika.

Butter a 4-cup [1-liter] mold and sprinkle it with the bread crumbs. Pack the fish mixture into the mold and cover it. Place the mold in a large saucepan filled with enough water to come halfway up the sides of the mold; cover the saucepan and steam for 45 minutes, or until the fish mixture is firm to the touch. Alternatively, cook the mixture in a water bath in a preheated 350° F. [180° C.] oven. To serve hot, unmold the pâté immediately. To serve cold, let it cool in the mold before unmolding.

ZOFIA CZERNY
POLISH COOKBOOK

Pâtés

Cheshire Pork Pie

Molding a raised crust of hot-water dough is demonstrated on pages 54-55. Melted gelatinous meat stock can be poured through the hole in the pastry lid after the cooked pie has been chilled overnight. The pie should then be rechilled to set the aspic before serving.

To make about 3 pounds [1 ½ kg.]

2 lb.	boneless pork shoulder, ground or finely chopped	1 kg.
1	medium-sized onion, finely chopped	1
1 tbsp.	brown sugar	15 ml.
	salt and freshly ground pepper	
	grated nutmeg	
1 lb.	hot-water crust dough (recipe, page 166)	½ kg.
3	medium-sized tart cooking apples, peeled, cored and sliced	3
⅔ cup	dry cider	150 ml.
1	egg, beaten	1

Mix the pork and the onion, and add the sugar and seasonings. Fry a piece of the mixture to test it for flavor. Use most of the dough to make a raised pie shell. Put a layer of the pork-and-onion mixture in the pie shell, then a layer of ap-

ple, and so on, until both are used up, finishing with a layer of pork. Pour the cider over the top and cover with a lid of dough. Decorate with dough scraps and cut a hole in the top. Brush the pie with the beaten egg. Bake it in a preheated 350° F. [180° C.] oven for one and one quarter hours.

SIMONE SEKERS
PÂTÉS, TERRINES AND POTTED MEATS

Raised Hare Pie

The technique of molding the dough for a raised pie is demonstrated on pages 54-55. To bone the hares, follow the technique used for rabbit shown on pages 66-67.

This raised pie may also be made with rabbit. Chicken livers may be substituted for hare or rabbit livers.

To make about 5 pounds [2½ kg.]

2 lb.	hot-water crust dough (recipe, page 166)	1 kg.
3 cups	fresh bread crumbs	¾ liter
two 3 lb.	hares, boned and sliced, the livers reserved and chopped	two 1 ½ kg.
1 tsp.	grated lemon peel	5 ml.
½ cup	port	125 ml.
12 tbsp.	butter, half melted, half diced	180 ml.
	salt and pepper	
2	eggs, 1 beaten	2
	grated nutmeg	
1	bay leaf	1
1¼ cups	gelatinous meat stock (recipe, page 162)	300 ml.
	fresh parsley sprigs	

While the dough is still warm, use it to mold a 2-quart [2-liter] raised pie, reserving enough dough for the lid. Make up a forcemeat by first mixing the bread crumbs with the livers and the lemon peel. Moisten the mixture with 5 tablespoons [75 ml.] of the port and the melted butter, season with salt and pepper and bind it with the unbeaten egg. Mix until thoroughly blended.

Line the sides and base of the molded pie with the forcemeat. Arrange the hare meat in the pie, season with salt, pepper and a pinch of nutmeg, and add the diced butter and the bay leaf. Cover with a dough lid, make a hole in the center and brush with the beaten egg. Bake the pie in a preheated 425° F. [220° C.] oven for one half hour; then turn down the oven to 325° F. [160° C.] and continue baking for another two hours. Remove the pie and let it cool. Heat the stock and add the remaining port. Pour the mixture into the cooled pie, and refrigerate to set the stock to an aspic. Serve the pie cold, garnished with parsley sprigs.

LIZZIE BOYD (EDITOR)
BRITISH COOKERY

Raised Tongue Pie

The technique of molding the dough for a raised pie is demonstrated on pages 54-55.

For this pie, mold the pie dough on a straight-sided round casserole, pan or soufflé dish that is about 6 inches [15 cm.] in diameter and 3 inches [8 cm.] deep and that will hold the coiled tongue snugly.

To make about 4½ pounds [2¼ kg.]

2 lb.	corned beef tongue, soaked for 3 hours in cold water	1 kg.
1½ lb.	hot-water crust dough (recipe, page 166)	¾ kg.
1½ lb.	basic forcemeat (recipe, page 163)	¾ kg.
	mace	
	cayenne pepper	
½ lb.	sliced bacon	¼ kg.
1	egg, beaten	1
1¼ cups	gelatinous meat stock, warmed (recipe, page 162)	300 ml.

Boil the tongue until tender (about two and one half hours), strip off the skin, and cut off the root end with its gristle and bone. Use three quarters of the warm dough to raise the pie around a mold. Let it set, then roll up the tongue and put it into the crust. Fill in the spaces with forcemeat, sprinkle with a pinch each of mace and cayenne pepper, and cover with the bacon slices.

Roll the remaining dough into a lid for the pie. Put the lid in place and make a hole in the center for steam to escape. Brush the lid with the beaten egg and bake it in a preheated 425° F. [220° C.] oven for half an hour. Turn down the heat to 325° F. [160° C.] and continue baking for another two hours. Remove the pie from the oven, let it cool slightly, then pour the warm stock through the hole in the pastry lid. Refrigerate the pie so that the stock sets to an aspic before serving.

LIZZIE BOYD (EDITOR)
BRITISH COOKERY

To Make a Goose Pye

This recipe is from an 18th Century English cookery book attributed to Hannah Glasse. The technique of boning a bird through the neck is demonstrated on pages 32-33. If the dough is difficult to roll out, you may press it onto the bird with your hands, as demonstrated on page 56. Instead of the seasoning used here, the birds can be marinated in a blend of dried herbs, salt, pepper and brandy. Basic forcemeat (recipe,
page 163) can be used to form additional layers by filling the gaps between the solid meats.

This pye is delicious, either hot or cold, and it will keep for a great while.

To make about 16 pounds [8 kg.]

1½ tsp.	ground mace	7 ml.
1½ tsp.	pepper	7 ml.
1 tbsp.	salt	15 ml.
12 to 14 lb.	goose, boned through the neck	6 to 7 kg.
4 lb.	chicken, boned through the neck	2 kg.
1	corned beef tongue, soaked in cold water for 1 hour, parboiled for 3 hours, or until tender, skinned and trimmed	1
½ lb.	butter	¼ kg.
8 lb.	hot-water crust dough (recipe, page 166)	4 kg.

Mix together the mace, pepper and salt, season your goose and fowl with it, then lay the tongue in the fowl and the fowl in the goose. Shape the goose in the same form as if whole. Spread the butter on top.

Roll out two thirds of the dough, place the goose in the center and raise up the sides around the goose. Roll out the rest of the dough to form a lid and place it over the goose. Crimp the edges, cut a hole in the top, and bake it in a preheated 400° F. [200° C.] oven for 15 minutes. Reduce the heat to 325° F. [160° C.] and bake for four hours more, covering the top with parchment paper if it browns too fast.

THE ART OF COOKERY, MADE PLAIN AND EASY

Touraine Easter Pâté

Pâté de Pâques en Croûte à la Tourangelle

To make about 1¾ pounds [875 g.]

½ lb.	fresh pork belly, ground	¼ kg.
½ lb.	veal scallops, cut into strips	¼ kg.
	salt and pepper	
1	shallot, very finely chopped	1
5	eggs, 4 hard-boiled, 1 lightly beaten	5
Dough		
1¾ cups	flour	425 ml.
7 tbsp.	butter	105 ml.
¼ cup	crème fraîche or heavy cream	125 ml.
½ tbsp.	salt	7 ml.
	gelatinous meat stock (recipe, page 162), made with a little port (optional)	

Place all of the dough ingredients in a bowl and knead with a wooden spatula to make a fairly stiff dough. Cover the dough with a damp cloth and refrigerate it. Mix together the pork, veal, salt, pepper and shallot. Fry a spoonful of the mixture and taste it for seasoning. Roll out the dough into a large rectangle. Form the meat mixture into a cylinder with the hard-boiled eggs in the center, and place the meat on the dough. Brush the edges of the dough with the beaten egg and fold up the long edges to enclose the meat. Press the ends with a rolling pin to seal them. Brush the top with the beaten egg, and decorate it with strips of surplus dough. Cut two holes in the top and insert foil chimneys.

Place the pâté on a baking sheet and bake it in a preheated 400° F. [200° C.] oven for 45 minutes, or until the top of the pastry is golden brown.

This pâté is best when served warm, but it may be surrounded with chopped port aspic and served cold.

PAUL-JACQUES LÉVÈQUE (EDITOR)
LES BONNES RECETTES DE LA CUISINE TOURANGELLE

Ham Baked in Pastry

Pasticcio di Prosciutto

This recipe is from the fifth book of the Works of Bartolomeo Scappi, published in 1570. This volume is devoted to the most important dishes of the great 16th Century cuisine: that is, to the pâtés.

To make about 2 pounds [1 kg.]

1 cup	red wine	¼ liter
	salt and pepper	
½ tsp.	ground cinnamon	2 ml.
1	whole clove, ground	1
½ tsp.	freshly grated nutmeg	2 ml.
1 lb.	boneless ham, in a rectangular block, about 3 by 3 by 6 inches [7 ½ by 7 ½ by 15 cm.]	½ kg.
½ lb.	boneless lean veal, thinly sliced	¼ kg.
4 tbsp.	butter	60 ml.
½ lb.	short-crust dough (recipe, page 167)	¼ kg.

Heat the wine with half of the seasonings in a nonreactive saucepan. When the wine begins to boil, put in the ham and simmer it for about 30 minutes, turning the ham several times. Drain the ham and sprinkle it on all sides with the remaining seasonings. Cook the veal in the butter for a few minutes, basting with a few spoonfuls of the wine in which the ham was cooked. Cool.

Roll out the dough thin. Grease a 4-cup [1-liter] loaf pan and line it with the dough, reserving some for the lid. Cover

the dough with veal slices. Place the ham on top, baste it with the veal cooking juices and cover it with the remaining veal slices. Cover with the rest of the dough and seal the edges. Cut a hole in the top of the dough and insert a foil or cardboard chimney.

Bake the ham in a preheated 375° F. [190° C.] oven for 45 minutes, or until golden brown. Let it cool before slicing.

MASSIMO ALBERINI
CENTO RICETTE STORICHE

Alsatian Pâté

Pâté Alsacien

To make about 3½ pounds [1¾ kg.]

1 lb.	boneless lean ham, half cut into strips, half chopped	½ kg.
½ lb.	boneless lean veal, cut into strips	¼ kg.
	salt	
	mixed spices	
6 tbsp.	white wine	90 ml.
¼ cup	Madeira	50 ml.
5	shallots, finely chopped	5
⅓ lb.	fresh pork fat	150 g.
1¼ lb.	short-crust dough (recipe, page 167)	600 g.
1¼ cups	gelatinous meat stock (recipe, page 162)	300 ml.

Place the strips of ham and veal in a nonreactive bowl and season them with salt and mixed spices; add the wine and Madeira and three of the chopped shallots. Cover and let the meats marinate in the refrigerator for 24 hours.

Combine the chopped ham, pork fat, salt, mixed spices and the remaining shallots. Pass the mixture twice through a food grinder. Fry a spoonful of this forcemeat and taste for seasoning.

Roll out half of the dough into a rectangle 12 by 6 inches [30 by 15 cm.]. Spread half of the forcemeat on the dough, leaving a margin of 2 inches [5 cm.]. Arrange the marinated meats on top of the forcemeat so that the layer is 2 inches high. Cover with the remaining forcemeat, and fold over the edges of dough so that the meat is partly covered.

Roll out the remaining dough. Moisten the folded edges of the first rectangle with water and place the second rectangle of dough over the first, pressing the edges so that they adhere. Cut a small hole in the middle of the lid of dough, and insert a small rolled card to act as a chimney.

Bake the pâté in a preheated 400° F. [200° C.] oven for 45 minutes, or until the pastry is golden. When the pâté has cooled, insert a funnel into the chimney and fill the pâté with the stock. Let the stock set.

PAUL BOUILLARD
LA CUISINE AU COIN DU FEU

Chicken Pâté

Pâté de Volaille

The technique of larding is shown on page 74. The technique of boning a bird through the back is shown on pages 79-81.

To make about 5 pounds [2½ kg.]

2 lb.	short-crust dough (recipe, page 167)	1 kg.
1 lb.	boneless lean veal, ground	½ kg.
1 lb.	fresh pork belly with the rind removed, ground	½ kg.
	salt	
	mixed spices	
2½ lb.	chicken, boned through the back	1¼ kg.
½ lb.	fresh pork fatback, half cut into lardons, half sliced into bards	¼ kg.
1	bay leaf	1
1	egg yolk, beaten with 1 tbsp. [15 ml.] water	1

Roll out three quarters of the dough into an oval shape ¾ inch [2 cm.] thick. Lift up the ends to form a purse shape. Line an 8-inch [20-cm.] oval hinged mold with the dough, pressing well against the bottom and sides; the dough walls should be ¾ inch higher than the rim of the mold. Take care to maintain an even thickness, lest the pâté leak during cooking. Roll out the remaining dough for the lid; set it aside.

Season the veal and ground pork belly with salt and mixed spices. Pound the mixture in a mortar to obtain a smooth forcemeat. Fry a spoonful of this mixture and taste it for seasoning. Spread the chicken out, skin side down. Season the lardons with salt and spices, and use them to lard the inside of the chicken. Spread the surface with a layer of forcemeat. Roll up the chicken into a cylinder.

Put a ¾-inch layer of forcemeat into the dough-lined mold. Put in the rolled-up chicken and sprinkle it with two pinches of salt and spices. Cover it with another layer of forcemeat, mounding it up in the center and leaving the dough edges free. Lay the bards of fatback over the forcemeat and put the bay leaf on top.

Moisten the edges of the dough, put the dough lid on top and seal the edges, pressing them together with your thumb and forefinger. Trim off the surplus and crimp the edges of the dough. Gather the dough trimmings into a ball and roll them ¼ inch [6 mm.] thick. Cut out a 7-inch [17-cm.] oval for the second lid. Moisten the first lid and put the second lid on top. Make a hole through both lids and brush the top of the dough with the beaten egg yolk. With the point of a knife, cut deep grooves in the lid for decoration.

Bake the pâté in a preheated 350° F. [180° C.] oven for two hours. If the lid browns too quickly, cover it with foil. To test for doneness, insert a trussing needle through the hole in the lid; it should slide in easily and come out hot.

JULES GOUFFÉ
LE LIVRE DE CUISINE

Ferdinand Wernert's Free-form Pâté

Pâté Pantin Ferdinand Wernert

To make about 5 pounds [2½ kg.]

1 lb.	veal tenderloin, 8 thin 6-inch [15-cm.] strips sliced off, the rest cubed	½ kg.
1 lb.	fresh pork fatback, 8 thin 6-inch [15-cm.] strips and 2 large bards sliced off, the rest cubed	½ kg.
½ lb.	prosciutto, 8 thin 6-inch [15-cm.] strips sliced off, the rest cubed	¼ kg.
	mixed spices	
	salt and freshly ground black pepper	
	dried thyme leaves	
	powdered bay leaf	
1 cup	Cognac or Madeira	¼ liter
6 oz.	boneless lean pork, ground	175 g.
2	eggs, beaten	2
2 lb.	short-crust dough (recipe, page 167)	1 kg.
1	egg yolk, beaten with 1 tsp. [5 ml.] salt	1

Combine the strips of veal, fatback and prosciutto in a shallow dish; season them with mixed spices, salt, pepper and a pinch each of thyme and powdered bay leaf. Mix well and pour in the Cognac or Madeira. Let the meats marinate until ready for use, stirring them from time to time.

Combine the cubes of veal, fatback and prosciutto with the ground pork; season with mixed spices, salt and pepper, thyme and bay leaf. Grind the meats together using the finest disk of a food grinder. Pound the ground meats in a mortar and mix vigorously, adding the beaten eggs and any Cognac or Madeira that was not absorbed by the marinating meats. Poach a ball of this forcemeat in boiling water and taste it for seasoning.

Roll out three quarters of the dough to a 14-by-10-inch [35-by-25-cm.] rectangle and place it on a buttered baking sheet. Place one of the fatback bards in the center of the rectangle. Spread a layer of the forcemeat on top, then marinated meat strips, then a second layer of the forcemeat; continue layering in the same way until you have used up all of the meats, arranging them symmetrically. Finish with a layer of forcemeat and cover with the other fatback bard.

Moisten lightly all around the edges of the dough and lift the two long sides of the rectangle of dough up over the top fatback bard so that the two edges meet. With a rolling pin, roll out the two ends of dough until they are about ⅛ inch [4 mm.] thick, cut off any excess and lift them up so that their moistened edges meet each other, pressing lightly with your fingers to ensure their sticking together.

Brush the surface of the pâté with a wet brush or cloth. Roll out the remaining dough, cut out a rectangle the size of the pâté and place it on top of the moistened surface. Pinch the edges together with a pastry wheel or with your thumb and forefinger; brush the surface with the beaten yolk. Decorate the top with designs incised in the dough. With a knife, make two openings in the center of the decorated dough, and insert into each a little piece of buttered parchment paper rolled like a chimney to let the steam escape.

Bake the pâté in a preheated 350° F. [180° C.] oven for one hour and 20 minutes. If the pastry browns too fast, cover it with foil or lightly dampened parchment paper. The pâté is done when thick, coagulated juices ooze around the chimneys and the internal temperature has reached 160° F. [70° C.]. Remove the pâté from the oven, let it settle for 10 to 15 minutes, then carefully cut it into generous slices with a serrated knife. Eat the pâté while it is still hot.

LOUISETTE BERTHOLLE
SECRETS OF THE GREAT FRENCH RESTAURANTS

Pork and Dried-Fruit Tarts

Herbe-Blade

To bake the pastry shells called for in this recipe, roll out 1 pound [½ kg.] of short-crust dough (recipe, page 167) and use it to line two 8-inch [20-cm.] tart pans. Press parchment paper against the dough and fill the pans with dried beans or rice. Place the pans in a preheated 400° F. [200° C.] oven and bake for 10 minutes, or until the dough is set but not colored. Remove the beans and the paper, prick the bottom of the shells with a fork, and bake the empty shells for five minutes until they are dry. Let the shells cool.

To make two 8-inch [20-cm.] tarts

3 lb.	pork blade roast, cut into large pieces	1½ kg.
1 tsp. each	chopped fresh hyssop and sage leaves	5 ml. each
2 tbsp.	chopped fresh parsley	30 ml.
½ lb.	dates, pitted and finely chopped	¼ kg.
2 cups	dried currants, soaked in warm water for 15 minutes and drained	½ liter
¼ cup	pine nuts	50 ml.
8	egg yolks	8
2 tbsp.	sugar	30 ml.
1 tsp.	ground ginger	5 ml.
1 tbsp.	salt	15 ml.
¼ tsp.	powdered saffron, mixed with 1 tbsp. [15 ml.] water	1 ml.
2	partially baked tart shells	2

Cover the pork with water and simmer it for one and one half hours, or until the meat comes easily away from the bones. Bone and dice the meat.

Strain 1¼ cups [300 ml.] of the cooking liquid, bring it to a boil and add the chopped herbs. When the liquid returns to a boil, remove the herbs with a skimmer and add them to the pork. Add the dates, currants and pine nuts to the pork.

Beat the egg yolks with the sugar, ginger, salt and saffron. Add to the pork mixture and blend well. Fill the pastry shells with this mixture and bake them in a preheated 375° F. [190° C.] oven for 35 to 40 minutes, or until the filling is firm. Serve the pork tarts hot or cold.

THOMAS AUSTIN (EDITOR)
TWO FIFTEENTH-CENTURY COOKERY-BOOKS

Ham Pâté

Aufgesetzte Schinkenpastete

To make about 3 pounds [1 ½ kg.]

½ lb.	fresh pork fatback, ground	¼ kg.
1 lb.	boneless lean pork, or pork and veal, ground	½ kg.
3	eggs, 2 lightly beaten, 1 yolk separated from the white	3
½ tsp.	salt	2 ml.
1 tsp.	paprika	5 ml.
2 tsp.	brandy or Madeira	10 ml.
2	hard rolls, soaked in water and squeezed almost dry	2
1 tbsp.	butter	15 ml.
1 tsp.	chopped onion	5 ml.
1 tsp.	chopped fresh parsley	5 ml.
1 lb.	short-crust dough (recipe, page 167) or rough puff dough (recipe, page 167)	½ kg.
⅓ lb.	ham, sliced	150 g.

Combine the fatback and the pork or pork and veal with the two beaten eggs, salt, paprika and brandy or Madeira. Cook the squeezed bread in the butter, with the onion and parsley, for about five minutes. Add to the meat mixture. Fry a spoonful of this forcemeat mixture and taste it for seasoning.

Roll out one third of the dough to form a rectangle 10 by 6 inches [25 by 15 cm.], and place it on a damp baking sheet. Spread a layer of forcemeat on the dough base, leaving a ¾-inch [2-cm.] margin all around the rectangle. Cover the forcemeat with a layer of ham slices. Repeat these layers until all of the meat is used.

Roll out the remaining dough, cut another, somewhat larger rectangle and use it to cover the pâté. Decorate with dough scraps. Brush the borders of the dough with the egg white and press them together. Make one or two small holes in the top and insert buttered paper funnels. Brush the pâté with the egg yolk. Bake it in a preheated 350° F. [180° C.] oven for one hour, or until golden brown. Serve hot or cold.

HENRIETTE DAVIDIS
PRAKTISCHES KOCHBUCH

Veal and Ham Pie

Traditionally there is a layer of hard-boiled eggs in the center of this pie, but if the pie is served hot, the egg is inclined to go crumbly, so it can quite well be omitted.

To make about 2 pounds [1 kg.]

1 lb.	boneless veal stew meat, trimmed and diced, trimmings reserved	½ kg.
⅓ lb.	boneless ham with the rind removed and reserved, diced	150 g.
1 or 2	eggs, hard-boiled and sliced (optional)	1 or 2
	salt and pepper	
½ tsp.	grated lemon peel	2 ml.
2	small bay leaves	2
2 cups	cold water	½ liter
1 lb.	short-crust dough (recipe, page 167), made with a mixture of lard and butter	½ kg.
2 tbsp.	milk	30 ml.
1	small onion, halved	1
1	carrot, sliced	1
6	peppercorns	6

Put half of the veal as a layer in the bottom of a 4-cup [1-liter] pie dish; then cover with a layer of the diced ham. Next add a layer of sliced hard-boiled eggs, if using. Season lightly with salt and well with pepper, and sprinkle with lemon peel. Repeat the layers of meats, and again season with salt and pepper and sprinkle with lemon peel. Place the bay leaves on top and pour in one third of the cold water.

Roll out the dough fairly thick. Dampen the rim of the pie dish. Cut a strip of dough to go around the rim; press it into place. Cover the pie with the rest of the dough, pressing it down onto the strip at the edge and crimping to make a wavy sealed border. Insert a pie funnel through the dough in the center of the dish, or cut two small slits for the steam to escape. Decorate the top, if desired, with the dough trimmings. Brush the dough with milk. Stand the pie dish on a baking sheet and place it in a 400° F. [200° C.] oven.

Place the veal trimmings and ham rind in an ovenproof pot with the onion, carrot, peppercorns and remaining cold water. Boil this stock gently for about 15 minutes. When the pie has been in the oven for 30 minutes, reduce the heat to 350° F. [180° C.] and place the stock in the oven with the pie. Cover the dough with oiled parchment paper if it browns too fast. Bake the pie for one and one quarter hours more.

Strain the stock, reduce it to ¾ cup [175 ml.], and pour it into the pie through the funnel or the slits in the pastry. The stock will make a well-flavored gravy if the pie is served hot or will set to an aspic if served cold. To serve cold, leave the pie in a cool place, not the refrigerator, for 24 hours.

AUDREY PARKER
COTTAGE AND COUNTRY RECIPES

Green Goose Pie

The technique of boning a bird through the neck is demonstrated on pages 32-33.

To make about 4 pounds [2 kg.]

two 4 lb.	geese, boned through the neck	two 2 kg.
	salt and pepper	
	ground mace	
	ground allspice	
8 tbsp.	butter, softened	120 ml.
½ lb.	short-crust dough (recipe, page 167) (optional)	¼ kg.
	gelatinous meat stock (recipe, page 162) (optional)	

Season the geese well with salt and pepper, mace and allspice. Put one inside the other, and press them as close as you can, drawing the legs inward. Put them in a pie dish, put the butter over them, and cover them with a tight-fitting lid or a top crust of dough with a small hole cut in the center.

Bake them in a preheated 325° F. [160° C.] oven for two hours, or until the pastry is golden brown and the pie reaches an internal temperature of 160° F. [70° C.]. Allow it to cool and, if desired, pour in melted gelatinous stock and chill to set it before serving.

MRS. RUNDELL
DOMESTIC COOKERY

Pâté of Leftover Chicken

Pâté Froid de Volaille à la Ménagère

To make about 4 pounds [2 kg.]

1 lb.	boneless cooked chicken, skinned and finely sliced	½ kg.
	salt and pepper	
1⅓ cups	chopped fresh mushrooms, cooked in 2 tbsp. [30 ml.] butter	325 ml.
¼ lb.	ham, cut into strips	125 g.
½ lb.	boneless lean pork, ground	¼ kg.
½ lb.	fresh pork fat, ground	¼ kg.
	mixed spices	
1¾ lb.	short-crust dough (recipe, page 167), made with butter and lard and 4 egg yolks	875 g.
1	egg, beaten with 2 tbsp. [30 ml.] water	1
1 cup	gelatinous meat stock (recipe, page 162)	¼ liter

Season the chicken slices with salt and pepper, and combine them with the mushrooms and ham strips. Pound the ground pork and pork fat together in a mortar, season with salt, pepper and mixed spices, and pass this forcemeat through a sieve. Fry a spoonful of forcemeat and taste it for seasoning.

Butter a round or oval 7-cup [1¾-liter] pâté mold and line it with dough. Line the bottom and sides with a ½-inch [1-cm.] layer of pork forcemeat. Put a layer of the chicken mixture in the bottom, then a layer of forcemeat. Continue these layers until the mold is full. Put on a lid of dough, moisten the edges and crimp them together to seal. Decorate the top with dough scraps and glaze it with the beaten egg. Cut a small hole in the center.

Bake the pâté in a preheated 350° F. [180° C.] oven for one and one half hours. Unmold the pâté and let it cool. Pour the stock through the hole in the lid and chill it to set.

LE CORDON BLEU

Duck Pâté with Olives

Croûte au Canard et aux Olives

The technique of boning a bird is shown on pages 22-23.

To make about 3 pounds [1 ½ kg.]

3 lb.	duck, boned and ground	1½ kg.
¼ lb.	pork tenderloin, ground	125 g.
½ tsp. each	salt, pepper, paprika, dried thyme leaves, grated nutmeg and powdered bay leaf	2 ml. each
¼ cup	marc or brandy	50 ml.
½ lb.	green olives, pitted	¼ kg.
2	eggs, 1 separated	2
1 lb.	short-crust dough *(recipe, page 167)*	½ kg.
2	slices fresh pork fatback	2

Mix the ground duck and pork with all of the seasonings, the marc or brandy, olives, one egg and the egg yolk. Fry a spoonful of the mixture and taste it for seasoning.

Butter a 6-cup [1½-liter] loaf pan. Roll out the dough ¼ inch [6 mm.] thick. Cut out a rectangle large enough to line the bottom and come two thirds of the way up the sides of the loaf pan; cut another, smaller rectangle for the lid. Line the pan with the large rectangle of dough, pleating the corners. Place a slice of fatback in the bottom, then put in the duck mixture. Cover with the remaining slice of fatback, then with the dough lid. Dampen the edges and crimp them together. Make a slit in the lid and brush the lid with the egg white. Bake the pâté in a preheated 375° F. [190° C.] oven for 45 minutes. Serve it cold, with a salad of lamb's lettuce or dandelion greens.

ÉLIANE THIBAUT COMELADE
LA CUISINE CATALANE

Traditional Hare Pâté

Pâté de Lièvre

To bone the hare, follow the technique used for rabbit shown on pages 66-67. The original version of this recipe called for the hare's blood to bind the terrine and the liver to flavor it; both are drawn from the animal when it is eviscerated, and both must be used at once. In this recipe, an egg is substituted for the blood.

To make about 5 pounds [2 ½ kg.]

⅓ lb.	fresh pork fatback, 1 bard sliced off, the rest cut into lardons	150 g.
	salt	
	mixed spices	
4 lb.	hare, boned, the saddle and legs cut into strips, the trimmings reserved	2 kg.
10 oz.	boneless lean veal, ground	300 g.
10 oz.	fresh pork belly with the rind removed	300 g.
1	egg	1
2 lb.	short-crust dough *(recipe, page 167)*	1 kg.
2	bay leaves	2
1	egg yolk, beaten with 1 tbsp. [15 ml.] water	1

Season the lardons with salt and mixed spices, and use them to lard the strips of hare. Season the hare trimmings and the ground veal and pork belly. Grind them together, then pound them in a mortar with the egg to obtain a smooth forcemeat. Fry a spoonful of it and taste it for seasoning.

Roll out three quarters of the dough into an oval ¾ inch [2 cm.] thick. Lift up the edges to form a purse shape, and press the dough into a hinged 2-quart [2-liter] oval mold, letting the edges rise above the edges of the mold. Roll out the remaining dough for the lid.

Line the dough with a layer of forcemeat. Cover it with strips of hare. Add another layer of forcemeat, then one of hare, then a final layer of forcemeat. Sprinkle the top with salt and mixed spices, cover it with the barding fat and top with the bay leaves. Moisten the edges of the dough, cover it with the lid and seal the edges. Trim off any surplus dough. Roll out the dough trimmings to a thickness of ¼ inch [6 mm.] and cut out an oval slightly smaller than the dish. Moisten the first dough lid and place the second lid on top. Make a hole in the middle of the double lid and brush the lid with the beaten egg yolk. Score the surface with a knife to make a decorative pattern. Bake the pâté in a preheated 375° F. [190° C.] oven for about one and three quarters hours, protecting the top of the pâté with parchment paper, if necessary, to keep it from browning too much. The pâté is done when the crust is golden brown and a meat thermometer, inserted though the hole in the lid, registers 160° F. [70° C.].

JULES GOUFFÉ
LE LIVRE DE CUISINE

Pâté of Small Game

Pâté de Petite Venaison

To bone the hare and the snipe, follow the techniques used for the rabbit and the quail on pages 66-67.

If this dish is destined to appear several times at family meals, bake it simply in a terrine. If it is to be served at a formal luncheon, fortify it with a wall of golden pastry.

To make about 5 pounds [2½ kg.]

4 lb.	hare, boned, the bones and liver reserved	2 kg.
1	snipe (optional), boned, the meat cut into strips and the bones reserved	1
4 cups	gelatinous meat stock *(recipe, page 162)*	1 liter
¾ lb.	boneless veal, ½ lb. [¼ kg.] ground, the rest cut into strips	350 g.
¼ lb.	boneless fatty pork, ground	125 g.
1¾ lb.	fresh pork fatback, 1 lb. [½ kg.] finely diced, 2 oz. [60 g.] cut into small lardons, the rest sliced into bards	875 g.
1	onion, finely chopped	1
5	shallots, 4 finely chopped	5
1	garlic clove, chopped	1
2	truffles, peeled and diced, the peelings reserved	2
	salt and pepper	
	dried thyme and savory leaves	
2	bay leaves, crumbled	2
	mixed spices	
	freshly grated nutmeg	
4	eggs	4
⅔ cup	eau de vie or other brandy	150 ml.
1 tbsp.	chopped fresh parsley	15 ml.
1 lb.	short-crust dough *(recipe, page 167)* (optional)	½ kg.
⅓ lb.	boneless chicken breast, cut into strips	150 g.

Break up the hare bones and place them in a saucepan with any trimmings of meat, the snipe carcass, if used, and the stock. Simmer for two hours to make a strong game stock.

Combine the foreleg meat and liver of the hare with the ground veal and pork, and grind them together. Add most of the diced fatback, the onion, whole shallot, garlic and truffle peelings. Put this mixture through the grinder. Season it with salt and pepper, thyme, savory, one crumbled bay leaf, mixed spices and a little nutmeg. Place the mixture in a large mortar, add the eggs and brandy, and pound it to ob-

tain a smooth forcemeat. Stir in the remaining diced fatback for a marbled effect. Fry a spoonful and taste it for seasoning.

Cube the meat from the saddle and hind legs of the hare. Lard the cubes with the fatback lardons and season them with salt and pepper, the parsley, one chopped shallot, a little thyme, the remaining bay leaf, and mixed spices.

Line a buttered 2½-quart [2½-liter] mold with the short-crust dough, if using; cover the dough, or an unlined mold, with half of the fatback bards. Put in a layer of forcemeat, then a layer of hare cubes, strips of veal, chicken and snipe, if using, and truffles. Repeat these layers, filling the gaps with forcemeat. Finish with a layer of forcemeat mixed with the remaining shallots. Cover with the remaining bards. Put on a lid of dough, if using; cut a hole in the top and insert a rolled paper chimney. Otherwise, cover the mold with a lid.

Bake the pâté in a preheated 400° F. [200° C.] oven for about one hour, or until a skewer inserted in the center for one half minute is hot to the touch when removed. Let it cool for at least 30 minutes, then strain the reduced stock and pour it into the chimney through a funnel or pour it over the terrine. Refrigerate until the stock sets to an aspic.

E. AURICOSTE DE LAZARQUE
CUISINE MESSINE

Duck Pie

This recipe is adapted from a classic English cookery book, first published in 1808. The technique of boning a bird through the neck is demonstrated on pages 32-33.

To make about 5 pounds [2½ kg.]

4 lb.	duck, boned through the neck	2 kg.
3 lb.	chicken, boned through the neck	1½ kg.
	salt and pepper	
	ground mace	
	ground allspice	
1	corned calf's tongue, blanched for 10 minutes, simmered until tender and skinned	1
½ lb.	basic forcemeat *(recipe, page 163)* (optional)	¼ kg.
1 lb.	short-crust dough *(recipe, page 167)* or hot-water crust dough *(recipe, page 166)*	½ kg.

Season the birds with salt, pepper, mace and allspice. Put the tongue inside the chicken and the chicken inside the duck. Press the whole closed; the skin of the legs should be drawn inward so that the body of the fowls may be quite smooth. If approved, the space between the fowls and the crust may be filled with forcemeat. Put the fowls into a pie dish lined with short-crust dough or into a raised hot-water crust. Cover with a lid of dough and decorate it with scraps. Bake in a preheated 325° F. [160° C.] oven for two and one half hours, or until the juices run clear. If the pastry browns too quickly, cover it with damp parchment paper.

MRS. RUNDELL
DOMESTIC COOKERY

Hare Pâté

Hasenpastete

To make about 4 pounds [2 kg.]

1	saddle of hare, boned, the bones reserved	1
¼ lb.	fresh pork fatback, cut into strips	125 g.
5 tbsp.	Madeira	75 ml.
	salt and pepper	
	paprika	
1	leg of hare, boned, the meat finely ground and the bones reserved	1
1¼ lb.	fresh pork belly with the rind removed, finely ground	600 g.
½ lb.	boneless lean veal, finely ground	¼ kg.
10 oz.	boneless lean pork, finely ground	300 g.
2	eggs	2
¼ cup	Cognac or brandy	50 ml.
	mixed spices	
	gelatinous meat stock (recipe, page 162), made with the hare bones and reduced until syrupy	
1 lb.	short-crust dough (recipe, page 167) or rough puff dough (recipe, page 167)	½ kg.
1	goose liver, trimmed, or ½ lb. [¼ kg.] chicken livers, trimmed, cut into thin strips	1
1 or 2	truffles or large fresh mushrooms, sliced	1 or 2
2	egg yolks, lightly beaten	2

Cut the saddle of hare into pieces the length and breadth of two fingers. Cut two of the fatback strips into small slivers and use these to lard the saddle. Place the larded saddle in a bowl with 2 tablespoons [30 ml.] of the Madeira and some salt, pepper and paprika. Marinate the saddle for one hour.

For the forcemeat, first mix together the ground hare, pork belly, veal and pork. Add the eggs, Cognac or brandy, salt, mixed spices and enough stock to make a smooth mixture. Fry a spoonful and taste it for seasoning.

Roll out the dough and use two thirds of it to line a 2-quart [2-liter] loaf pan or ovenproof dish. Spread the base and sides of the mold with the forcemeat, then make layers of the marinated saddle, the forcemeat, fatback strips, goose liver and truffles or mushrooms. Continue these layers, ending with fatback strips. Cover with the remaining dough. Crimp the edges together. Cut one or two holes in the lid and insert parchment paper funnels. Decorate the pâté with dough scraps and brush it with the beaten egg yolks. Bake it in a preheated 400° F. [200° C.] oven for one and one half hours. Cover the top with parchment paper if the dough browns too quickly.

When the pâté is cooked, add the remaining Madeira through the paper funnels. Once the pâté has cooled completely, refrigerate it.

HENRIETTE DAVIDIS
PRAKTISCHES KOCHBUCH

Pheasant Pâté

Pâté de Faisan

The technique of boning a bird is shown on pages 22-23.

To make about 3 pounds [1½ kg.]

4 lb.	pheasant, boned, the liver reserved	2 kg.
⅔ cup	Cognac	150 ml.
	salt and pepper	
1	shallot, chopped	1
7 tbsp.	butter	105 ml.
½ lb.	veal liver, trimmed and sliced	¼ kg.
⅔ cup	Madeira	150 ml.
¾ lb.	short-crust dough (recipe, page 167)	350 g.
½ cup	truffle pieces	125 ml.
1	egg, beaten	1

Cut the pheasant meat into pieces and place them in a bowl. Add the Cognac, salt, pepper and the chopped shallot. Let the meat marinate for two hours.

Melt the butter in a skillet and add the pheasant liver and veal liver. Sauté them for five minutes, or until they are browned. Remove the livers and set them aside. Pour the Madeira into the skillet and let it reduce a bit. Remove one quarter of the pheasant meat from the marinade. Drain the meat, add it to the skillet, and cook it for 10 minutes. Remove the skillet from the heat. Grind the cooked pheasant meat and the reserved livers and season with a little pepper. Taste this forcemeat for seasoning.

Roll out two thirds of the dough and use it to line the bottom and sides of a 6-cup [1½-liter] loaf pan. Form a ½-inch [1-cm.] layer of the forcemeat in the lined pan. Cover it with the remaining marinated pheasant pieces and the truffles, and with the remaining forcemeat. Roll out the remaining dough and cover the pâté with it. With moistened fingers, press the lid onto the bottom pastry. Use the point of a knife to score a design on the lid and cut a small hole in it. Place a rolled card in the hole to serve as a steam chimney.

Glaze the top of the pâté with the beaten egg. Bake the pâté in a preheated 375° F. [190° C.] oven for one and three quarters hours.

MYRETTE TIANO
300 RECETTES DU GIBIER

Sweetbread Pie or Pâté

To prepare the sweetbreads for this recipe, soak them for two hours in cold water, changing the water twice, drain, then blanch them for four minutes. Refresh and drain them, peel off their membranes and cool them under a weighted board.

If you decide to make a terrine rather than a pâté, omit the dough. Cover the forcemeat with a double layer of foil, removing it for the last 20 minutes of cooking time to brown the top. Cool the terrine under a light weight overnight.

To make about 4 pounds [2 kg.]

¾ lb.	boneless lean pork, or pork and veal mixed, finely ground	350 g.
½ lb.	fresh pork fatback, finely ground	¼ kg.
2	slices salt pork, finely ground	2
2	large eggs, beaten	2
1½ tbsp.	flour	22½ ml.
½ cup	heavy cream	125 ml.
1¼ cups	coarsely chopped fresh mushrooms	300 ml.
2 tbsp.	finely chopped onion	30 ml.
1	garlic clove, crushed to a paste	1
6 tbsp.	butter	90 ml.
	salt and pepper	
	dried thyme leaves	
1 lb.	short-crust dough *(recipe, page 167)*, made with butter and lard and 1 tbsp. [15 ml.] confectioners' sugar	½ kg.
1 lb.	sweetbreads, soaked, drained, blanched, trimmed, weighted and separated into uniform pieces	½ kg.
1	egg yolk, beaten with 1 tbsp. [15 ml.] water	1

Mix all of the ground meats together and add the eggs, flour and cream. Cook the mushrooms, onion and garlic in the butter slowly for 15 minutes. Add them to the forcemeat, season well with salt, pepper and thyme, and mix well.

Line a 5-cup [1¼-liter] loaf pan or terrine mold with short-crust dough, keeping aside enough dough for the lid. Pack in about one third of the forcemeat; arrange half of the sweetbreads on top in two parallel rows. Use another third of the forcemeat to tuck around and over the sweetbreads. Arrange the rest of the sweetbreads on top and cover them with the last of the forcemeat. Mound it up above the rim of the loaf pan or mold to support the dough lid. Moisten the dough rim, lay on the lid and crimp the edges. Brush with the beaten egg yolk and decorate with leaves made from dough. Cut a hole in the lid to let steam escape. Cook in a preheated 350° F. [180° C.] oven for one and a half hours; cover the lid with parchment paper when it browns. Eat warm.

JANE GRIGSON
GOOD THINGS

Eel Pâté

Pâté d'Anguille

To keep the juices of the filling from seeping into the pastry, you may line the dough with barding fat. The technique of preparing an eel is demonstrated on pages 58-69.

To make about 6 pounds [3 kg.]

10 tbsp.	butter	150 ml.
3 lb.	eel, filleted, skinned and cut into strips the length of the mold, the bones reserved	1½ kg.
1¼ cups	chopped fresh mushrooms	300 ml.
3 tbsp.	chopped shallots	45 ml.
2 tbsp.	chopped fresh parsley	30 ml.
1 tbsp.	salt	15 ml.
1 tsp.	white pepper	5 ml.
½ tsp.	grated nutmeg	2 ml.
3 tbsp.	white wine	45 ml.
3 tbsp.	Cognac	45 ml.
3 tbsp.	oil	45 ml.
1 lb.	forcemeat mousseline *(recipe, page 164)*, made with fish, preferably pike, the bones reserved	½ kg.
2	salt anchovies, filleted, soaked in water for 30 minutes, drained, patted dry and pounded with 4 tbsp. [60 ml.] butter	2
1½ lb.	short-crust dough *(recipe, page 167)*	¾ kg.
1	egg yolk, beaten with 1 tbsp. [15 ml.] water	1
1 cup	fish aspic *(recipe, page 163)*, made with the eel and pike bones, melted	¼ liter

Melt 8 tbsp. [120 ml.] of the butter in a frying pan and cook the eel, mushrooms, shallots and parsley for about five minutes, or just until the fillets are stiff. Transfer to a bowl and add the salt, white pepper, nutmeg, wine, Cognac and oil. Cover and let the mixture cool.

Mix the fish mousseline with the anchovy butter. Add the liquid from the eel marinade.

Line a buttered 2½-quart [2½-liter] rectangular mold with dough. Make a layer of mousseline on the bottom and sides, then put in a layer of eel strips. Continue these layers until the mold is full, finishing with a layer of mousseline. Melt the remaining butter and sprinkle it over the top.

Moisten the edges of the dough lining, put on a lid of dough and pinch the edges to seal them. Decorate the pâté with leaves of leftover dough. Make a hole in the middle for steam to escape. Brush with the egg yolk. Bake the pâté in a preheated 350° F. [180° C.] oven for about one and one half hours. If the crust browns too quickly, cover it with dampened parchment paper.

When the pâté has cooled, pour in the fish aspic through the hole in the top. Chill to set the aspic before serving.

P. E. LALOUE
LE GUIDE DE LA CHARCUTERIE

Trout Pâté

Le Pâté de Poissons en Croûte

Serve this pâté with whipped *crème fraîche* or heavy cream flavored with sherry vinegar and a few drops of lemon juice. If you wish to serve the pâté warm, replace the fish aspic with butter cooked until it is nut brown and then flavored with strained fresh lemon juice.

To make about 4 pounds [2 kg.]

2 lb.	lake trout with the head removed, cleaned, skinned and cut into pieces	1 kg.
	salt and pepper	
1 lb.	short-crust dough (recipe, page 167)	½ kg.
2 tbsp.	finely cut chives	30 ml.
¼ cup	pistachios, blanched and peeled	50 ml.
1 lb.	forcemeat mousseline (recipe, page 164), made with fish, preferably pike	½ kg.
⅓ cup	fish aspic (recipe, page 163)	75 ml.
Marinade		
1 cup	olive oil	¼ liter
1	bouquet garni	1
3 tbsp.	strained fresh lemon juice	45 ml.
1	onion, sliced	1
2	carrots, sliced	2
1 tsp. each	tarragon, basil and chervil	5 ml. each

Mix together all of the marinade ingredients, put in the fish and marinate it for several hours. Strain the marinade into a nonreactive saucepan, bring to a simmer and poach the fish in it for five minutes; the fish should be firm but not browned. Remove the fish pieces, bone them and season with salt and pepper.

Line a 2-quart [2-liter] terrine with the dough. Make a layer of fish pieces, sprinkle with chives and pistachios, and spread with mousseline. Continue these layers, finishing with the mousseline. Cover the terrine with a layer of dough, make a hole in the center and insert a cardboard or foil chimney. Bake in a preheated 350° F. [180° C.] oven for about one hour, or until golden brown. Pour the melted fish aspic through the chimney in the top and let the terrine cool. Chill and serve.

RAYMOND THUILIER AND MICHEL LEMONNIER
LES RECETTES DE BAUMANIÈRE

Tuna Pâté

Pâté de Thon

To poach fresh tuna for this recipe, simmer it for five to 10 minutes in a pan of water containing a bouquet garni, an onion and a carrot. Alternatively, use oil-packed, canned tuna, but drain it well.

To make about 4 pounds [2 kg.]

1 lb.	tuna, lightly poached, skinned and boned	½ kg.
2 lb.	forcemeat mousseline (recipe, page 164), made with fish	1 kg.
1 lb.	short-crust dough (recipe, page 167)	½ kg.
3	truffles, cooked in white wine and diced	3
½ cup	Madeira	125 ml.

Roll out two thirds of the dough and use it to line a 2-quart [2-liter] terrine. Line the base and sides with a layer of fish mousseline and scatter over a few pieces of truffle. Put in the tuna and cover it with the remaining mousseline. Arrange the remaining pieces of truffle in a circle on top. Pour in the Madeira. Roll out the remaining dough to form a lid. Cover the pâté with the lid, moistening the edges and crimping them together to seal them. Cut a small hole in the top.

Bake the pâté in a preheated 350° F. [180° C.] oven for two hours, covering the top with damp parchment paper if it browns too fast. Unmold the pâté when cool; serve it cold.

JULES BRETEUIL
LE CUISINIER EUROPÉEN

Pork Cake

To make about 2 pounds [1 kg.]

½ lb.	rough puff dough (recipe, page 167)	¼ kg.
1 lb.	boneless cooked pork, diced	½ kg.
3	small onions, parboiled and chopped	3
1	large apple, peeled, cored and thinly sliced	1
	salt and pepper	
1 tsp.	sugar	5 ml.

Grease a 3-cup [¾-liter] oblong, shallow baking pan and line it with rolled-out dough. Spread the pork over the dough, the onions over the pork and lastly add a layer of apple slices; season liberally with salt and pepper and scatter in the sugar. Wet the edges of the dough and cover with a thin dough top. Mark with a knife into 3-inch [8-cm.] squares. Bake the cake in a preheated 375° F. [190° C.] oven for 45 minutes, or until the pastry is golden. Serve hot or cold.

MRS. ARTHUR WEBB
FARMHOUSE COOKERY

Little Fish Pastries

Petits Pâtés de Poisson

To make eighteen 3½-inch [9-cm.] pastries

1 lb.	salmon, whiting, pike, haddock or other well-flavored fish fillets, skinned	½ kg.
2 cups	dry white bread crumbs	½ liter
1 cup	heavy cream	¼ liter
2 tsp.	salt	10 ml.
¼ tsp.	grated nutmeg	1 ml.
2	shallots, finely chopped	2
3 tbsp.	finely chopped fresh parsley	45 ml.
2	scallions, finely chopped	2
2	egg yolks	2
2 tbsp.	butter, softened	30 ml.
1½ lb.	puff-pastry dough *(recipe, page 167)*	¾ kg.
1	egg, beaten with ½ tsp. [2 ml.] salt	1

Chop the fish and mix it with the crumbs, cream, salt, pepper, nutmeg, shallots, parsley and scallions. A little at a time, purée the mixture in a blender or processor until smooth, and transfer it to a bowl. Alternatively, pound the fish, crumbs and seasonings in a mortar and gradually work in the cream. Taste the mixture—it should be highly seasoned. Beat in the egg yolks and butter.

Roll out the puff-pastry dough to a thickness of ¼ inch [6 mm.], and stamp out a dozen 3-inch [8-cm.] rounds and a dozen 3½-inch [9-cm.] rounds. Lay the dough trimmings one on top of the other, roll the dough out again, and stamp out six more rounds of each size. Line small tartlet pans with the large rounds, fill them with fish mixture, and moisten the inside edges with the beaten egg. Cover with the smaller rounds and press the edges gently together to seal them. Brush the tops with beaten egg and chill the pastries for 15 minutes. Set the tartlet pans on a baking sheet and bake them in a preheated 400° F. [200° C.] oven for one half hour, or until a skewer inserted in the center of a pastry for half a minute is hot to the touch when withdrawn. Serve the fish pastries as soon as possible.

ANNE WILLAN
GREAT COOKS AND THEIR RECIPES

Lovely Aurora's Pillow

L'Oreiller de la Belle Aurore

This pâté, shaped like a pillow, is named in honor of Claudine Aurore-Recamier, the mother of Jean Anthelme Brillat-Savarin—the eminent 19th Century French gastronome and author. The pâté was served regularly at l'Hôtel de la Côte d'Or, Alexandre Dumaine's restaurant in Saulieu, Burgundy. Dumaine's version calls for ½ pound [¼ kg.] each of chicken livers and fresh foie gras—the liver of a specially fattened goose. This recipe calls for 1 pound [½ kg.] of chicken livers because fresh foie gras is not available in America.

The technique of boning a bird is shown on pages 22-23.

To make about 12 pounds [6 kg.]

3 lb.	chicken, boned, the breast meat cut into strips, the leg meat ground, and the liver and bones reserved	1½ kg.
1 lb.	boneless lean veal, half cut into strips, half ground	½ kg.
½ lb.	boneless ham, cut into strips	¼ kg.
	salt and pepper	
	mixed spices	
1 tbsp.	chopped shallots	15 ml.
½ cup	white wine	125 ml.
1 tsp.	anisette	5 ml.
3 tbsp.	strained fresh lemon juice	45 ml.
2 tbsp.	olive oil	30 ml.
two 3 lb.	partridges, boned, the breast meat cut into strips, the leg meat ground and the livers and bones reserved	two 1½ kg.
4 lb.	duck, boned, the breast meat cut into strips, the leg meat ground and the liver and bones reserved	2 kg.
1	saddle of hare, boned and cut into strips, the trimmings ground and the bones reserved	1
½ cup	Cognac	125 ml.
½ cup	Madeira	125 ml.
1 lb.	fresh pork belly, rind removed, ground	½ kg.
¼ lb.	fresh pork fat, cut into matchsticks	125 g.
2 tbsp.	butter	30 ml.
1 lb.	chicken livers, trimmed	½ kg.
1 lb.	fresh pork fatback, sliced into bards	½ kg.
⅓ cup	pistachios, blanched, peeled and chopped	75 ml.
2 oz.	truffles, diced	60 g.
2½ lb.	puff-pastry dough or rough puff dough *(recipes, page 167)*	1¼ kg.
1	egg, beaten with 2 tbsp. [30 ml.] water	1
	gelatinous meat stock *(recipe, page 162),* made with the game and poultry bones	

Combine the chicken, veal and ham strips. Season with salt and mixed spices, and add the shallots, white wine, anisette, lemon juice and 1 tablespoon [15 ml.] of the olive oil.

In another bowl, combine the partridge, duck and hare strips. Season them with salt and add half of the Cognac, half of the Madeira and the remaining olive oil. Cover and refrigerate both of these mixtures for 24 hours, turning the meats occasionally in the marinades.

For the white forcemeat, combine the ground chicken and veal, and half of the ground pork belly. Season with salt.

For the dark forcemeat, combine the ground hare trimmings, leg meat from the duck and the partridges, and the remaining pork belly. Season with salt.

In a nonreactive pan, sauté the matchsticks of pork fat in the butter until they are golden. Remove them from the pan and, in the rendered fat, cook the reserved game livers and all of the chicken livers until they are brown outside but still pink inside. Season with salt and pepper. Drain off the excess fat, pour in the remaining Cognac and ignite it. Add the remaining Madeira, cover the pan and let the livers cool. Pound the liver mixture in a mortar and pass it through a sieve. Incorporate half of this mixture into the white forcemeat and half into the dark forcemeat. Fry a spoonful of each mixture and taste for seasoning.

Line a 6-quart [6-liter] square or rectangular mold with bards of fatback. Spread the base with a layer of dark forcemeat. Arrange a layer of chicken, veal and ham strips interspersed with pistachios and truffle pieces. Make a layer of white forcemeat, then a layer of duck, partridge and hare strips, truffles and pistachios. Continue these layers, arranging them carefully so that each kind of meat is above another kind, to form a mosaic when the pâté is sliced vertically. Finish with a layer of forcemeat. Cover the top with fatback bards, cover the mold and cook it in a water bath in a preheated 325° F. [160° C.] oven for four hours, or until the juices run clear.

After the terrine has cooled, refrigerate it for two to three days. The day before serving the pâté, unmold the terrine and remove all of the fat and aspic from its surfaces. Roll out the dough, place half of it on a baking sheet and place the terrine on it. Brush the edges with beaten egg and then cover with the remaining dough. Pinch the edges to seal. Decorate the rim and one corner with scraps of dough to resemble an embroidered pillow. Brush the pâté with beaten egg and make five holes in the top for the steam to escape. Place a paper chimney in each hole.

Bake the pâté in a preheated 425° F. [220° C.] oven for five to 10 minutes, then reduce the heat to 375° F. [190° C.] and bake it for one and one half hours, or until the pastry is golden brown and well puffed.

Let the pâté cool until tepid, then pour the melted gelatinous stock through the holes in the top. When the pâté has cooled completely, chill it in the refrigerator to set the aspic.

To serve, cut the pâté in half lengthwise, then cut each half into crosswise slices.

ALEXANDRE DUMAINE
MA CUISINE

Ground Pork Pie
Gâteau à la Berrichonne

Use a deep pie dish for this recipe so that you are able to have a good 1 inch [2½ cm.] of filling. If you are making an enormous cartwheel of a pie for a party, you will need proportionately more bread crumbs — ½ cup [125 ml.] to every ½ pound [¼ kg.] of meat is about right — and another 30 minutes of cooking time.

As an alternative to including salt pork, buy neck or shoulder of pork, which has a high proportion of fat to lean, and brine it (recipe, page 166). This very mild curing improves the flavor.

You can layer the meat with grated apple, onion and potato, as they do in the North of England. Some people add peas so that a whole meal is eaten in a convenient form — it is ideal for picnics, and it tastes nicer warm than very hot. Good, solid open-air food, though I always omit the potato as that makes it too solid for most people these days.

To make about 2½ pounds [1¼ kg.]		
½ lb.	boneless fatty pork, ground	¼ kg.
¾ lb.	boneless lean pork, ground	350 g.
¼ lb.	lean salt pork with the rind removed, blanched for 3 minutes and ground	125 g.
3 tbsp.	chopped fresh parsley	45 ml.
1 tbsp.	dried thyme leaves	15 ml.
	salt and freshly ground pepper	
	quatre épices or ground mace	
2 to 4 tbsp.	fine dry bread crumbs	30 to 60 ml.
1 lb.	puff-pastry dough (recipe, page 167) or rough puff dough (recipe, page 167)	½ kg.
1	egg white, lightly beaten	1
1	egg yolk, beaten with ¼ cup [50 ml.] water	1

Mix the ground meats together with the parsley, thyme, salt and pepper. Add a little quatre épices or mace, but the main seasoning should be the herbs. Add the bread crumbs. Fry a spoonful of the mixture and taste it for seasoning.

Roll out the dough. Line a 9-inch [23-cm.] pie dish with just over half of the dough, and brush the dough with the egg white: This keeps the pie from becoming too soggy. Pack in the filling, cover with the rest of the dough, decorate, crimp the edges and brush with the egg-yolk-and-water glaze.

Bake the pie in a preheated 425° F. [220° C.] oven for 15 minutes, then reduce the heat to 350° F. [180° C.] and bake for another 30 minutes.

JANE GRIGSON
THE ART OF MAKING SAUSAGES, PÂTÉS AND OTHER CHARCUTERIE

Galantines and Aspic Presentations

Burgundian Parslied Ham

Jambon Persillé de Bourgogne

To make about 3 pounds [1½ kg.]

4 lb.	ham	2 kg.
1	calf's foot or 3 pig's feet	1
1	veal hindshank	1
8	peppercorns	8
1	bouquet garni	1
4 cups	dry white wine or half water and half wine	1 liter
1 tbsp.	white wine vinegar	15 ml.
1½ cups	chopped fresh parsley	375 ml.
	salt and pepper	

Cover the ham generously with water, bring to a boil and simmer for 45 minutes. Cut the meat into chunks and put them into a large, nonreactive pot with the calf's foot or pig's feet, the veal hindshank, the peppercorns and the bouquet garni. Pour in the wine until it covers the contents of the pot. Simmer gently until the ham is very well cooked. Drain off the liquid through layers of cheesecloth or a muslin-lined strainer. Taste and adjust the seasoning. Add the vinegar and leave the liquid to set slightly in a cool place.

Crush the ham into a roomy bowl. Keep the rest of the meat to make a separate dish of brawn (headcheese). Add the parsley to the setting aspic, pour it over the ham in the bowl and mix well. If you are intending to turn it out later on, keep some of the parsley aspic to melt slightly and brush over it in a green layer. When the ham is cut, it has a beautifully marbled appearance. Serve it with good bread and unsalted or lightly salted butter.

JANE GRIGSON
GOOD THINGS

Suckling Pig Galantine

Galantine de Cochon de Lait

The technique of boning and stuffing a suckling pig is demonstrated on pages 75-77.

To make about 11 pounds [5½ kg.]

2 lb.	veal liver, trimmed and ground	1 kg.
2 lb.	fresh pork belly, ground	1 kg.
2	eggs	2
	salt	
	mixed spices	
	mixed dried herbs	
12 lb.	suckling pig, boned, the head left intact, the bones reserved	6 kg.
½ lb.	fresh pork fatback, cut into long, narrow strips	¼ kg.
1 lb.	boneless game or chicken meat, thinly sliced (optional)	½ kg.
¼ lb.	truffles, sliced (optional)	125 g.
9	carrots	9
4	medium-sized onions	4
1	large bouquet garni	1
2	calf's feet, split	2
4 cups	white wine	1 liter
	gelatinous meat stock (recipe, page 162)	

Combine the ground veal liver and pork belly, add the eggs, and season with salt, mixed spices and herbs. Fry a spoonful of this forcemeat and taste it for seasoning. Spread out the suckling pig on a table and cover it with half of the prepared forcemeat. Add a layer of fatback strips, then the game or chicken and truffles, if using, and cover with the remaining forcemeat. Sew up the pig's stomach and pat the pig into its natural shape. Wrap it in a cloth and tie it up, taking care not to force it out of shape.

Put the pig into a long, nonreactive pan, preferably a fish kettle, with the carrots, onions, bouquet garni, the reserved bones and the calf's feet. Add the wine and enough stock to cover the pig, and simmer gently, covered, for eight hours. Drain the galantine, let it cool, then remove the cloth. Serve the galantine cold on a napkin-covered serving dish. The cooking liquid may be degreased, reduced and chilled to make an accompanying aspic.

GOMBERVAUX (EDITOR)
LA BONNE CUISINE POUR TOUS

Cold Ham Loaf

Polpettone Freddo di Prosciutto

To make about 1 ½ pounds [¾ kg.]

1 ¼ lb.	boneless ham, ground	600 g.
⅓ cup	chopped fresh parsley	75 ml.
1 tbsp.	finely chopped onion	15 ml.
6 tbsp.	grated grana or Parmesan cheese	90 ml.
3	eggs, lightly beaten	3
	salt	
	grated nutmeg	
1 tbsp.	pistachios, blanched and peeled	15 ml.
1 or 2	carrots, parboiled for 5 minutes	1 or 2
5 cups	gelatinous meat stock *(recipe, page 162)*	1 ¼ liters

Combine the ham, parsley, onion, cheese and eggs. Season with a little salt and nutmeg. Add the pistachios. Shape the mixture into a thick cylinder. Make a slit in the top, put in the carrots and close the slit. Wrap the cylinder in a cloth and tie it securely. Bring the stock to a boil, put in the wrapped cylinder and simmer it for 20 minutes, or until firm when pressed with a finger. Drain and cool the loaf. Boil down the stock until it will set to an aspic, then let it cool and set. Cut the loaf into thin slices; arrange them on a serving dish. Chop the aspic and use it to garnish the dish.

CIA ERAMO
SEGRETI E NO DELLA CUCINA MANTOVANA

Veal Breast Galantine

Pancetta di Vitello Ripiena

To make about 3 pounds [1 ½ kg.]

⅓ cup	ground ham	75 ml.
⅓ cup	ground mortadella	75 ml.
⅔ lb.	boneless pork, ground	300 g.
3	eggs, lightly beaten	3
⅔ cup	freshly grated Parmesan cheese	150 ml.
	salt and pepper	
2 lb.	boneless veal breast, with a pocket cut for stuffing	1 kg.
1	onion	1
2	carrots	2
2	celery ribs	2
1	bouquet garni	1

Combine the ground meats. Add the eggs, cheese, salt and pepper, and mix well. Stuff the veal breast with this mix-

ture, then sew up the edges to enclose the stuffing. Wrap the veal tightly in a cloth. Put the vegetables and the bouquet garni into a large pot of water and bring to a boil. Add the veal to the pot and simmer it for two hours, or until it is tender. Drain the veal and let it cool. Unwrap the galantine and serve it cut into slices.

PIER ANTONIO SPIZZOTIN (EDITOR)
LA CARNE CONVENIENTE

Veal Roll

Rifreddo di Vitella di Latte

To make about 1 ½ pounds [¾ kg.]

1 lb.	boneless lean veal in 1 slice, flattened to ½ inch [1 cm.]	½ kg.
2 oz.	ham, thinly sliced	60 g.
2 oz.	mortadella, thinly sliced	60 g.
1	boneless chicken breast, skinned and thinly sliced	1
	salt and pepper	
2 tbsp.	butter	30 ml.
6 cups	gelatinous meat stock *(recipe, page 162)*	1 ½ liters

Forcemeat

¼ lb.	boneless lean veal, ground	125 g.
¼ cup	ground ham	50 ml.
⅓ cup	freshly grated Parmesan cheese	75 ml.
1 ½ tbsp.	butter	22 ½ ml.
1	egg	1
	salt and pepper	

For the forcemeat, pound the ground veal and ham together in a mortar. Add the remaining forcemeat ingredients and work the mixture to a smooth paste. Fry a spoonful of the mixture and taste it for seasoning.

Spread the flattened slice of veal with some of the forcemeat. On it place layers of sliced ham, mortadella and chicken. Cover with forcemeat, and continue these layers until all of the meats are used. Roll up the veal slice with the filling inside and tie the cylinder as you would a sausage. Season the roll with a little salt and pepper.

Brown the veal roll in the butter in a large saucepan. When the roll is golden, pour off the butter and add just enough stock to immerse the roll. Cover and simmer for about three hours, or until the roll is tender. Remove the veal roll from the stock and let it cool. When it is cold, remove the string and slice it. If you wish, chill the stock until it sets and garnish the veal with this aspic.

PELLEGRINO ARTUSI
LA SCIENZA IN CUCINA E L'ARTE DI MANGIAR BENE

147

Stuffed Breast of Veal
Cima Ripiena

The technique of preparing brains is demonstrated on pages 30-31. To prepare the sweetbreads called for in this recipe, soak them for two hours in a bowl of cold water, changing the water once or twice, drain, then blanch them for four minutes. Refresh and drain them, peel off their membranes and cool the sweetbreads under a weighted board.

To make about 4 pounds [2 kg.]

3 lb.	veal breast, boned to form a pocket	1½ kg.
1	garlic clove, halved	1
2 quarts	gelatinous meat stock (recipe, page 162)	2 liters
1	onion	1
1	carrot	1
1	celery rib	1
1	bay leaf	1
	Veal stuffing	
¼ lb.	boneless veal, cubed	125 g.
¼ lb.	calf's sweetbreads, soaked, drained, blanched, trimmed and weighted	125 g.
¼ lb.	calf's brains, soaked, drained, blanched for 3 minutes, membranes and red veins removed	125 g.
4 tbsp.	butter	60 ml.
½ oz.	dried mushrooms, soaked in warm water for 30 minutes, drained, stems cut off (optional)	15 g.
3 tbsp.	freshly shelled peas	45 ml.
¼ tsp.	dried marjoram leaves	1 ml.
	salt and pepper	
3 tbsp.	freshly grated Parmesan cheese	45 ml.
6	eggs, beaten	6

Rub the inside of the veal breast with the garlic.

To make the stuffing, brown the cubed veal, sweetbreads and brains in the butter. Chop the meats and mushrooms, if using, and mix with the remaining stuffing ingredients. Pour the mixture (it will be almost liquid) into the pocket of the veal breast, filling it by two thirds. Sew up the opening. Prick the meat lightly with a fork to prevent it from bursting during cooking.

Bring the stock to a boil and put in the vegetables and the bay leaf. When the stock returns to a boil, add the stuffed veal. Simmer it gently for two hours, or until it is tender. Drain it and let it cool between two plates, with a weight on top. Serve sliced.

STELLA DONATI (EDITOR)
IL GRANDE MANUALE DELLA CUCINA REGIONALE

Russian Veal Aspic
Aspic de Poitrine à la Russe

If it is necessary to clarify the cooking liquid for this aspic presentation, follow the directions for clarifying gelatinous meat stock (recipe, page 162).

To make about 4 pounds [2 kg.]

6	calf's feet, blanched for 8 minutes	6
3 lb.	veal breast, blanched for 8 minutes and cut into even-sized pieces	1½ kg.
1	onion	1
1	carrot	1
1	celery rib	1
1	bouquet garni	1
	salt and pepper	
	grated nutmeg	
	croutons	
	Horseradish sauce	
1⅓ cups	grated fresh horseradish	325 ml.
2 tbsp.	white wine vinegar	30 ml.
1¼ cups	sour cream	300 ml.
2 tbsp.	chopped fresh parsley	30 ml.
1 tbsp.	chopped fresh fennel or dill leaves	15 ml.
½ tsp.	sugar	2 ml.
	salt	

Place the calf's feet and veal in a large pot with the vegetables and the bouquet garni. Cover generously with water, bring to a boil, cover, and simmer for one and one half hours, or until the meat begins to fall off the bones. Drain the meats, reserving the cooking liquid. Bone and dice the meats. Season them to taste with salt, pepper and nutmeg.

Strain and degrease the cooking liquid; clarify it if necessary. Chill a 2-quart [2-liter] mold, line it with a little of the cooking liquid, and chill it again to set the liquid to an aspic. Place the diced meats in the mold and fill the mold with the liquid. Chill until the liquid sets, about two hours.

About 10 minutes before serving, combine all of the ingredients for the horseradish sauce and add a pinch of salt. Unmold the aspic onto a serving dish and surround it with croutons. Serve accompanied by the sauce in a sauceboat.

A. PETIT
LA GASTRONOMIE EN RUSSIE

Homemade Galantine
Galantina Casalinga

To make about 1 1/2 pounds [3/4 kg.]

1 lb.	boneless veal or lean beef, ground	1/2 kg.
1/4 lb.	boneless ham, ground	125 g.
1/4 lb.	cooked beef tongue, half ground, half cubed	125 g.
1	thick slice bacon, ground	1
1/3 cup	Marsala	75 ml.
2 tbsp.	pistachios, blanched and peeled	30 ml.
2	eggs	2
	salt and pepper	
	gelatinous meat stock *(recipe, page 162)*, chilled to set, and chopped	

Mix the ground meats in a bowl. Stir in the Marsala and pistachios. Add the cubed tongue, eggs, salt and pepper. Mix well. Fry a spoonful of the mixture and taste it for seasoning.

Shape the mixture into a loaf, wrap it in parchment paper and tie it securely. Place the loaf in a pot of lightly salted water, bring to a boil and simmer it gently for one and one half hours. Remove the loaf from the pot, and place it on a dish with a light weight on top. When it is cool, refrigerate until firm—about three hours. Cut the loaf into slices, arrange them on a dish and garnish with the chopped aspic.

IL CUCCHIAIO D'ARGENTO

Galantine of Pork
Galantina di Maiale

To make about 3 pounds [1 1/2 kg.]

1 lb.	boneless pork tenderloin, cubed	1/2 kg.
1/2 lb.	fresh pork fatback, half cubed, half ground	1/4 kg.
1/2 lb.	boneless ham, cubed	1/4 kg.
1/4 lb.	cooked beef tongue, cubed	125 g.
3 tbsp.	pistachios, blanched and peeled	45 ml.
1	truffle, diced	1
	salt and pepper	
1/3 cup	dry Marsala	75 ml.
3/4 lb.	boneless pork loin, ground	350 g.
1	large piece pork caul, soaked and drained	1
	gelatinous meat stock *(recipe, page 162)*	

Place in a bowl the cubed pork tenderloin, fatback, ham and tongue. Add the pistachios and truffle. Season with salt and pepper, add the Marsala, and let the mixture marinate for at least one hour.

In a large mortar, combine the ground pork loin and fatback. Pound the mixture, then press it through a sieve. Alternatively, grind the meats together two times. Add the pounded or ground meats to the marinated mixture, and work all of the ingredients together with your hands until the Marsala is completely absorbed. Fry a spoonful of the mixture and taste it for seasoning.

Spread the caul out on a large square of muslin or a double thickness of cheesecloth. Place the mixture on the caul and shape the meats into a cylinder. Tightly wrap the caul around the meats and fold over the ends of the caul. Wrap this galantine in the cloth, and tie the cloth at the ends and in the center. Place it in a pan, cover it with stock, bring to a boil and simmer it for about two hours, or until firm.

FERNANDA GOSETTI
IN CUCINA CON FERNANDA GOSETTI

Sausage in a Boot
Saucisson en Brodequin

The technique of boning a bird is shown on pages 22-23.

To make about 2 1/2 pounds [1 1/4 kg.]

1 lb.	boneless lean lamb, ground	1/2 kg.
1	old partridge, boned and ground	1
1/2 lb.	fresh pork belly, ground	1/4 kg.
2 or 3	eggs	2 or 3
	salt	
	mixed spices	
3 tbsp.	pistachios, blanched, peeled and coarsely chopped	45 ml.
1/4 lb.	fresh pork fatback, diced	125 g.
1/4 lb.	boneless ham, diced	125 g.
2	truffles, diced	2
1	piece pork caul, soaked and drained	1
1/2 cup	white wine	125 ml.
	gelatinous meat stock *(recipe, page 162)*	

Combine all of the ingredients except the caul, wine and stock, and work together until thoroughly blended. Fry a spoonful of the mixture and taste it for seasoning. Form the mixture into a sausage shape and wrap it in the caul, folding over the ends of the caul securely.

Place four thin slats of wood lengthwise along the sausage, and tie them with string so that the sausage is surrounded by the slats of wood, forming a long rectangle. Place the encased sausage in a nonreactive oval pan or fish kettle, cover it with stock and wine, and bring it to a boil. Simmer for about one hour, or until the sausage is firm. Let it cool in the stock before removing the string and wood.

MENON
LE MANUEL DES OFFICIERS DE BOUCHE

Easter Sunday Galantine

To make about 1¾ pounds [875 g.]

1 lb.	boneless lamb, ground	½ kg.
½ lb.	bacon, ground	¼ kg.
2 cups	fresh bread crumbs	½ liter
2	eggs, well beaten	2
½ tsp.	salt	2 ml.
	pepper	
5 cups	gelatinous meat stock *(recipe, page 162)*	1¼ liters

Place the meats in a large bowl. Stir in the bread crumbs, eggs, salt, pepper and 1¼ cups [300 ml.] of the stock. Fry a spoonful of the mixture and taste it for seasoning. Turn the mixture onto a lightly floured board and shape it into a large sausage. Tie it in a floured cloth napkin, sew the edges of the cloth together, and tie the ends firmly with tape or string.

Heat the remaining stock in a pot. Put in the galantine, cover, and simmer it for two hours. Remove the galantine and, if the cloth is loose, retie it. Place the galantine on a dish with another dish on top and weight it. Refrigerate it when cooled. The next day, remove the weight and cloth. Skim the stock and reduce it until it will set to an aspic. Brush the galantine with stock and serve it when the aspic has set.

MRS. ARTHUR WEBB
FARMHOUSE COOKERY

Brawn

Presskopf

To make about 4 pounds [2 kg.]

1	pig's head with tongue	1
1	pork heart	1
	salt and pepper	
2 tsp.	grated lemon peel	10 ml.
½ tsp.	ground cloves or mace	2 ml.
⅔ cup	white wine	150 ml.
⅔ cup	white wine vinegar	150 ml.

Cover the pig's head and heart with cold water, bring to a boil, cover, and simmer until soft—about two and one half hours. When tender, bone the meat and cut it into small pieces. In a nonreactive pan, boil down the liquor, reducing it by about one half. Season the sauce with salt, pepper, lemon peel and cloves or mace; add the wine and the vinegar. Stir the meat into the sauce and bring to a simmer. Rinse a 2-quart [2-liter] mold out with cold water and pour the mixture into it. Cool, chill overnight and turn it out to serve.

ANDRÉ L. SIMON
A CONCISE ENCYCLOPAEDIA OF GASTRONOMY

Somerset Pig's-Head Brawn

To make about 4 pounds [2 kg.]

1	pig's head, with tongue	1
4 quarts	brine *(recipe, page 166)*	4 liters
2	carrots, sliced	2
1	onion, sliced	1
2	turnips, sliced	2
3	shallots, sliced	3
1	bouquet garni	1
2	blades mace	2
12	whole allspice	12
4	peppercorns	4
4	whole cloves	4
	salt and pepper	

Lay the pig's head in the brine, cover and refrigerate it overnight. Rinse the head well; put it in a pot and cover it with cold water. Boil it for two hours, or until the meat will easily leave the bone. Bone the head and cut the meat into dice—also the ears and tongue after skinning the latter. Return the bones to the liquor; boil up. Add the vegetables, bouquet garni, spices and seasoning, and boil for one hour, or until only 1 quart [1 liter] of liquor remains. Strain it into another pot. Lay in the pieces of meat, season them with salt and pepper, if required, and let the liquor come to a boil. Rinse a 2½-quart [2½-liter] mold with cold water and pour in the meat and liquor. When cold and set, the brawn is ready.

KATHLEEN THOMAS
A WEST COUNTRY COOKERY BOOK

Pork Galantine

Galantina di Maiale

To make about 2 pounds [1 kg.]

¼ lb.	corned beef tongue, half diced	125 g.
¼ lb.	boneless ham, lean part diced	125 g.
10	pistachios, blanched and peeled	10
	salt and pepper	
	freshly grated nutmeg	
⅓ cup	Marsala	75 ml.
1¼ lb.	boneless lean pork	600 g.
¼ lb.	fresh pork fat	125 g.
¼ lb.	pork caul, soaked and drained	125 g.
1	bouquet garni	1

Put the diced tongue and ham in a bowl with the pistachios, salt and pepper, a pinch of nutmeg, and the Marsala. Mix the ingredients well. Grind together the pork, the remaining tongue, ham fat and pork fat. Add to the ingredients in the bowl and mix until thoroughly blended. Fry a spoonful and taste it for seasoning. Spread out the pork caul, put the mixture in the middle and wrap the caul around it to form a large sausage. Wrap it in a cloth and tie the middle and both ends.

Bring a large pot of salted water to a boil, add the bouquet garni and put in the galantine. Simmer it for one and one half hours, or until it is firm. Drain, place the galantine on a dish with a weight on top and let it cool.

PIER ANTONIO SPIZZOTIN (EDITOR)
LA CARNE CONVENIENTE

Pork or Pig's-Head Cheese

To make about 4 pounds [2 kg.]

½	pig's head with tongue, brains removed, head and tongue brined (recipe, page 166), then soaked in cold water for 2 hours	½
1	pig's foot, brined (recipe, page 166), then soaked in cold water for 2 hours	1
1 lb.	beef foreshank or ox cheek	½ kg.
1	large onion	1
4	large carrots	4
1	bunch fresh parsley	1
2	bay leaves	2
8 to 10	black peppercorns	8 to 10
1	large leek or 2 celery ribs	1
2	small garlic cloves	2
	salt and freshly ground pepper	
2 tbsp.	strained fresh lemon juice	30 ml.

Put all the meats in a very large pot with the other ingredients except the salt, pepper and lemon juice, cover with water and simmer very, very gently for a minimum of four hours. The slower the meats are cooked, the better the result will be; if they are boiled too fast, both the pig's head and the beef will be ragged and stringy.

When the head and foot are cooked—the meat should come away from the bones at a touch—remove them, with the beef, to a bowl. Strain the stock. As soon as the meats are cool enough to handle, skin the tongue and also the rough parts of the head around the ear and snout where the skin is coarse. Remove all gristle. (What you leave out of a brawn is as important as what you put in.)

Chop all the head meat and the skin which is left on it, the foot and the beef. Cut the tongue into neat little slices.

Taste to see if extra salt is needed. A brawn should always be fairly highly seasoned or it will be insipid and cloying; it will probably need extra pepper, freshly ground, possibly salt, and lemon juice. This last ingredient is a highly important one in cold dishes made with fat meat.

Now mix the sliced tongue with the other chopped meats. There will be enough to fill a 2-quart [2-liter] mold, terrine or cake pan or, if you prefer, two smaller ones.

Add about 2 cups [½ liter] of the hot stock and leave the whole thing to cool. Then cover it with a piece of parchment paper, weight it with a plate that just fits inside the mold or pan, and refrigerate it until the next day. It can be kept for several days. Before unmolding it, stand the mold or pan in a bowl of hot water for a few minutes.

ELIZABETH DAVID
SPICES, SALT AND AROMATICS IN THE ENGLISH KITCHEN

Pig's Head in Aspic
Tête de Porc en Gelée

Serve this with vinaigrette as a first course, or with potatoes boiled in their skins as a main course.

To make about 5 pounds [2½ kg.]

½	pig's head with tongue	½
1	pig's foot	1
1	calf's foot	1
1 lb.	boneless pork loin	½ kg.
1	bouquet garni	1
1	whole clove	1
2	leeks, finely chopped	2
1	onion, finely chopped	1
3	garlic cloves, finely chopped	3
2 tbsp.	finely chopped fresh parsley	30 ml.
	freshly grated nutmeg	
1	bay leaf	1

Place the meats in a large pot, breaking the bones of the head and folding it to fit it in. Add the bouquet garni and the clove, cover with water and bring to a boil. Skim the surface and simmer for two hours, or until the meat begins to come off the bones. Remove the meats and let them cool.

Strain off the cooking liquid into a saucepan and add the leeks, onion, garlic, parsley, nutmeg and bay leaf. Boil for three to five minutes to soften the vegetables slightly.

Bone and chop all of the meats. Stir them into the cooking liquid, return to a boil and cook for two minutes more. Correct the seasoning and remove the bay leaf.

Pour the mixture into bowls or terrines, distributing the meat and liquid evenly. Refrigerate to set the aspic.

JOSEPH KOSCHER AND ASSOCIATES
LES RECETTES DE LA TABLE ALSACIENNE

Pig's Head and Feet in Aspic

Stoudiène ou Kholodetz

To make about 4 pounds [2 kg.]

½	pig's head	½
4	pig's feet	4
3 quarts	water	3 liters
1 tbsp.	salt	15 ml.
15	juniper berries	15
6	bay leaves	6

Place all of the ingredients in a pot, bring to a boil and simmer gently for four hours. Remove all of the bones and cut the meat into small pieces. Strain the stock. Place the meat in a 3-quart [3-liter] mold and cover it with the strained stock. Refrigerate until set, then unmold to serve.

H. WITWICKA AND S. SOSKINE
LA CUISINE RUSSE CLASSIQUE

Breakfast Brawn

If the pig's tongue is also boiled and then skinned, it can be placed in the center of the mold with the meat around it; this adds greatly to the appearance and flavor of the brawn.

To make about 4 pounds [2 kg.]

½	pig's head, brains and tongue removed, head soaked in salted water and rinsed	½
2 lb.	boneless beef shank	1 kg.
1 tbsp.	mixed pickling spices	15 ml.
2	small onions, sliced	2
	salt and pepper	
1 tsp.	Demerara sugar	5 ml.
	freshly grated nutmeg	
	fresh parsley sprigs	

Place the pig's head in a large pot with the beef. Cover with water; bring slowly to a boil, boil quickly for five minutes, then skim. Tie the pickling spices and sliced onions in a piece of muslin and add them to the pot. Sprinkle in 1 teaspoon [5 ml.] of salt and the sugar. Cover, and simmer until all the meat is quite tender (about two hours). Lift the meat out carefully onto a large dish. Remove all the bones, large and small. Sprinkle the meat generously with salt and pepper, and sparingly with nutmeg. Finely chop the meat, then add a few spoonfuls of the broth and bring the meat just to the boiling point in a saucepan. (Be very careful that it does not burn.) Turn the meat into a wet 2-quart [2-liter] mold, put a plate on the top and weight it down. Turn out the brawn when cold and garnish it with fresh parsley.

MRS. ARTHUR WEBB
FARMHOUSE COOKERY

Family-Style Brawn

Terrine Familiale

To make about 3½ pounds [1¾ kg.]

1 lb. each	boneless beef, veal and pork	½ kg. each
1	calf's foot	1
½ lb.	fresh pork belly with the rind removed	¼ kg.
1	bouquet garni	1
2	garlic cloves	2
1	onion, sliced	1
1¼ cups	red wine	300 ml.
	salt and pepper	
¼ cup	Madeira	50 ml.

Put the beef, veal and pork into a nonreactive pot with the calf's foot, pork belly, bouquet garni, garlic and onion. Add the wine, cover with water and bring to a boil. Cover; simmer for one and one half hours, or until the meats are tender.

Drain all of the meats, reserving the cooking liquid. Bone the calf's foot and grind it with the other meats. Season the mixture with salt and pepper, add the Madeira and work the mixture until it is smooth. Taste for seasoning. Pack the mixture into a 7-cup [1¾-liter] terrine. Make holes in the meat mixture with a fork. Pour in enough of the cooking liquid just to cover the meat. Cool, then refrigerate.

ROBERT J. COURTINE
LES DIMANCHES DE LA CUISINE

A Small Brawn

Once tried, this recipe lends itself to numerous variations. Other spices and herbs may be added to your taste.

To make about 2 pounds [1 kg.]

2	pig's feet	2
2	chicken quarters	2
½ tsp.	black peppercorns	2 ml.
¼ tsp.	freshly grated nutmeg	1 ml.
1	bay leaf	1
1	sprig marjoram (optional)	1
1	onion (optional)	1
	salt and pepper (optional)	

Put the pig's feet and the chicken quarters into a large, heavy pot, and cover them with cold water. Bring slowly to a boil. Let them boil for five minutes. Skim well. Add the peppercorns, nutmeg, bay leaf and marjoram, if using. Then put on the lid and simmer for three hours, or until the meat falls from the bones. (Add the onion, if used, after about one hour.)

Lift out the meat. Strain the stock; let it cool for a little while. Remove all of the bones and cut the meat into small pieces. Skim off the fat from the stock and mix the stock with the meat, adding salt and pepper if necessary. Boil the meat and the stock together for a few minutes. Now put the meat and enough stock to cover it well into a 5-cup [1¼-liter] mold that has been rinsed out with cold water (or divide the mixture between smaller molds). Remove any fat from the surface as soon as possible. Leave the brawn in a cool place to set firm. It can go into the refrigerator when set and cold.

To turn out the brawn, dip the mold into hot water for a few moments.

AUDREY PARKER
COTTAGE AND COUNTRY RECIPES

Polish Meat Galantine

Galantyna z Mięsa

To make about 1½ pounds [¾ kg.]

1	hard roll, crumbled	1
½ lb.	boneless veal, cubed	¼ kg.
½ lb.	boneless pork, cubed	¼ kg.
1	egg	1
1	garlic clove	1
	salt and pepper	
¼ tsp.	dried marjoram leaves	1 ml.
¼ tsp.	grated nutmeg	1 ml.
¼ cup	water	50 ml.
⅔ cup	diced ham	150 ml.
¼ cup	diced sour gherkins	50 ml.
¼ lb.	bacon, diced	125 g.
2 or 3	egg whites, lightly beaten	2 or 3
1	tomato or ½ cucumber, sliced	1
Stock		
1½ lb.	calf's feet, cut into chunks	¾ kg.
1	carrot	1
¼	medium-sized celeriac	¼
1	onion	1
1	parsnip	1
1	bay leaf	1
4 or 5	dried hot chilies	4 or 5
	peppercorns	
6 cups	water	1½ liters
	salt	

Put all of the stock ingredients except the salt in a large pot. Bring to a boil, cover and cook over low heat for four hours, adding salt to taste after three and one half hours. Strain.

Soak the roll in a little of the stock until it is soft. Put the roll, veal and pork through a food grinder three times, using the finest disk the third time. Add the egg. Crush the garlic with salt and add it to the meat mixture with pepper, marjoram and nutmeg. Mix well until fluffy, adding the water as you mix. Fry a spoonful and taste it for seasoning.

Rub a piece of muslin with butter, and spread the meat mixture on it in a rectangle. Sprinkle the ham, sour gherkins and bacon down the center and roll the meat around this garnish with the help of the cloth. Wrap a string around the galantine at intervals and tie the ends tightly.

Bring the stock to a boil, put in the galantine and simmer it for one hour. Let it cool in the stock, then put it on a plate, weight it with a board and refrigerate it overnight.

Boil the stock until it has reduced to 3 cups [¾ liter]. Add the egg whites and whisk while it returns to a boil. Strain the stock through a colander lined with muslin or a double thickness of cheesecloth. Unwrap the galantine and place it on an oblong dish. Decorate it with tomato or cucumber slices. Spoon the stock over it, chilling each layer so that it sets to an aspic before repeating. Alternatively, chill the stock to set it and dice the aspic to use as a garnish.

HELENA HAWLICZKOWA
KUCHNIA POLSKA

Quimper Terrine

Terrine Quimpéroise

To make about 1½ pounds [¾ kg.]

1 lb.	fresh pork rind	½ kg.
1	calf's foot, split in half	1
3 lb.	pork shoulder, boned, bones reserved	1½ kg.
	salt and pepper	
4 or 5	onions, chopped	4 or 5
⅓ cup	finely chopped mixed fresh chives, parsley and chervil	75 ml.
1 tsp.	mixed spices	5 ml.

Place the pork rind and calf's foot in a large pot with the pork bones. Cover with cold water, season with salt and pepper, bring to a boil, cover and simmer for two hours. Strain.

Mix together the onions and herbs. Place the piece of pork on a flat surface and season it with salt, pepper and the mixed spices. Cover with the onion-and-herb mixture, leaving margins at the edges. Roll up and tie the pork.

Place the pork in an oval terrine somewhat larger than the roll and cook it, uncovered, in a preheated 425° F. [220° C.] oven for about 10 minutes, or until the surface begins to brown. Turn the meat and brown the other side for 10 minutes. Pour the strained cooking liquid into the terrine; it should come about three quarters of the way up the meat. Cover the terrine and return it to the oven for one and one half hours, or until the pork is quite tender. Serve it cold.

LA CUISINE BRETONNE

Larded and Glazed Pork Liver
Foie de Porc, Piqué et Glacé
To make about 3 ½ pounds [1 ¾ kg.]

one 3 lb.	pork liver, trimmed	one 1 ½ kg.
½ lb.	salted pork fatback, cut into lardons	¼ kg.
	gelatinous meat stock (recipe, page 162)	

Lard the liver generously, inserting the lardons symmetrically across the grain of the liver. Place the liver on a board just large enough to hold it, and tie it to the board with string, giving the liver a nice, round shape.

Bring a large pot of stock to a simmer. Put in the liver on its board and cook it over very low heat, with the stock just trembling, for 40 to 50 minutes, or until the liver is firm. Let the liver cool in the stock.

Remove the liver and untie it from the board. Heat a little stock and dip the liver in it to cleanse it. Pat the liver dry, place it in a deep 7-cup [1 ¾-liter] oval dish and refrigerate it. Clarify the cooking stock, cool it almost to the setting point and use it to glaze the liver. Refrigerate the liver until the aspic is firm. Serve it cut into slices.

P. E. LALOUE
LE GUIDE DE LA CHARCUTERIE

Green Chicken Terrine
La Terrine "Chiquetaille" de Poule Verte
To make about 3 pounds [1 ½ kg.]

6	leeks, chopped	6
6	large stems chard, tough ribs removed, leaves chopped	6
1 cup	chopped fresh parsley	¼ liter
4	leafy celery ribs, chopped	4
2 ¼ cups	freshly shelled young peas, parboiled for 5 minutes	550 ml.
3 ½ lb.	chicken	1 ½ kg.
	salt and pepper	
½ cup	water	125 ml.
1 tbsp.	unflavored powdered gelatin, softened in 2 tbsp. [30 ml.] water	15 ml.
½ cup	crème fraîche or heavy cream	125 ml.
	green mayonnaise (recipe, page 164)	

Mix all of the chopped vegetables, and place a layer of them in the bottom of an oiled casserole. Put in the chicken and cover with the remaining vegetables. Season with salt and pepper and add the water. Cover the casserole and cook over low heat for one and three quarters to two hours, or until the chicken is very tender.

Skin and bone the chicken and dice the meat. Strain off the cooking liquid and add the dissolved gelatin to it. Purée the cooked vegetables in a blender, a small batch at a time. Mix the diced chicken, vegetable purée, cooking liquid, peas and cream. Correct the seasoning. Turn the mixture into a 7-cup [1 ¾-liter] terrine, cover and refrigerate overnight.

ODETTE REIGE
LES TERRINES DE VIANDES, DE COQUILLAGES ET POISSONS, DE LEGUMES

Galantine of Chicken or Capon
Galantine de Poulard ou de Chapon

The technique of boning a bird through the back is demonstrated on pages 79-81.

The galantine may be served either hot or cold; if you serve it hot, mask it with chopped truffles stewed in butter or with a velouté sauce *(recipe, page 165)*, made from the cooking liquid.

To make about 6 pounds [3 kg.]

two 5 to 6 lb.	chickens or capons, boned through the back	two 2 ½ to 3 kg.
1 lb.	fresh pork fatback, ½ lb. [¼ kg.] cut into strips, ¼ lb. [125 g.] sliced into bards	½ kg.
½ lb.	beef marrow	¼ kg.
1 ¼ cups	chopped fresh mushrooms	300 ml.
2 oz.	truffles or truffle peelings, finely chopped	60 g.
5	slices firm-textured white bread, crusts removed, soaked in cream and squeezed dry	5
3 or 4	egg yolks	3 or 4
1 tsp.	fines herbes	5 ml.
	mixed spices	
2 tbsp.	finely chopped fresh parsley	30 ml.
2 or 3	scallions, finely chopped	2 or 3
	salt and pepper	
½ lb.	boneless ham, cut into strips	¼ kg.
⅓ cup	pistachios, blanched and peeled	75 ml.
4	large slices boneless lean beef, flattened to ¼ inch [6 mm.]	4
2	onions, chopped	2
2	carrots, chopped	2
1	parsnip, chopped	1
	gelatinous meat stock (recipe, page 162) or water	

Remove the meat from the chickens or capons, leaving a thin layer attached to the skin. Grind the meat with the ¼ pound

[125 g.] of uncut fatback, the beef marrow, mushrooms and truffles. Pound the mixture in a mortar, working in the bread and egg yolks and seasoning with fines herbes, mixed spices, parsley, scallions, salt and pepper. Fry a spoonful of this forcemeat and taste it for seasoning.

Spread the chicken or capon skins out on a table, skin side down, and spread each with a layer of forcemeat. Season the meat strips by rolling them in fines herbes and mixed spices. On top of the forcemeat, make a layer of lengthwise rows of seasoned strips of fatback, ham, fatback and pistachios, then another layer of forcemeat, and so on in the same order until all these ingredients are used up.

Roll up the galantines so that the stuffing is completely enclosed in the skins. Wrap each galantine in a cloth and tie it firmly at intervals.

Take a saucepan or oval casserole large enough to hold both of the galantines and line it with fatback bards, the slices of beef and chopped onions, carrots and parsnip. Season with herbs, spices, salt and pepper. Put in the galantines and cover them with a layer of seasonings, vegetables, beef and fatback. Pour in enough stock or water to cover the galantines. Bring to a boil and simmer for one and one half hours, or until the galantines feel firm when pinched gently.

Drain the galantines and unwrap them to serve hot. If serving cold, cool them under weights. Strain and degrease the cooking stock, cool, chill, and chop the resulting aspic for use as a garnish.

MASSIALOT
LE NOUVEAU CUISINIER ROYAL ET BOURGEOIS

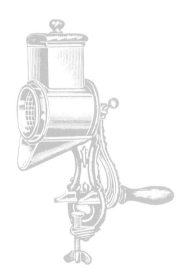

Classic Chicken Galantine

Galantine de Poularde

The technique of boning a bird through the back is demonstrated on pages 79-81; reserve the chicken bones, heart and gizzard for stock-making. An alternative, layered method of assembling the filling is shown on page 80. If the galantine has kept its shape well during cooking, it need not be unwrapped and rewrapped before weighting.

To make about 5 pounds [2½ kg.]

½ lb.	boneless pork, finely ground	¼ kg.
½ lb.	boneless veal, finely ground	¼ kg.
	salt and pepper	
	mixed spices	
4 lb.	chicken, boned through the back, most of the meat removed and diced	2 kg.
⅓ lb.	fresh pork fatback, diced	150 g.
⅓ lb.	boneless lean ham, diced	150 g.
⅓ lb.	corned beef tongue, blanched for 10 minutes and diced	150 g.
⅓ lb.	truffles, diced	150 g.
3 tbsp.	pistachios, blanched and peeled	45 ml.
½ cup	brandy	125 ml.
2	eggs	2
5 quarts	gelatinous meat stock (recipe, page 162), made with 2 cups [½ liter] Madeira	5 liters
	salt	

Make the forcemeat by pounding together the pork and veal in a mortar; season with salt, pepper and mixed spices. (To obtain a very fine forcemeat, rub the mixture through a sieve.) Combine the diced chicken, fatback, ham, tongue, truffles and pistachios. Add the forcemeat, brandy and eggs. Mix well, then fry a spoonful and taste it for seasoning.

Spread out the chicken skin on the table, skin side down. Knead the forcemeat into a ball and lay it on the chicken. Spread the forcemeat evenly, forming it into a rectangle. Fold over the chicken skin.

Dip a large coarse linen cloth about 20 inches [50 cm.] square in water and wring it out, then spread it out on the table. Place it so that a flap about 10 inches [25 cm.] wide hangs over the edge of the table. Place the galantine lengthwise on this cloth, about 4 inches [10 cm.] from the table edge, with the chicken breast upward. Wrap the galantine in the cloth as tightly as possible. Tie both ends of the cloth securely. Wrap the galantine with string to keep it in shape.

Heat the stock to a simmer, lay the galantine in it and simmer gently for one and three quarters hours. Remove the galantine. Let it rest for 15 minutes before unwrapping it. Remove the cloth, rinse it in lukewarm water and wring it thoroughly. Wrap the galantine in it as before, taking care to keep the slit part of the chicken skin underneath. Tie the galantine. Press it on a large plate covered with a weighted board. Let it cool and then refrigerate it for at least 12 hours.

Strain the stock, clarify it if necessary and let it cool. Chill this aspic and chop it to decorate the galantine.

PROSPER MONTAGNÉ
THE NEW LAROUSSE GASTRONOMIQUE

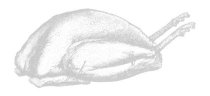

Truffled Galantine

Galantine Truffée

The technique of boning a bird through the back is demonstrated on pages 79-81.

I added the truffles to this recipe, which was originally created by Raymond Oliver for his friend Jean Cocteau.

To make about 5 pounds [2½ kg.]

2 tbsp.	butter	30 ml.
2 tbsp.	oil	30 ml.
1	onion, sliced	1
2	carrots, sliced	2
1	celery rib, sliced	1
4 to 5 lb.	roasting chicken, boned through the back, bones and giblets reserved, the neck crushed	2 to 2½ kg.
1	calf's foot, split	1
1 lb.	boneless lean veal	½ kg.
1 lb.	boneless lean pork	½ kg.
	salt and pepper	
¼ cup	Cognac	50 ml.
2 or 3	truffles, diced	2 or 3
1	large bard of fresh pork fatback	1
½ cup	Madeira	125 ml.

Heat the butter and oil, and lightly brown the onion, carrots and celery. Break up the chicken bones and add them, along with the neck. Cover, and stew gently for 15 minutes. Add the calf's foot and cover generously with water. Cover, and simmer for two hours.

Spread out the boned chicken on a cloth. With a boning knife, carefully cut most of the meat away from the skin, including the breast and thigh meat. Grind the meat with the veal and pork. Season the inside of the chicken skin generously with pepper and lightly with salt, and sprinkle it with the Cognac. Keep it cool. Season the forcemeat and combine it with the diced truffles. Fry a spoonful of the forcemeat and taste it for seasoning.

Trim and finely chop the liver, heart and gizzard of the chicken, season them, and roll them in the bard of fatback to make a roll the length of the chicken.

Spread half of the forcemeat on the inner surface of the chicken skin, put the roll of fat on top, and cover it with the remaining forcemeat. Roll up the chicken, giving it approxi-

mately its original form, wrap it in a cloth and tie both ends and the middle.

Strain the bone stock. Return it to the pot and put in the wrapped chicken. Simmer it for one and one half hours and let it cool in the stock. Take out the galantine, unwrap it, rinse the cloth and rewrap the galantine, tying the ends. Cool the galantine under a weight for two hours. Place the galantine in the refrigerator.

Clarify the stock if necessary and simmer it, uncovered, for one hour. Strain it through a cloth. Stir in the Madeira and let the stock cool. Refrigerate it until it sets to an aspic.

Slice the galantine, and serve it surrounded by coarsely chopped aspic.

ROBERT COURTINE
ZOLA À TABLE

Majorcan Truffled Turkey

Pavo Trufado

The technique of boning a bird through the back is demonstrated on pages 79-81.

To make about 11 pounds [5½ kg.]

2½ cups	sherry	625 ml.
2½ tsp.	freshly grated nutmeg	12 ml.
	salt and pepper	
12 lb.	turkey, boned through the back, the bones reserved	6 kg.
¼ lb.	truffles, chopped, the liquid reserved if canned truffles are used	125 g.
2 lb.	boneless pork, cut into strips	1 kg.
2 oz.	boneless ham, cut into strips	60 g.
3 slices	lean bacon, cut into strips	3 slices
1	carrot	1
1	onion	1
2	bay leaves	2
1 tbsp.	unflavored powdered gelatin, softened in 2 tablespoons [30 ml.] water	15 ml.
1	egg white	1

Put half of the sherry into a shallow dish large enough to hold the turkey when it is laid flat. Add half of the nutmeg and some pepper, and put in the turkey, meat side down.

Combine the remaining sherry with the remaining nutmeg, salt and pepper, and the truffle liquid, if using. Pour this marinade over the pork, ham and bacon. Let both mixtures marinate for one hour.

Drain the turkey and place it skin side down on a board. Drain the remaining meats, reserving the marinade, and fill the turkey with alternate layers of pork, bacon, ham and truffles. Join the edges of the turkey around the filling and sew it up. Wrap this galantine in a cloth and tie it securely.

Place the turkey bones in a large pot with the carrot, onion, bay leaves and a little sherry from the reserved marinade. Put in the galantine and cover it with water. Bring to a boil and simmer it for about one and one half hours, or until it feels firm when lightly pinched.

Remove the galantine from the pot, unwrap it and re-wrap it tightly in a clean cloth. Tie both ends and place the galantine under a weighted board until it is completely cold. Refrigerate it.

Strain about 2 cups [½ liter] of the turkey stock and reheat it in a saucepan with the gelatin and the egg white. When the stock reaches a boil, strain it through a cloth to clarify it. Cool the stock, then chill it until it sets to an aspic. Decorate the galantine with the aspic to serve.

GABRIEL SASTRE RAYO AND ANTONIA ORDINAS MARI (EDITORS)
LIBRE DE CUINA DE C'AN CAMES SEQUES

Turkey Galantine

Galantine de Dinde

The technique of boning a bird through the back is demonstrated on pages 79-81.

Other birds may be made into galantines in the same way, with the amount of forcemeat and the cooking time adjusted in proportion to their size.

To make about 7 pounds [3½ kg.]

7 lb.	turkey, boned through the back, the meat removed without tearing the skin	3½ kg.
2 lb.	boneless fatty pork, ground	1 kg.
	salt and pepper	
	quatre épices	
¼ lb.	fresh pork fatback, thinly sliced and cut into long strips	125 g.
½ lb.	fresh pork rind	¼ kg.
	gelatinous meat stock (recipe, page 162) or water	
2	carrots	2
2	onions, stuck with 3 whole cloves	2
	peppercorns	
1	large bouquet garni	1
¼ cup	port	50 ml.

Cut the breast and thigh meat of the turkey into strips. Chop the remaining meat very fine, mix it with the ground pork, and season well with salt, pepper and *quatre épices*. Fry a spoonful of this forcemeat and taste it for seasoning.

Spread out the turkey skin and cover the inner side with alternate strips of light and dark meat. Season with salt and pepper. Cover with the strips of fatback, then with the force-

meat. Fold in the skin of the wings and legs, then sew up the edges of the skin to form a large sausage.

Line a large saucepan with the pork rind. Put in the galantine, cover it generously with stock or water, and add the carrots, onions, peppercorns and the bouquet garni. Season lightly with salt and pepper. Bring to a boil, cover, and simmer gently for three hours, or until the galantine is firm when lightly pinched. Let it cool until lukewarm in the cooking liquid. Remove the galantine and place it under a board with a 2- to 4-pound [1- to 2-kg.] weight on top. Cool the galantine completely.

Strain and degrease the cooking liquid. Boil to reduce it until it will set to an aspic; cool, stir in the port, and refrigerate the aspic to set it. Refrigerate the cooled galantine for 48 hours, then serve it surrounded by chopped aspic.

ZETTE GUINAUDEAU-FRANC
LES SECRETS DES FERMES EN PÉRIGORD NOIR

Goose Brawn

Fromage d'Oie

As you pack the meats into the terrine, you may distribute among the layers some finely chopped parsley, chives and tarragon. Serve this brawn with sour gherkins and other pickled vegetables.

To make about 4 pounds [2 kg.]

2 lb.	goose, cut into pieces	1 kg.
1	calf's foot, halved	1
4 cups	dry white wine	1 liter
2	onions, sliced	2
3	carrots, sliced	3
2	garlic cloves, sliced	2
1	bouquet garni with savory	1
	salt and pepper	

Place all of the ingredients in a nonreactive pot, adding a little water if the liquid does not completely cover the meats. Bring to a boil, cover, and simmer for two hours, or until the meat is falling away from the bones.

Line a 2-quart [2-liter] terrine with foil. Skin the pieces of goose and place the skin at the bottom of the terrine, the outside pressed against the foil. Bone the meats and dice the meat from the calf's foot. Pack the meats into the terrine, interspersed with the carrot slices. Press the mixture down firmly. Strain the cooking liquid slowly into the terrine so that it fills in all the gaps. Put a weighted plate on top of the meat. Let it cool and then chill it overnight. To serve, unmold and slice the brawn.

JACQUELINE GÉRARD
BONNES RECETTES D'AUTREFOIS

Rabbit in Aspic

Lapin de Garenne en Gelée

To make about 1 ½ pounds [¾ kg.]

3 lb.	rabbit, cut into pieces	1½ kg.
	dry white wine	
	salt	
	mixed spices	
¼ lb.	fresh pork belly with the rind, cut into small strips	125 g.
2	shallots, chopped	2
1	bouquet garni	1
1	bard of fresh pork fatback	1

Cut the meaty parts of the rabbit (the saddle and the legs) into large pieces. Place them in a bowl with white wine to cover, salt and mixed spices. Let them marinate for several hours. Place the pieces of rabbit in a 4-cup [1-liter] terrine with the pork-belly strips. Pour in enough of the marinade to come up to the level of the rabbit pieces, adding a little water and more wine if necessary. Add the shallots and the bouquet garni. Cover with the bard of fatback and put on the lid. Cook the terrine in a water bath in a preheated 300° F. [150° C.] oven for three to three and one half hours. Without removing the lid, let the rabbit cool, then refrigerate it for 48 hours. Unmold to serve.

ALEXANDRE DUMAINE
MA CUISINE

Molded Rabbit Galantine

Le Pâté de Lapin

The technique of boning a rabbit is shown on pages 66-67.

To make about 4 pounds [2 kg.]

3 lb.	wild rabbit, boned and cut into strips	1½ kg.
1 lb.	boneless veal, cut into strips	½ kg.
1 lb.	boneless pork, cut into strips	½ kg.
½ lb.	fresh pork belly, cut into strips	¼ kg.
½ lb.	salt pork, cut into strips	¼ kg.
2 or 3	truffles, sliced	2 or 3
2 tbsp.	salt	30 ml.
1½ tbsp.	pepper	22½ ml.
3 quarts	gelatinous meat stock (recipe, page 162)	3 liters

Mix together the strips of meat, the truffles, the salt and the pepper. Line a 2½-quart [2½-liter] terrine mold with a large piece of cloth, letting the edges hang over the sides. Put in the meat mixture, fold the cloth over to tightly enclose it and sew up the edges of the cloth. Lift the wrapped meat mixture out of the mold.

In a large pot, bring the stock to a boil. Put in the wrapped meat, cover, and simmer it gently for four hours.

Lift out the wrapped meat, unwrap it and slide it back into the mold used for shaping. Strain and degrease the cooking liquid; taste it for seasoning. Pour it over the meat and let it cool. Refrigerate the galantine until the aspic is set.

70 MÉDECINS DE FRANCE
LE TRÉSOR DE LA CUISINE DU BASSIN MÉDITERRANÉEN

Rabbit with Vegetables in Aspic

Lapin de Garenne en Gelée

To make about 3 pounds [1½ kg.]

2	large pieces fresh pork rind	2
4 lb.	rabbit, cut into pieces	2 kg.
½ lb.	lightly salted pork belly with the rind removed, cut into small pieces	¼ kg.
1	calf's foot, boned and cut into small pieces	1
3	onions, sliced	3
2	carrots, sliced	2
1	bay leaf, crumbled	1
1 tsp.	dried thyme leaves	5 ml.
	salt and pepper	
2 cups	dry white wine	½ liter
½ cup	gelatinous meat stock (recipe, page 162)	125 ml.
	flour-and-water paste	

Line the bottom of a 7-cup [1¾-liter] terrine with one of the pork rinds. Layer rabbit pieces, pork belly and calf's foot pieces, then add half of the vegetables, herbs and seasonings. Repeat with the remaining meats, vegetables and seasonings. Pour in the wine and stock and cover with the remaining pork rind.

Cover the terrine and seal on the lid with the flour-and-water paste. Place in a water bath and cook the terrine in a preheated 350° F. [180° C.] oven for approximately one and three quarters hours. Allow the terrine to cool completely before serving it.

JACQUELINE GÉRARD
LES MEILLEURES RECETTES DE GIBIER

Galantines of Young Rabbit

Galantines de Lapereaux Froids

The technique of boning a rabbit is shown on pages 66-67.

To make about 5 pounds [2½ kg.]

1 lb.	boneless lean veal, ground	½ kg.
½ lb.	beef marrow or suet	¼ kg.
6	eggs, 2 lightly beaten, 4 hard-boiled and cut into strips	6
	salt and pepper	
	mixed spices	
	fines herbes	
two 2½ lb.	rabbits, boned, the bones broken up	two 1¼ kg.
½ lb.	ham, cut into strips	¼ kg.
½ lb.	fresh pork fatback, cut into strips	¼ kg.
⅓ cup	pistachios, blanched and peeled	75 ml.
½ cup	almonds, blanched, peeled and split	125 ml.
2	truffles, cut into julienne	2
1	onion, coarsely chopped	1
2	carrots, coarsely chopped	2
1	bouquet garni	1
	gelatinous meat stock (recipe, page 162)	

Mix together the ground veal and marrow or suet. Work in most of the beaten eggs and season well with salt and pepper, mixed spices and fines herbes. Fry a spoonful of this mixture and taste it for seasoning.

Spread some of this mixture inside the rabbits, then make a layer of alternating lengthwise rows of the ham and fatback strips, pistachios, hard-boiled eggs, split almonds and truffle julienne. Season this layer and continue alternating layers of forcemeat and garnish until all of the ingredients are used up, finishing with a layer of forcemeat. Roll the rabbits into sausage shapes, sealing the edges with the remaining beaten eggs.

Tie each stuffed rabbit tightly in a cloth. In a large oval casserole, make a bed of the chopped vegetables, bouquet garni and broken-up rabbit carcasses. Put in the rolled rabbits, cover them with stock and bring to a boil. Cover and simmer for about one and one half hours.

Remove the galantines from the liquid and weight them between two plates to cool. Unwrap them, place them in a deep dish, degrease the cooking stock and strain it over the rabbits. Chill thoroughly to set the aspic before serving.

MARIN
LES DONS DE COMUS

Jellied Rabbit

Compote de Lapin

To make about 2½ pounds [1¼ kg.]

4 lb.	rabbit, cut into pieces	2 kg.
2 tbsp.	oil	30 ml.
1	bouquet garni	1
1	garlic clove	1
	salt and pepper	
1 cup	water	¼ liter
1	calf's foot	1
Marinade		
2	onions, chopped	2
3 or 4	carrots, sliced	3 or 4
1	garlic clove	1
1	whole clove	1
1	bouquet garni with plenty of thyme	1
4 cups	red, white or rosé wine	1 liter
⅓ cup	vinegar	75 ml.
	salt	
1 tsp.	black peppercorns	5 ml.

Combine the marinade ingredients in a large, nonreactive bowl. Add the rabbit pieces to the bowl and let them marinate for several hours.

Heat the oil in a nonreactive saucepan. Drain the rabbit pieces, pat them dry and brown them in the oil. Add the sliced carrots from the marinade and, when they have browned, strain the marinade liquid into the pan. Cook until the liquid is reduced by one half. Add the bouquet garni, garlic, salt and pepper, water and calf's foot. Cover the pan tightly. Cook over low heat for one and one half hours. Let the mixture cool slightly, then remove and bone the rabbit. Boil the cooking liquid until it is reduced to a syrupy sauce. Remove the bouquet garni, garlic and the calf's foot.

Place the rabbit meat in a 5-cup [1¼-liter] terrine, pour the sauce over it and decorate the top with a few carrot pieces. Refrigerate for several hours until the sauce sets to an aspic before serving the rabbit from the terrine.

FLORENCE DE ANDREIS
LA CUISINE PROVENÇALE D'AUJOURD'HUI

Galantine of Pheasant à la Lorenzo

Galantine de Faisan à la Lorenzo

To bone the partridges, follow the technique of boning a bird shown on pages 22-23. To bone the pheasant, follow the technique of boning a bird through the back demonstrated on pages 79-81.

To make about 4 pounds [2 kg.]

1 lb.	large chicken livers, trimmed	½ kg.
2 tbsp.	butter	30 ml.
3	partridges, boned, the bones reserved and the meat ground	3
1 lb.	boneless fatty pork, ground	½ kg.
	salt	
	freshly grated nutmeg	
	cayenne pepper	
4	egg yolks	4
2 tbsp.	finely chopped fresh parsley	30 ml.
3 to 4 lb.	pheasant, boned through the back, the bones reserved	1½ to 2 kg.
¼ lb.	truffles, quartered	125 g.
3 lb.	veal hindshank	1½ kg.
2	onions, 1 chopped and lightly sautéed in butter, 1 stuck with 2 whole cloves	2
1	bouquet garni	1
1	carrot, quartered	1
	gelatinous meat stock (recipe, page 162)	
	aspic cream (recipe, page 165)	
	diced truffles (optional)	
	blanched and peeled pistachios (optional)	
	cooked tongue (optional)	
	hard-boiled egg whites (optional)	

Sauté the chicken livers in the butter for two minutes, or until just firm but not brown. Reserve half of the livers and thoroughly pound the other half.

Combine the ground partridge and pork, and season highly with salt, nutmeg and cayenne pepper. Add the egg yolks and the pounded liver, and press this forcemeat through a sieve. Add the sautéed onion and the parsley. Fry a spoonful of the forcemeat and taste it for seasoning.

Spread out the pheasant on the table, skin side down. Cut away half the thickness of the breast fillets and arrange this meat on the skin to make an even layer. Spread with one third of the forcemeat and make a layer of half of the reserved livers and quartered truffles. Make another layer of forcemeat, another layer of livers and truffles, and a final layer of forcemeat. Enclose the layers well in the pheasant skin, sew it together and roll the galantine in a large cloth napkin; tie it firmly at both ends and in the center.

Place the game carcasses in a large pot with the veal hindshank, onion stuck with cloves, bouquet garni, carrot and the galantine. Cover with stock, bring to a boil and simmer gently for two and one half hours. Let the galantine cool in the stock for one hour, then unwrap and rewrap it and place it under a weighted board to cool completely.

Refrigerate the galantine. To serve, unwrap it and trim the ends nicely. Coat it with aspic cream and chill it until the coating has set. Decorate it as desired with diced truffles, pistachios, tongue and egg white.

CHARLES RANHOFER
THE EPICUREAN

To Collar a Hare

To bone the hare, follow the demonstration of boning a suckling pig on pages 75-77. Cut off the head of the hare, remove the forelegs completely, remove the lower joints of the hind legs and bone the thighs by opening them out.

To make about 3 pounds [1½ kg.]

4 lb.	hare, boned	2 kg.
½ lb.	salt pork with the rind removed, half cut into lardons, half thinly sliced	¼ kg.
	mixed spices	
	salt	
¾ lb.	basic forcemeat (recipe, page 163) (optional)	350 g.
½ lb.	boneless veal, thinly sliced	¼ kg.
1¼ cups	white wine	300 ml.
2½ cups	gelatinous meat stock (recipe, page 162)	625 ml.

Lard the hare with the lardons, season the inside of it with mixed spices and salt, and spread with the forcemeat, if using. Roll up the hare tightly and tie it with string. Line a deep 2-quart [2-liter] casserole with the veal slices, put in the hare, pour in the wine and stock, and cover with the salt-pork slices. Bring to a simmer and cook gently for two hours, or until the hare is tender, adding more stock if necessary.

Remove the string and place the hare in a deep serving dish. Strain and degrease the cooking liquid, pour it over the hare and refrigerate until the stock has set to an aspic.

F. COLLINGWOOD AND J. WOOLAMS
THE UNIVERSAL COOK

Venison and Pork Galantine

A type of mold rather than a true galantine, this dish originated in the 14th Century, when the venison would probably be supplemented with meat from wild boar.

To make about 2 pounds [1 kg.]

2 lb.	thick venison flank	1 kg.
1 each	sprig thyme and marjoram	1 each
2	peppercorns	2
	salt and pepper	
¼ lb.	boneless ham, cubed	125 g.
½ lb.	boneless fatty pork, ground	¼ kg.
1	large garlic clove, crushed to a paste	1
2	eggs, hard-boiled and sliced	2

Bone the venison and cut away any gristle. Put the venison bones in a pan and cover them with 5 cups [1¼ liters] of water; add the thyme, marjoram, peppercorns and salt, and cook for 30 minutes.

Mix the ham with the pork and the garlic. Fry a spoonful of this forcemeat and taste it for seasoning. Place the boned venison on a board and spread over it half of the forcemeat. Top with the sliced hard-boiled eggs, season with salt and pepper, and cover with the remaining forcemeat. Roll the venison up carefully in a floured napkin, and tie it at both ends and at intervals to secure its shape. Strain the venison stock, add the galantine and simmer it gently for three to four hours, or until it feels firm when lightly pinched.

Let it cool in the liquid, then remove it from the stock, take off the cloth and put the galantine in a dish that just fits it. Place a heavy weight on top and press it for several hours.

LIZZIE BOYD (EDITOR)
BRITISH COOKERY

Tuna Loaf

Pasticcio di Tonno

To make about 2½ pounds [1¼ kg.]

1¼ cups	canned oil-packed tuna, drained and finely ground	300 ml.
8	medium-sized starchy potatoes	8
3	eggs	3
	salt	
	mayonnaise (recipe, page 164)	

Boil the potatoes, unpeeled, until they are tender, then peel and mash them. Add the tuna and the eggs, season with salt

and work the mixture to obtain a smooth paste. Shape the mixture into a loaf, wrap it in a cloth, tie with string and lower it into a pot of cold water. Bring to a boil and simmer it for about one hour, or until it is firm. Drain, unwrap the loaf and let it cool. Refrigerate it.

Slice and serve it covered with mayonnaise.

IL CUCCHIAIO D'ARGENTO

Tuna Roll

Fiambre de Bonito o Atun

To make about 3 pounds [1½ kg.]

2 lb.	tuna, skinned, boned and ground	1 kg.
2 tbsp.	fresh bread crumbs	30 ml.
1 cup	dry sherry	¼ liter
2	eggs, lightly beaten	2
	salt	
¼ lb.	lean salt pork with the rind removed, blanched for 3 minutes and cut into strips	125 g.
¼ lb.	ham, cut into strips	125 g.
5	large carrots, cut into thick strips and parboiled for 7 minutes	5
1	onion, quartered	1
1	sprig parsley	1
1	garlic clove	1
⅔ cup	white wine	150 ml.
1	small bay leaf	1

Mix the tuna with the bread crumbs, sherry and eggs. Season lightly with salt.

Spread out a clean cloth on a table. In the center, place one third of the tuna mixture. Cover it with layers of half of the salt pork, ham and carrot strips. Cover with another third of the tuna, the remaining salt pork, ham and carrots, and then the remaining tuna. Fold the cloth around the preparation, press the cloth firmly to make a compact roll, and tie the ends.

Place the roll in a nonreactive pot, add the remaining ingredients, season with a little salt and cover with water. Bring to a boil, cover, and simmer for one hour, or until the roll is firm. Drain the roll and let it cool slightly. Place the roll between two boards, weight the top board and let the roll cool completely.

To serve, slice the roll and decorate it with chopped lettuce or slices of hard-boiled egg.

MARIA LUISA GARCÍA
EL ARTE DE COCINAR

Pike and Salmon Galantine with Sorrel Sauce

To make about 2 ½ pounds [1 ¼ kg.]

1 ½ lb.	pike fillets, skinned and ground	¾ kg.
3	eggs	3
4 tsp.	coarse salt	20 ml.
	cayenne pepper	
¼ tsp.	freshly ground black pepper	1 ml.
	freshly grated nutmeg	
1 ¾ cups	heavy cream	425 ml.
2	truffles, cut into ⅜-inch [9-mm.] cubes	2
¼ cup	brine-packed green peppercorns, drained	50 ml.
½ lb.	salmon fillet, skinned and cut into ½-inch [1-cm.] cubes	¼ kg.
	olive oil	
5 tbsp.	finely cut fresh dill	75 ml.
Sorrel sauce		
1 ¼ cups	mayonnaise *(recipe, page 164)*	300 ml.
½ cup	heavy cream, whipped	125 ml.
2 tbsp.	imported green-herb Dijon mustard	30 ml.
1 cup	shredded fresh sorrel leaves, ½ cup [125 ml.] cooked in 1 tsp. [5 ml.] butter until wilted, then puréed through a sieve	¼ liter
	freshly ground black pepper	

Place the pike in the work bowl of a food processor fitted with the metal blade. With the machine running, add the eggs, one by one. Then add the salt, a large pinch of cayenne, the black pepper, a pinch of nutmeg and the cream, and process the mixture until it is smooth. Transfer it to a large bowl. Fold in the truffles, 2 tablespoons [30 ml.] of the green peppercorns and the salmon cubes. Cover and chill for one hour.

Place a piece of plastic wrap 20 inches [50 cm.] long on your work surface. Brush with olive oil a center area of the wrap about 10 by 14 inches [25 by 35 cm.]. Scatter 3 tablespoons [45 ml.] of the dill and the remaining green peppercorns over the oiled surface. Spoon the fish mixture along the center of the prepared area to form a cylinder about 4 inches [10 cm.] wide and 14 inches [35 cm.] long. Roll the plastic wrap around the cylinder, tie the ends with string and wrap the cylinder again in plastic to make it watertight.

In a pot broad enough to hold the roll flat, bring to a boil enough water to cover the galantine. Reduce the heat to a simmer and add the galantine. Simmer for 45 minutes.

While the galantine is cooking, make the sorrel sauce by first combining the mayonnaise, whipped cream, mustard and puréed sorrel. Add the shredded leaves and season with

pepper. Set aside. Remove the galantine from the water and let it cool. Unwrap, slice, and serve it with the sorrel sauce.

TOM MARGITTAI AND PAUL KOVI
THE FOUR SEASONS

Standard Preparations

Gelatinous Meat Stock

To make about 3 quarts [3 liters] stock

2 lb.	veal hindshank	1 kg.
2	calf's feet, halved lengthwise and blanched for 5 minutes	2
2 lb.	chicken backs, necks and wing tips	1 kg.
½ lb.	fresh pork rind	¼ kg.
about 5 quarts	water	about 5 liters
1	bouquet garni, including leek and celery	1
1	garlic bulb	1
2	medium-sized onions, 1 stuck with 2 whole cloves	2
4	large carrots	4
	salt	

Place a round, metal pastry cutter or trivet in the bottom of a large stockpot to prevent the ingredients from sticking. Fit all of the meat and chicken pieces into the pot, and add enough water to cover them by about 2 inches [5 cm.]. Bring slowly to a boil and, with a slotted spoon, skim off the scum that rises. Keep skimming, occasionally adding a glass of cold water, until no scum rises—after 10 to 15 minutes.

Add the bouquet garni, garlic, onions and carrots, and skim once more as the liquid returns to a boil. Reduce the heat to very low, cover the pot with the lid ajar, and simmer for four to five hours, skimming at intervals.

Ladle the stock into a colander lined with several layers of dampened muslin or cheesecloth and set over a large bowl. Cool the strained stock, then refrigerate it for 12 hours. When the stock has set, spoon off the solidified fat. Wipe off traces of fat with a towel dipped in water and squeezed dry.

If the stock is not as clear as desired, melt it over high heat. Add six lightly beaten egg whites and six crushed egg shells, and whisk constantly until the mixture comes to a boil. Cook undisturbed until the egg-white foam rises to the surface, then remove the pot from the heat. Let the stock settle for a minute or so, then boil it up two more times. Strain the stock through a cloth-lined colander.

Tightly covered, the stock can safely be kept refrigerated for up to a week if brought to a boil every two days. Or, the stock may be melted and poured into freezer containers.

Fish Stock

2 lb.	fish heads, bones and trimmings, rinsed and broken up	1 kg.
1 each	onion, carrot and leek, sliced	1 each
1	celery rib, diced	1
1	bouquet garni	1
2 quarts	water	2 liters
2 cups	dry white wine	½ liter

Place the fish, vegetables and bouquet garni in a large non-reactive pot. Add the water. Bring to a boil slowly over low heat. Skim the top until no more scum rises, then cover the pot and simmer the mixture for 15 minutes. Add the wine and simmer, covered, for another 15 minutes. Strain the stock into a deep bowl through a colander lined with muslin or a double thickness of cheesecloth. Cool the stock, then cover it and chill it overnight, or until the stock has set to an aspic. With a spoon, remove any fat from the surface.

Fish aspic. In a nonreactive saucepan, warm 2 cups [½ liter] of the refrigerated stock over low heat. Soften 2 tablespoons [30 ml.] of powdered gelatin in 4 tablespoons [60 ml.] of cold water for five minutes. Add a little of the warm stock, then slowly stir the gelatin mixture into the pan of stock. Refrigerate a spoonful of the stock; it should set within 10 minutes. If it does not, soften a little more gelatin and add it to the saucepan. Add 1 tablespoon [15 ml.] of Madeira or other fortified wine if desired.

Clarified fish aspic. Add one egg shell and one whisked egg white to the warmed stock with the gelatin. Whisking constantly, bring the mixture to a boil over high heat. When the egg-white foam rises to the surface, remove the pan from the heat. Let it settle for a minute or so, then boil it up two more times. Strain the stock through a cloth-lined colander.

Court Bouillon

2	onions, thinly sliced	2
2	carrots, thinly sliced	2
1	bouquet garni	1
6 cups	water	1½ liters
	salt	
1 cup	dry white wine (optional)	¼ liter

Put the vegetables, bouquet garni and water into a large nonreactive pot, and season with a pinch of salt. Bring to a boil, then reduce the heat, cover and simmer for about 15 minutes. Pour in the wine, if using, and simmer for an additional 15 minutes. Strain the court bouillon through a sieve into a bowl or a clean pan before using it.

Basic Forcemeat

For a more flavorful forcemeat, you may substitute a bread-and-stock panada for the bread crumbs. To make the panada, first sprinkle 1 cup [¼ liter] of fresh bread crumbs into 1 cup of hot gelatinous meat stock *(recipe, page 162)*. Then, stirring constantly, cook until the stock has reduced slightly and the mixture has formed a thick, smooth paste.

¾ lb.	boneless veal, finely ground or chopped	350 g.
¾ lb.	boneless pork, finely ground or chopped	350 g.
¾ lb.	fresh pork fatback, finely ground or chopped	350 g.
2	chicken livers, trimmed and finely ground or chopped	2
2	eggs	2
1 cup	fresh bread crumbs	¼ liter
2 tbsp.	brandy, Madeira, pastis, sherry, port, or red or white wine	30 ml.
	mixed dried herbs	
	mixed spices	
	salt and pepper	

Combine all of the ground or chopped meats; add the eggs and bread crumbs. Add the remaining ingredients and blend them until thoroughly combined. Fry a spoonful of this mixture and taste it for seasoning.

Chicken Liver Purée

This quantity is sufficient to enrich a forcemeat made with 2½ pounds [1¼ kg.] of meat.

1 tbsp.	finely chopped shallots	15 ml.
2 tbsp.	butter	30 ml.
⅓ lb.	chicken livers, trimmed	150 g.
1 tbsp.	brandy	15 ml.

Gently stew the shallots in the butter for about five minutes, without letting them color. Add the chicken livers, increase the heat and cook for two minutes. Pour in the brandy, ignite it and stir constantly until the flames die.

Let the mixture cool until tepid. Pour the contents of the pan, including the juices, into a mortar. Pound with a pestle to make a rough purée. Force the purée through a sieve. Alternatively, purée the contents of the pan in a food processor or blender.

Forcemeat Mousseline

For a contrast of texture and flavor, any of the following can be added to the mousseline after the cream has been incorporated: blanched, peeled and chopped pistachios; chopped poached shrimp or steamed mussels; sautéed chopped mushrooms; or chopped truffles.

To make about 4 cups [1 liter] mousseline

1 lb.	fish fillets, skinned and chopped, or boneless chicken breasts, cubed	½ kg.
	salt and pepper	
	freshly grated nutmeg	
	cayenne pepper (optional)	
2	large egg whites	2
2 cups	heavy cream	½ liter

In a mortar or a food processor, purée the fish or the chicken. Season with salt, pepper, nutmeg and cayenne pepper, if using. Gradually add the egg whites, beating by hand with a wooden spoon until they are completely incorporated. A little at a time, rub the purée through a fine-meshed sieve, using a plastic pastry scraper for a drum sieve or a wooden pestle for any other sieve. Pack the purée into a glass or metal bowl and cover it with plastic wrap. Place the bowl in a larger bowl containing crushed ice, and refrigerate for at least one hour.

Remove the bowls from the refrigerator. Replenish the crushed ice, if necessary. Using a wooden spoon, work a little heavy cream into the mixture. Return the bowls to the refrigerator for 15 minutes. Continue beating in small quantities of cream, refrigerating for 15 minutes between each addition. Beat the mixture vigorously as soon as it becomes soft enough. When all of the cream has been incorporated, poach a spoonful of the mixture and taste it for seasoning. Cover the mousseline and refrigerate it until ready for use.

Flour Panada

To produce a forcemeat mousseline with greater body and a smoother texture, this panada can be incorporated into the purée as demonstrated on pages 10-11.

To make about 3 cups [¾ liter] panada

1¼ cups	milk	300 ml.
¾ cup	flour	175 ml.
	salt and white pepper	
	grated nutmeg	
4	egg yolks	4
6 tbsp.	butter, melted	90 ml.

Bring the milk to a boil and let it cool slightly. Sift the flour, salt, pepper and nutmeg into a mixing bowl. Make a well in the center of the flour mixture and drop in the egg yolks. Mixing from the center, work the yolks into the flour. Gradually stir in the hot milk and the melted butter, and continue stirring to blend thoroughly.

In a small saucepan, cook the panada over medium heat, stirring with a whisk, until the mixture starts to thicken. Beating with a wooden spoon, continue to cook the mixture until it pulls away from the sides of the pan. Spread the panada on a plate to cool.

Watercress Mousse

To make about 3 cups [¾ liter] mousse

6	bunches watercress, stems removed, parboiled for 2 minutes, squeezed dry and finely chopped	6
⅔ cup	gelatinous meat or fish stock *(recipes, pages 162 and 163)*	150 ml.
⅔ cup	heavy cream, lightly whipped	150 ml.
	salt and pepper	

Melt the stock and pour it into a metal bowl. Force the watercress through a fine-meshed sieve into the stock. Set the bowl in ice and stir the mixture until it begins to thicken. Remove the bowl from the ice, fold in the cream and season to taste. Spoon the mousse into a serving bowl, cover and refrigerate until serving time.

Sorrel mousse. Gently stew 10 ounces [300 g.] of sorrel in 2 tablespoons [30 ml.] of butter, stirring, for 20 minutes, or until it is reduced to a fairly dry purée. Add about two thirds of the melted stock and reduce the mixture by about one half. Force it through a fine-meshed sieve into a bowl and stir in the remaining stock. Add salt and pepper. Stir over ice until the mixture begins to thicken, then stir in the cream.

Tomato mousse. Stew a finely chopped onion in 1 tablespoon [15 ml.] of butter until soft. Add 6 tablespoons [90 ml.] of white wine and reduce the mixture over high heat until the pan is nearly dry. Add four medium-sized tomatoes that have been peeled, seeded and coarsely chopped. Season with a little sugar, salt, pepper and cayenne pepper. Simmer uncovered, stirring occasionally, for about 30 minutes, or until the tomatoes are reduced to a purée. Add about half of the melted stock and boil the mixture, stirring, until reduced by half. Sieve the mixture into a bowl and add the remaining stock. Stir over ice until the mixture begins to turn syrupy; just as the setting point is reached, fold in the cream.

Mayonnaise

To prevent curdling, the egg yolks, oil and vinegar or lemon juice should be at room temperature and the oil should be added very gradually at first. The ratio of egg yolks to oil may be varied according to taste. The prepared mayonnaise will keep for several days in a covered container in the refrigerator. Stir it well before use.

To make about 1½ cups [375 ml.] mayonnaise		
2	egg yolks	2
	salt and white pepper	
2 tsp.	wine vinegar or strained fresh lemon juice	10 ml.
1 to 1½ cups	oil	250 to 375 ml.

Put the egg yolks in a warmed dry bowl. Season with salt and pepper and whisk for about a minute, or until the yolks become slightly paler in color. Add the vinegar or lemon juice and whisk until thoroughly mixed.

Whisking constantly, add the oil, drop by drop to begin with. When the sauce starts to thicken, pour in the remaining oil in a thin, steady stream, whisking rhythmically. Add only enough oil to give the mayonnaise a soft but firm consistency. It should just hold its shape when lifted in a spoon. If the mayonnaise is too thick, whisk in 1 to 2 teaspoons [5 to 10 ml.] of additional vinegar or lemon juice, or warm water.

Green mayonnaise. Parboil ¼ pound [125 g.] of spinach leaves for two minutes; drain the spinach in a strainer, plunge it into cold water to stop the cooking, and squeeze the spinach dry with your hands. Finely chop the spinach, then purée it in a food mill or a food processor. Stir the purée into the prepared mayonnaise, along with 1 tablespoon [15 ml.] of fines herbes.

Tartar sauce. Add 1 tablespoon each (or more to taste) of finely chopped sour gherkins, capers and fines herbes to 1½ cups [375 ml.] of prepared mayonnaise.

Vinaigrette

The proportion of vinegar to oil may be varied according to the acidity of the vinegar used and the tartness of the food to be dressed. However, one part vinegar to four parts oil is a good mean ratio. Despite its name, this dressing may be made with lemon juice instead of vinegar.

Any vinaigrette may be enhanced with chopped fresh herbs (parsley, fines herbes, basil, mint, marjoram or hyssop), capers, chopped shallots or finely sliced sour gherkins.

To make about ⅔ cup [150 ml.] vinaigrette		
1 tsp.	salt	5 ml.
¼ tsp.	freshly ground pepper	1 ml.
2 tbsp.	wine vinegar	30 ml.
½ cup	oil	125 ml.

Put the salt and pepper into a small bowl. Add the vinegar, and stir until the salt dissolves. Then stir in the oil.

Tomato vinaigrette. Add 2 tablespoons [30 ml.] of puréed raw tomato or of cooked, reduced puréed tomato to the prepared vinaigrette.

Basic White Sauce

To make about 2 cups [½ liter] sauce		
2 tbsp.	butter	30 ml.
2 tbsp.	flour	30 ml.
2½ cups	milk	625 ml.
	salt	
	white pepper (optional)	
	freshly grated nutmeg (optional)	
	heavy cream (optional)	

Melt the butter in a heavy saucepan over low heat. Stir in the flour and cook, stirring, for two or three minutes. Pour in all of the milk at once, whisking constantly to blend the mixture completely. Increase the heat and continue whisking while the sauce comes to a boil. Reduce the heat to very low and simmer, uncovered, for about 40 minutes, stirring occasionally to prevent the sauce from forming a skin or sticking to the bottom of the pan. Season to taste with salt and, if desired, white pepper and a pinch of nutmeg. Whisk again until the sauce is perfectly smooth. Add a little heavy cream if you prefer a richer sauce.

Velouté Sauce

For a fish velouté, replace the meat stock with fish stock *(recipe, page 163)*.

To make about 2 cups [½ liter] sauce		
2 tbsp.	butter	30 ml.
2 tbsp.	flour	30 ml.
2 cups	gelatinous meat stock (recipe, page 162)	½ liter
	salt and pepper	

Melt the butter in a heavy saucepan over low heat. Stir in the flour and cook, stirring, for two to three minutes. When this roux stops foaming and is a light golden color, pour in all of the stock, whisking constantly to blend the mixture smooth. Increase the heat and continue to whisk until the sauce comes to a boil. Reduce the heat to very low and move the pan so that one side of it is off the heat. Simmer the sauce for about 30 minutes, skimming occasionally. Season to taste with salt and pepper before using the sauce.

Aspic cream. When the velouté sauce is finished, stir in 1 cup [¼ liter] of gelatinous meat stock, a spoonful at a time. Stirring constantly, cook over low heat until the sauce is reduced to about 1½ cups [375 ml.]. Gradually stir in ½ cup [125 ml.] of heavy cream and reduce the sauce again. Set the pan over a bowl of ice and stir the sauce until it cools and starts to thicken.

White Butter Sauce

To make about 1 to 1 ½ cups [250 to 375 ml.] sauce

⅓ cup	dry white wine	75 ml.
⅓ cup	white wine vinegar	75 ml.
3	shallots, very finely chopped	3
	salt	
	pepper	
½ to ¾ lb.	unsalted butter, chilled and finely diced	250 to 350 g.

In a heavy stainless-steel or enameled saucepan, boil the wine and the vinegar with the shallots and a pinch of salt until only enough liquid remains to moisten the shallots. Remove the pan from the heat and let the mixture cool for a few minutes. Season it with pepper.

Place the pan on a heat-diffusing pad over very low heat and whisk in the butter, a handful at a time, whisking after each addition until the mixture has a creamy consistency. Remove the sauce from the heat as soon as all of the butter has been incorporated. Serve at once.

Tomato Sauce

When fresh, ripe summer tomatoes are not available, use drained, canned Italian-style or home-canned tomatoes.

To make about 1 ¼ cups [300 ml.] sauce

6	medium-sized very ripe tomatoes, quartered	6
1	bay leaf	1
1	large sprig dried thyme	1
	coarse salt	
1	onion, sliced	1
2	garlic cloves, lightly crushed (optional)	2
2 tbsp.	butter, cut into small pieces (optional)	30 ml.
	freshly ground pepper	
1 to 2 tsp.	sugar (optional)	5 to 10 ml.
1 tbsp.	finely chopped fresh parsley (optional)	15 ml.
4	fresh basil leaves, torn into small pieces (optional)	4

Place the tomatoes in a nonreactive saucepan with the bay leaf, thyme and a pinch of coarse salt. Add the onion and the garlic, if using. Bring to a boil, crushing the tomatoes lightly with a wooden spoon, and cook, uncovered, over fairly brisk heat for 10 minutes, or until the tomatoes have disintegrated into a thick pulp. Tip them into a plastic or stainless-steel sieve placed over a pan. Using a wooden pestle, push the tomatoes through the sieve. Cook, uncovered, over low heat until the sauce is reduced to the required consistency. Remove the pan from the heat. If you like, whisk in the pieces of butter to enrich the sauce. Season the sauce with pepper and, if desired, with sugar, chopped parsley and basil.

Chunky tomato sauce. Peel and seed the tomatoes, and cut them into chunks. Lightly sauté a finely chopped onion and a chopped garlic clove in a little oil and butter. Add the tomatoes and cook over brisk heat, stirring occasionally, for 10 minutes, or until they are reduced to a pulp. Season and add herbs to taste. About 2 tablespoons [30 ml.] of butter can be added at the end of the cooking to enrich the sauce.

Brine

To make about 4 cups [1 liter] brine

4 cups	water	1 liter
1 ¼ cups	coarse salt	300 ml.
2 tbsp.	white or brown sugar	30 ml.
1 tbsp.	juniper berries	15 ml.
4 or 5	whole cloves	4 or 5
3	bay leaves	3
1	blade mace	1
2 or 3	sprigs thyme	2 or 3

Bring the water to a boil with the salt and sugar. Wrap the remaining ingredients in cheesecloth and add them to the pot. Boil for two minutes. Remove the pot from the heat and let the brine cool completely. Discard the cloth package.

Hot-Water Crust Dough

Depending on how much dough is required, the amounts specified in this recipe may be doubled, tripled—or even multiplied by eight.

To make about 1 pound [½ kg.] dough

2 cups	flour	½ liter
	salt	
1 tsp.	confectioners' sugar (optional)	5 ml.
6 tbsp.	butter or lard	90 ml.
7 tbsp.	water	105 ml.

Sift the flour into a bowl with the salt and the sugar, if using. Make a well in the middle. Put the butter or lard and the water in a saucepan and bring to a boil. Pour this mixture into the well in the flour and mix together quickly, stirring until a smooth dough is formed. Cover and let the dough stand in a warm place for 30 minutes, or until it is firm but still warm and pliable. Roll it out on a floured board or shape it with your hands for a raised pie.

Short-Crust Dough for Pâtés

Depending on how much dough is required, the amounts specified in this recipe may be doubled or tripled. For pâtés, the chilled dough is usually rolled to a thickness of ¼ to ⅓ inch [6 mm. to 1 cm.].

To make about 1 pound [½ kg.] dough

2½ cups	flour	625 ml.
1 tsp.	salt	5 ml.
10 tbsp.	butter or 5 tbsp. [75 ml.] butter and 5 tbsp. lard, chilled and cubed	150 ml.
1	small egg	1
	cold water	

Sift the flour and the salt into a large mixing bowl. Add the cubed butter, and cut it into the flour with two knives until the mixture is coarse and crumbly. Break the egg into the bowl and stir with a fork until it is absorbed by the flour. Add cold water, one spoonful at a time, until the dough begins to cohere.

Knead the dough lightly, then gather it into a ball, wrap it tightly in plastic wrap, foil or wax paper, and refrigerate it for at least one hour before rolling it out. The wrapped dough can be safely kept in the refrigerator for two or three days.

Rough Puff Dough

Depending on how much dough is required, the amounts specified in this recipe may be doubled or tripled. For pâtés, the chilled dough is usually rolled to a thickness of ¼ to ⅓ inch [6 mm. to 1 cm.].

To make about 1 pound [½ kg.] dough

2 cups	flour	½ liter
½ tsp.	salt	2 ml.
½ lb.	cold unsalted butter, cut into small cubes	¼ kg.
5 to 6 tbsp.	cold water	75 to 90 ml.

Sift the flour and salt into a mixing bowl. Add the butter and, using two table knives, rapidly cut it into the flour until the butter is in tiny pieces. Do not work the mixture for more than a few minutes. Add 2 tablespoons [30 ml.] of the water and, with a fork, quickly blend it into the flour-and-butter mixture. Add just enough of the rest of the water to allow you to gather the dough together into a firm ball with your hands. Wrap the dough tightly in plastic wrap, foil or wax paper and refrigerate it for at least one hour, or put it in the freezer for 20 minutes until the surface is slightly frozen.

Place the dough on a cool, lightly floured surface and smack it flat with a rolling pin. Turn the dough over to make sure that both sides are well floured, and rapidly roll out the dough into a rectangle about 12 inches [30 cm.] long and 5 to 6 inches [12 to 15 cm.] wide. Fold the two short ends to meet each other in the center, then fold again to align the folded edges. Following the direction of the fold lines, roll the dough into a rectangle again, fold again in the same way, rewrap the dough and refrigerate it for at least 30 minutes. Repeat this process two or three more times—letting the dough rest in the refrigerator each time—before using the dough. Tightly wrapped, the dough can safely be kept in the refrigerator for two or three days.

Puff-Pastry Dough

To make about 2 pounds [1 kg.] dough

3 cups	all-purpose flour	¾ liter
1 cup	cake flour	¼ liter
2 tsp.	salt	10 ml.
1 lb.	unsalted butter	½ kg.
10 to 12 tbsp.	water	150 to 180 ml.

Sift the flours and the salt into a bowl. Cut a quarter of the butter into small pieces and add them to the bowl. Using your finger tips, rub the butter into the flour. Add just enough cold water—a few tablespoonfuls at a time—to bind the ingredients, and work the dough into a ball. Wrap the dough in floured plastic wrap and chill it in the refrigerator for about 30 minutes.

Meanwhile, place the remaining butter between two sheets of parchment or wax paper and, with a rolling pin, flatten the butter into a slab about 6 inches [15 cm.] square and ½ inch [1 cm.] thick. Chill the butter in the refrigerator for about 30 minutes.

Place the dough on a lightly floured board and roll it into a 12-inch [30-cm.] square. Place the square of butter diagonally in the center of the dough and fold the corners of the dough over the butter so that they meet in the center. Roll the dough into a rectangle 12 by 18 inches [30 by 45 cm.].

Fold the dough in thirds and give it a quarter turn. Roll the dough again into a rectangle and fold it again into thirds. Wrap and chill the dough for at least one hour. Roll and turn the dough twice more, refrigerate for a few hours, and repeat, giving it six turns in all. After a final turn, refrigerate for four hours before using it. Tightly wrapped, the dough can safely be kept in the refrigerator for two or three days, or in the freezer for two or three months. If frozen, defrost it in the refrigerator overnight.

Recipe Index

All recipes in the index that follows are listed by their English titles. Entries are also organized by the major ingredients specified in the recipes. Foreign recipes are listed by country of origin. Recipe credits appear on pages 174-176.

Recipe Credits

The sources for the recipes in this volume are shown below. Page references in parentheses indicate where the recipes appear in the anthology.

Académie des Gastronomes, Académie Culinaire de France, *La Haute Cuisine Française.* © Jean-Pierre Delarge, Le bélier prisme, 1975. Published by Jean-Pierre Delarge, Éditeur, Paris. Translated by permission of Jean-Pierre Delarge, Éditeur(87).
Ahern, Mrs. Robert L. M., (Editor), *The Fine Arts Cookbook.* Copyright © 1970 by Museum of Fine Arts, Boston, Massachusetts. Published by Museum of Fine Arts. By permission of Museum of Fine Arts, Massachusetts(97).
Alberini, Massimo, *Cento Ricette Storiche.* Copyright Sansoni Editore, Firenze. Published by Sansoni Editore, Florence, 1974. Translated by permission of G. C. Sansoni Editore Nuova S.p.A.(135).
Allen, Jana and Margaret Gin, *Innards and Other Variety Meats.* Copyright © 1974 by Jana Allen and Margaret Gin. Published by 101 Productions, San Francisco. By permission of 101 Productions(102).
The Art of Cookery, Made Plain and Easy. By a Lady. London, 1747(134).
Artusi, Pellegrino, *La Scienza in Cucina e l'Arte di Mangiar Bene.* Copyright © 1970 Giulio Einaudi Editore S.p.A., Torino. Published by Giulio Einaudi Editore S.p.A.(120, 147).
Austin, Thomas (Editor), *Two Fifteenth-Century Cookery-Books.* Published by the Oxford University Press, London. By permission of The Council of the Early English Text Society, Oxford(137).
Barry, Naomi, *International Herald Tribune.* December 28, 1978 (article on "Eating Out"). By permission of Naomi Barry, Paris(125).
Beck, Simone and Michael James, *New Menus from Simca's Cuisine.* Copyright © 1979, 1978 by Simone Beck and Michael James. By permission of Harcourt Brace Jovanovich, Inc.(84).
Benoit, Félix and Henry Clos Jouve, *La Cuisine Ly-*

onnaise. © Solar, 1975. Published by Solar, Paris. Translated by permission of Solar(100).
Bertholle, Louisette, *250 Recettes de Sologne et d'Ailleurs.* © 1962 by Éditions de la Pensée Moderne. Published by Éditions de la Pensée Moderne, Paris. Translated by permission of the author, Neuvy sur Barangeon(95). *Secrets of the Great French Restaurants.* Copyright © 1974 by Macmillan Publishing Co., Inc. By permission of Macmillan Publishing Co., Inc.(128, 136).
Bisson, Marie, *La Cuisine Normande.* © Solar, 1978. Published by Solar, Paris. Translated by permission of Solar(111, 114).
Bocuse, Paul and Louis Perrier, *Le Gibier.* © 1973, Flammarion. Published by Flammarion et Cie, Paris. By permission of Flammarion et Cie(121).
Bouillard, Paul, *La Cuisine au Coin du Feu.* Copyright 1928 by Albin Michel. Published by Éditions Albin Michel, Paris. Translated by permission of Éditions Albin Michel(105, 135).
Boulestin, X. M. and A. H. Adair, *Savouries and Hors-d'Oeuvre.* © Marcel Boulestin and A. H. Adair, 1956. Published by William Heinemann Limited, London, 1932. By permission of William Heinemann Limited(105).
Boyd, Lizzie (Editor), *British Cookery.* 1976 by British Tourist Authority and British Farm Produce Council. Published by Croom Helm Ltd., London. By permission of The British Tourist Authority, London(87, 133, 134, 161).
Brazier, Eugénie, *Les Secrets de la Mère Brazier.* © Solar, 1977. Published by Solar, Paris. Translated by permission of Solar(91, 93).
Breteuil, Jules, *La Cuisinier Européen.* Published by Garnier Frères Libraires-Éditeurs, Paris, 1860(143).
Břízová, Joza and Maryna Klimentová, *Tschechische Küche.* Published by Verlag Práca, Prague and Verlag für die Frau, Leipzig. Translated by permission of Dilia, Authors' Agency, Prague, for the authors(99, 123).
Carrier, Robert, *The Connoisseur's Cookbook.* Copyright © 1965, by Robert Carrier. Published by Random House, Inc., New York. Originally published as *The Robert Carrier Cookbook* in London, by Thomas Nelson & Sons Ltd. By permission of the author, Suffolk(99).
Cavalcanti, Ippolito, Ducca di Buonvicino, *Cucina Teorico-Pratica.* Second Edition, 1839 Naples(127).
Charretton, Bernard and Christine, *Les Bonnes Recettes du Chasseur.* © Bordas, Paris 1980. Published by Édi-

tions Bordas. Translated by permission of Éditions Bordas(112, 121).
Clark, Morton G., *French-American Cooking from New Orleans to Quebec.* Copyright © 1967 by Morton Clark. By permission of Harper & Row, Publishers, Inc.(124).
Collingwood, F. and J. Woolams, *The Universal Cook.* Fourth Edition, 1792. Published by Scatchward and Whitaker(120, 160).
Comelade, Eliane Thibaut, *La Cuisine Catalane.* © Éditions CLT J. Lanore. Published by Éditions Jacques Lanore, Paris 1978. Translated by permission of Éditions Jacques Lanore(139).
Conran, Caroline (Editor), *Michel Guérard's Cuisine Gourmande.* English translation copyright © 1976 by William Morrow and Company, Inc. Originally published in French, under the title *La Grande Cuisine Gourmande,* copyright © 1976 by Éditions Laffont S.A. By permission of William Morrow(100, 132).
Le Cordon Blue. Published by Le Cordon Bleu de Paris, 1929, 1934. Translated by permission of Le Cordon Bleu de Paris(119, 138).
Courtine, Robert J., *Les Dimanches de la Cuisine.* © Éditions de la Table Ronde, 1962. Published by Les Éditions de la Table Ronde, Paris. Translated by permission of Les Éditions de la Table Ronde(152). *Zola à Table.* © 1978 by Éditions Robert Laffont. Published by Éditions Robert Laffont, Paris. Translated by permission of Éditions Robert Laffont(156).
Il Cucchiaio d'Argento. Published by Editoriale Domus S.p.A., Milan 1950. Translated by permission of Editoriale Domus S.p.A.(149, 161).
La Cuisine Bretonne, *(L'Encyclopédie de la Cuisine Régionale).* © Presses Pocket, 1979. Published by Presses Pocket. Translated by permission of Solar(104, 125, 153).
Cutler, Carol, *The Six-Minute Soufflé and Other Culinary Delights.* Copyright © 1976 by Carol Cutler. By permission of Clarkson N. Potter, Inc.(106).
Czerny, Zofia, *Polish Cookbook.* Copyright © 1961, 1975 Państwowe Wydawnictwo Ekonomiczne. Published by Państwowe Wydawnictwo Ekonomiczne, Warsaw. By permission of Agencja Autorska, Warsaw(87, 132).
David, Elizabeth, *Spices, Salt and Aromatics in the English Kitchen.* Copyright © Elizabeth David, 1970. Published by Penguin Books Ltd., London. By permission of Penguin Books Ltd.(85, 151). *Summer Cooking.* © Elizabeth David,

950, 1951, 1955, 1965, 1980. Published in 1980 under the [tit]le *Elizabeth David Classics* comprising *A Book of Mediter-*[ra]*nean Food*, *French Country Cooking* and *Summer Cook-*[in]g, by Jill Norman Ltd., London. By permission of Jill Nor[m]an Ltd.(86, 88).

[D]avidis, Henriette, *Praktisches Kochbuch*. Newly re[vi]sed by Luise Holle. Published in Bielefeld and Leipzig, [1]898(96, 137, 141).

[d]e Andreis, Florence, *La Cuisine Provençale Aujourd'Hui*. © Rivages 1980. Published by Éditions Ri[va]ges, Marseille. Translated by permission of Sarl Éditions [Ri]vages(92, 99, 159).

[d]e Aznar, Marina Pereyra and Nina Froud, *The [H]ome Book of Spanish Cookery*. Copyright Marina de Az[n]ar and Nina Froud 1956. Revised edition © Marina de [A]znar and Nina Froud 1967. Published by Faber and [Fa]ber Limited, London 1956. By permission of Faber and [Fa]ber Limited(90, 113).

[d]e Lazarque, E. Auricoste, *Cuisine Messine*. Published [b]y Sidot Frères, Libraires-Éditeurs, Nancy, 1927. Reprinted [b]y Laffitte Reprints, Marseille, 1979. Translated by permis[si]on of Laffitte Reprints(140).

[d]e Périgord, A.-B., *Le Trésor de la Cuisinière et de la [M]aîtresse de Maison*. Published by Garnier Frères, Paris, [1]852(118).

[D]onati, Stella (Editor), *Il Grande Manuale della Cucina [R]egionale*. Copyright 1979 Euroclub Italia S.p.A., Berga[m]o. Published by Sugar Co. Edizioni S.r.l., Milan. Translat[ed] by permission of Euroclub(148).

[D]ouglas, Joyce, *Old Derbyshire Recipes and Customs*. © [Jo]yce Douglas, 1976. Published by Hendon Publishing Co. [Lt]d., Nelson, Lancaster. By permission of Hendon Publish[in]g Co. Ltd.(93).

[D]umaine, Alexandre, *Ma Cuisine*. © 1972 by Pensée [M]oderne, Paris. Published by Éditions de la Pensée Mo[d]erne, Paris. Translated by permission of Jacques [G]rancher, Éditeur, Paris(144, 158).

[El]kon, Juliette, *A Belgian Cookbook*. Copyright © 1958 [b]y Farrar, Straus and Cudahy, Inc. Published by Farrar, [St]raus and Cudahy, New York. By permission of Farrar, [St]raus and Cudahy, New York. By permission of [Fa]rrar, Straus and Giroux, Inc.(116).

[Fe]ramo, Cia, *Segreti e No Della Cucina Mantovana*. Pub[lis]hed by Edizioni Citem, Mantova, 1980. Translated by [p]ermission of the author(88, 94, 147).

[F]ortin, Stanley, *The World Book of Pork Dishes*. © 1967 [b]y Stanley Fortin. First published in Great Britain by Pelham [Bo]oks Ltd., London 1967. By permission of Pelham Books [Lt]d.(91).

[Ga]rcía, Maria Luisa, *El Arte de Cocinar*. Copyright [1]977 Maria Luisa García. Eighth Edition. Published by Edi[to]l Ediciones, Valladolid. Translated by permission of the [a]uthor, Mieres (Asturias)(161).

[Gé]rard, Jacqueline, *Bonnes Recettes d'Autrefois*. © Li[b]rairie Larousse, 1980. Published by Librairie Larousse, [Pa]ris. Translated by permission of Société Encyclopédique [U]niverselle, Paris(109, 157). *Les Meilleures Recettes de Gi-*[b]ier. © 1978 Elsevier Séquoia, Bruxelles. Published by Else[vi]er Séquoia, Bruxelles. Translated by permission of Else[vi]er Séquoia(158).

[G]ombervaux (Editor), *La Bonne Cuisine pour Tous*. Pub[lis]hed by Presses de la Renaissance, Paris 1979(146).

[G]osetti, Fernanda, *In Cucina con Fernanda Gosetti*. © [1]978 Fabbri Editori, Milano. Published by Fabbri Editori, [Mi]lan, 1978. Translated by permission of Gruppo Editor[ial]e Fabbri Bompiani/Sonzogno/Etas S.p.A.(149).

[Go]uffé, Jules, *Le Livre de Cuisine*. Fifth Edition. Pub[lis]hed by Librairie Hachette, Paris, 1881(108, 136, 139).

[G]rigson, Jane, *Good Things*. Copyright © 1971 by Jane [G]rigson. Copyright © 1971 by Alfred A. Knopf, Inc. By per[m]ission of Alfred A. Knopf, Inc.(142, 146). *The Art of Mak-*[in]g Sausages, Pâtés and Other Charcuterie. Copyright © [1]967, 1968 by Jane Grigson. By permission of Alfred A. [Kn]opf, Inc.(112, 145).

[G]uérard, Michel, *Michel Guérard's Cuisine Minceur*. [En]glish translation copyright © 1976 by William Morrow [an]d Company, Inc. Originally published under the title *La [G]rande Cuisine Minceur*, copyright © 1976 by Éditions Laf[fi]nt S.A. By permission of William Morrow(130).

Guinaudeau-Franc, Zette, *Les Secrets des Fermes en Périgord Noir*. Published by Éditeur Berger-Levrault, Paris 1980. Translated by permission of the author(96, 116, 157).

Hawliczkowa, Helena, *Kuchnia Polska* (Editor: Maria Librowska). Copyright by Helena Hawliczkowa. Published by Państwowe Wydawnictwo Ekonomiczne, Warsaw, 1976. Translated by permission of Agencja Autorska, Warsaw, for the author(107, 153).

Holleman, Ria, *Pastei en Pâté*. © 1973 Unieboek B. V. Bussum—Holland. Published by C. A. J. Van Dishoeck, Bussum. Translated by permission of Unieboek B. V.(94, 98, 117, 122).

Hutchins, Sheila, *English Recipes and Others from Scotland, Wales and Ireland*. © 1967 by Sheila Hutchins. Published by Metheun & Co. Ltd. By permission of the author(122). *Pâtés & Terrines*. Copyright © 1978 by Sheila Hutchins. Published by Elm Tree Books/Hamish Hamilton Ltd., London 1978. By permission of Hamish Hamilton Ltd.(88, 101, 116).

Iribe, Maybelle and Barbara Wilder, *Pâtés for Kings and Commoners*. Copyright © 1977 by Barbara Wilder and Maybelle Iribe. By permission of Hawthorn Books, a division of Elsevier-Dutton Publishing Co., Inc.(103).

Isnard, Léon, *La Cuisine Française et Africaine*. © Albin Michel, 1949. Published by Éditions Albin Michel, Paris. Translated by permission of Éditions Albin Michel(118).

Ivens, Dorothy, *Pâtés & Other Marvelous Meat Loaves*. Copyright © 1972 by Dorothy Ivens. Published by J. B. Lippincott Company, New York. By permission of Harper & Row, Publishers, Inc., New York(100, 111).

Jans, Hugh, *Vrij Nederland*, October 1975 (magazine). Translated by permission of Hugh Jans(129, 131).

Koscher, Joseph and Associates, *Les Recettes de la Table Alsacienne*. © Librairie Istra/Saisons d'Alsace 1969. Published by Société Alsacienne d'Édition et de Diffusion, Strasbourg. Translated by permission of Librairie Istra(151).

Laloue, P. E., *Le Guide de la Charcuterie*. Copyright 1950 by P. E. Laloue. Published by Le Guide de la Charcuterie(142, 154).

Lévêque, Paul-Jacques (Editor), *Les Bonnes Recettes de la Cuisine Tourangelle*. Published by C. L. D., Normand and Cie., Éditeur. Translated by permission of Éditions C. L. D., Chambray-Les-Tours, France(102, 131, 134).

Margittai, Tom and Paul Kovi, *The Four Seasons*. Copyright © 1980 by Tom Margittai and Paul Kovi. By permission of Simon & Schuster, a division of Gulf & Western Corporation(104, 123, 162).

Marin, *Les Dons de Comus*. Vol. 2, Paris, c. 1742(120, 159).

Massialot, *Le Nouveau Cuisinier Royal et Bourgeois*. Published by Claude Prudhomme, Paris 1712(154).

70 Médecins de France, *Le Trésor de la Cuisine du Bassin Méditerranéen*. Published by Les Laboratoires du Dr. Zizine(158).

Menon, *Le Manuel des Officiers de Bouche*. Published by Le Clerc, Librairie, Paris 1759(149). *Les Soupers de la Cour, (ou L'Art de Travailler toutes Sortes d'Aliments)*. Originally published in 1755 by Guillyn, Libraire, Paris. Reprinted in 1978 by Librairie SOETE, Paris(89).

Montagné, Prosper, *The New Larousse Gastronomique*. English text copyright © 1977 by the Hamlyn Publishing Group. By permission of Crown Publishers, Inc.(155).

Morand, Simone, *Cuisine et Gastronomie du Maine, de la Touraine et de l'Anjou*. Published by Société d'Éditions Ouest-France, Rennes. Translated by permission of Société d'Éditions Ouest-France(102, 109, 110, 114).

Nignon, Édouard (Editor), *Le Livre de Cuisine de L'Ouest-Éclair*. Published in 1941 by L'Ouest-Éclair, Rennes. Translated by permission of Société d'Éditions Ouest-France, Rennes(106).

Olney, Judith, *Comforting Food*. Copyright © 1979 by Judith Olney. Published by Atheneum Publishers, New York. By permission of Atheneum Publishers(94). *Summer Food*. Copyright © 1978 by Judith Olney. Published by Atheneum Publishers, Inc., New York. By permission of Atheneum Publishers, Inc.(129).

Olney, Richard, *Simple French Food*. Copyright © 1974 by Richard Olney. Published by Atheneum Publishers, New

York. By permission of Atheneum Publishers(95, 103, 124).

Ortega, Simone, *Mil Ochenta Recetas de Cocina*. © Simone K. de Ortega, 1972 © Alianza Editorial, S. A., Madrid, 1972. Published by Alianza Editorial, S. A. Translated by permission of Alianza Editorial, S. A.(93, 97).

Parker, Audrey, *Cottage and Country Recipes*. © Audrey Parker 1975. Published by Faber and Faber Limited, London. By permission of Faber and Faber Limited(138, 152).

Petit, A., *La Gastronomie en Russie*. Published by the author and Émile Mellier, Paris, 1860(148).

Petits Propos Culinaires VII, February 1981. © Prospect Books 1981. Published by Prospect Books, London and Washington, D.C. By permission of the publisher(89, 108).

Petits Propos Culinaires VIII, June 1981. © Prospect Books 1981. Published by Prospect Books, London and Washington, D.C. By permission of the publisher(110).

Philippon, Henri, *Cuisine du Quercy et du Périgord*. © 1979, by Éditions Denoël, Paris. Published by Éditions Denoël. Translated by permission of Éditions Denoël(89).

Plucińska, Ida, *Ksiażka Kuchaiska Udoskonalona*. Copyright by author, Poznan, 1945. Translated by permission of Agencja Autorska, Warsaw(85).

Ranhofer, Charles, *The Epicurean*. Originally published by R. Ranhofer, New York 1893. Republished by Dover Publications, Inc., New York 1971(96, 160).

Read, Miss, *Miss Read's Country Cooking*. © 1969 by Miss Read. Published by Michael Joseph Ltd., London, 1969. By permission of Michael Joseph Ltd., for the author(104, 110).

Reige, Odette, *Les Terrines de Viandes, de Coquillages et Poissons, de Légumes*. © Les Cahiers de Fanny, Hubschmid et Bouret, Paris 1979. Translated by permission of Hubschmid and Bouret, Éditeurs, Paris(126, 128, 130, 154).

Renaudet, Benjamin, *60 Recettes pour Préparer le Lapin Domestique et le Lapin de Garenne à la Cuisine Bourgeoise*. Published by Albin Michel, Éditeur, Paris. By permission of Albin Michel, Paris(113).

Robaglia, Suzanne, *Margaridou: Journal et Recettes d'une Cuisinière au Pays d'Auvergne*. Published by Éditions CREER, F-63340 Nonette, 1977. Translated by permission of Éditions CREER(98).

Rubinstein, Helge, *French Cookery*. Published by Eyre Methuen, London. By permission of Associated Book Publishers Ltd., London(84, 107).

Rundell, Mrs., *Domestic Cookery*. Published by John Murray, London, February 1837(138, 140).

St. Clair, Lady Harriet (Editor), *Dainty Dishes*. Eleventh Edition. Published by John Hogg, London(90).

Sastre Rayo, Gabriel and Antonia Ordinas Mari (Editors), *Libre de Cuina de C'an Cames Seques (Cocina Mallorquina de Siempre)*. Published by Impreso por Antigua Imprenta Soler, Palma de Mallorca, 1977. Translated by permission of Antonia Ordinas Mari(156).

Sekers, Simone, *Pâtés, Terrines and Potted Meats*. Copyright Simone Sekers 1978. Published by B. T. Batsford Ltd., London. By permission of B. T. Batsford Ltd.(85, 97, 133).

Simon, André L., *A Concise Encyclopaedia of Gastronomy*. Published by William Collins Sons and Company Limited, London c. 1956. By permission of William Collins Sons and Company Limited(150).

Spizzotin, Pier Antonio (Editor), *La Carne Conveniente (Il Cuoco in Casa)*. © Copyright by Editoriale del Drago S.r.l. Milano 1979. Published by Editoriale del Drago S.r.l., Milan. Translated by permission of Editoriale del Drago S.r.l.(147, 150).

Tante Marguerite, *La Cuisine de la Bonne Ménagère*. Published by Éditions de L'Épi, Paris c. 1939(86, 114, 118).

Thomas, Kathleen, *A West Country Cookery Book*. © Kathleen Thomas 1961. Published by B. T. Batsford Ltd., London. By permission of the author and the publisher(150).

Thuilier, Raymond and Michel Lemonnier, *Les Recettes de Baumanière*. © 1980, Éditions Stock. Published by Éditions Stock, Paris. Translated by permission of Éditions Stock(112, 115, 143).

Tiano, Myrette, *Les Gibiers*. © Solar, 1979. Published by

Solar, Paris. Translated by permission of Solar(117). *300 Recettes du Gibier.* © Solar, 1973. Published by Solar, Paris(141).
Troisgros, Jean & Pierre, *The Nouvelle Cuisine of Jean & Pierre Troisgros.* English translation copyright © 1978 by William Morrow and Company, Inc. Originally published under the title *Cuisiniers à Roanne.* Copyright © by Éditions Laffont, S.A. By permission of William Morrow(127).
Urvater, Michèle and David Liederman, *Cooking the Nouvelle Cuisine in America.* Copyright © 1979 by Michèle Urvater and David Liederman. Published by the Workman Publishing Company Inc., New York. By permission of the Workman Publishing Company Inc.(126).
Vence, Céline, *Encyclopédie Hachette de la Cuisine Régionale.* © Hachette 1979. Published by Hachette,

Paris. Translated by permission of Hachette(92, 119).
Vernon, Anne, *111 Recettes Pour le Lapin.* © 1977 Éditions de Trévise. Published by Éditions de Trévise, Paris. Translated by permission of Éditions de Trévise(115).
Viola, Pauline and Knud Ravnkilde, *Cooking with a Danish Flavour.* Copyright © 1978 by Pauline Viola and Knud Ravnkilde. Published by Elm Tree Books for Danish Agricultural Producers, London. By permission of Hamish Hamilton Ltd., London(101).
Voegeling, François, *La Gastronomie Alsacienne.* © Copyright by Éditions des Dernières Nouvelles de Strasbourg. Published by Éditions des Dernières Nouvelles d'Alsace—ISTRA. Translated by permission of Éditions ISTRA(86).
Webb, Mrs. Arthur, *Farmhouse Cookery.* Published by

George Newnes Ltd., London c. 1930. By permission of Miss Gwyneth Webb, heir to the author(90, 143, 150, 152).
Weber, Dominique, *Les Bonnes Recettes des Provinces de France.* © Bordas, Paris, 1979. Published by Éditions Bordas. Translated by permission of Éditions Bordas(92).
Willan, Anne, *Great Cooks and Their Recipes.* A McGraw-Hill Book Co. Publication, 1977(144).
Willinsky, Grete, *Kulinarische Weltreise.* © 1961 by Mary Hahn's Kochbuchverlag, Berlin W. Published by Bü chergilde Gutenberg, Frankfurt/Main. Translated by permission of Mary Hahn's Kochbuchverlag, Munich(98).
Witwicka, H. and S. Soskine, *La Cuisine Russe Classique.* © Éditions Albin Michel, 1968 and 1978. Published by Éditions Albin Michel, Paris. Translated by permission Éditions Albin Michel(152).

Acknowledgments

The indexes for this book were prepared by Louise W. Hedberg. The editors are particularly indebted to Alain Binot, Dominique's Restaurant, Washington, D.C.; Gail Duff, Kent, England; Robert Greault, Le Bagatelle Restaurant, Washington, D.C.; Ray Greenfield, Betsy Crosby, U.S. Department of Agriculture, Agriculture Marketing Service, Washington, D.C.; Heinrich Hofmann, The Alibi Restaurant, Fairfax, Virginia; Milton Kaufman, Kaufco Sales, West Nyack, New York; Sarah Kelly, London; Francis Layrle, French Embassy, Washington, D.C.; Anton Mosimann, London; Ann O'Sullivan, Majorca, Spain; Jean Louis Palladin, Jean-Louis At Watergate,

Washington, D.C.; Dr. R. H. Smith, Aberdeen, Scotland; Dr. Dan Stillwell, U.S. Department of Agriculture, Livestock, Poultry and Feed Division, Washington, D.C.

The editors also wish to thank: Pat Alburey, Hertfordshire, England; R. Allen & Co., Ltd., London; Mary Attenborough, Essex, England; Jacques Bonnichon, Gourmet Francais, Hanover, Massachusetts; Marisa Centis, London; Dr. E. Ciolfi, U.S. Department of Agriculture, Standards and Procedure Division, Washington, D.C.; Liz Clasen, London; Lesley Coates, Essex, England; Emma Codrington, Surrey, England; W. J. Duncum, Hertfordshire, England; Mimi Errington,

Nottinghamshire, England; Nayla Freeman, London; Ann Hall, London; Mary Harron, London; Maggie Heinz, London; Wanda Kemp-Welch, Nottingham, England; Douglas McNeill, Four Seasons, Washington, D.C.; Marcus Leuw Ltd., London; George Mayo, Derek Walke Port City Seafood, Alexandria, Virginia; Philippa Millard, London; Sonya Mills, Kent, England; Norbert Moldan, Pietrus Foods, Inc., Sleepy Eye, Minnesota; Wendy Morri London; Maria Mosby, London; Dilys Naylor, Surrey, England; Jo Oxley, Surrey, England; Joyce Dodson Piotrowski, Burke, Virginia; Phyllis Richman, *The Washington Post,* Washington, D.C.; Sylvia Robertson, Surrey, England; Michael Schwab, London; Suzanne's, Washington, D.C.; Fiona Tillett, London; J. M. Turnell & Co., London; Tina Walker, London.

Picture Credits

The sources for the pictures in this book are listed below. Credits for each of the photographers and illustrators are listed by page number in sequence with successive pages indicated by hyphens; where necessary, the locations of pictures within pages are also indicated—separated from page numbers by dashes.

Photographs by John Elliott: 6—top, 7, 8—top, 9, 12—bottom, 13—right, 14—bottom left, 15—center, 18—top, bottom right, 19—top, bottom left, bottom center, 22-23, 24—top, bottom left, bottom right, 25, 26-27—top, 28—bottom center, bottom right, 29—top right, bottom, 30-31, 33—bottom right, 36—top right, 42, 48—bottom, 49—top center, top right, bottom, 50-51, 54-55, 72, 73—top, bottom left, 74—top, bottom left, bottom

center, 80-81—bottom, 82.
Other photographs (alphabetically): Tom Belshaw, cover, 4, 8—bottom center, bottom right, 10—top left, 11—bottom left, 13—left, center, 14—top left, bottom center, bottom right, 15—top center, top right, bottom left, 18—bottom left, 19—bottom right, 20, 21—top, bottom left, bottom right, 24—bottom center, 26-27—bottom, 32, 33—top, bottom left, 58-59, 60—top, bottom right, 61, 63—bottom right, 79, 80-81—top. Alan Duns, 6-7—bottom, 10—top right, bottom, 11—top, bottom, bottom right, 12—top, 14—top center, top right, 15—top left, bottom center, bottom right, 34, 36—top left, bottom, 37-39, 44-45, 48—top, 49—top left. Fil Hunter, 64-65. Louis Klein, 2. Bob Komar, 8—bottom left, 21—bottom center, 28—top, bottom left, 29—top left, top center, 52, 56-57, 60—bottom center, 62, 63—top, bottom left, 70, 73—bottom right, 74—bottom right, 75-78. Aldo Tutino, 16, 40-41, 46-47, 66-69.

Illustrations: From the Mary Evans Picture Library and private sources and *Food & Drink: A Pictorial Archive from Nineteenth Century Sources* by Jim Harter, published by Dover Publications, Inc., 1979, 90-167.

Library of Congress Cataloguing in Publication Data
Main entry under title:
Terrines, pâtés & galantines.
  (The Good cook, techniques & recipes)
  Includes index.
    1. Terrines. 2. Pâtés (Cookery) 3. Galantines.
I. Time-Life Books. II. Series.
TX749.T43   641.8'12   81-21310
ISBN 0-8094-2927-6   AACR2
ISBN 0-8094-2926-8 (lib. bdg.)
ISBN 0-8094-2925-X (retail ed.)